T0358906

Comparative Causal Mapping

This text has much to offer for both beginners and advanced practitioners of comparative causal mapping. It provides a thorough and systematic overview of the field with useful tips for researchers. An excellent addition to the methodologist's tool-kit.
Catherine Cassell, Leeds University Business School, UK

This book presents in a highly accessible yet scholarly form, an introduction to the theory and practice of comparative (cognitive) causal mapping (CCM), centred on the authors' CMAP3 software. Although the authors' main focus is on their own particular approach, there are many useful insights and lessons for all users of CCM techniques, novices and experienced users alike.
Gerard P. Hodgkinson, University of Warwick, UK

This book is the perfect gateway to causal mapping. Its hands-on approach will be invaluable for graduate students and scholars alike.
Daniela Stockmann, Leiden University, the Netherlands

Comparative Causal Mapping

The CMAP3 Method

MAURI LAUKKANEN
Department of Business, University of Eastern Finland

MINGDE WANG
Department of Politics and International Relations, University of Oxford

Routledge
Taylor & Francis Group

LONDON AND NEW YORK

First published 2015 by Gower Publishing

2 Park Square, Milton Park, Abingdon, Oxfordshire OX14 4RN
52 Vanderbilt Avenue, New York, NY 10017

Routledge is an imprint of the Taylor & Francis Group, an informa business

First issued in paperback 2019

Gower Applied Business Research
Our programme provides leaders, practitioners, scholars and researchers with thought provoking, cutting edge books that combine conceptual insights, interdisciplinary rigour and practical relevance in key areas of business and management.

British Library Cataloguing in Publication Data
A catalogue record for this book is available from the British Library

Library of Congress Cataloging-in-Publication Data
Laukkanen, Mauri.
   Comparative causal mapping : the CMAP3 method / by Mauri Laukkanen and Mingde Wang.
       pages cm
   Includes bibliographical references and index.
     ISBN 978-1-4724-3993-2 (hardback) -- ISBN 978-1-4724-3995-6 (ebook) -- ISBN 978-1-4724-3994-9 (epub) 1. Decision making. 2. Cognitive maps (Psychology) 3. Causation--Research. 4. Management. I. Wang, Mingde. II. Title.
   HD30.23.L3748 2015
   003'.56--dc23
                        2014031714

ISBN 13: 978-1-4724-3993-2 (hbk)
ISBN 13: 978-0-367-87965-5 (pbk)

Contents

List of Figures	*ix*
List of Tables	*xi*
About the Authors	*xiii*
Foreword	*xv*
Preface	*xxi*
Abbreviations	*xxv*

1   Introduction   **1**
1.1   What Are Causal Maps?   2
1.2   Visual vs. Non-Visual Presentation   4
1.3   Why Causal Maps?   7
1.4   Plan of the Book   9

2   Concepts in Comparative Causal Mapping   **11**
2.1   Models in the Mind   12
2.2   Formation of Causal Ideas   19
2.3   Stability and Change of Thinking   23
2.4   Impact of Knowledge   25
2.5   Towards Eliciting Knowledge and Mental Models   29

3   Comparative Causal Mapping   **37**
3.1   Data Acquisition   37
    3.1.1   Documentary Data   39
    3.1.2   Low-structured Interviewing   42
    3.1.3   Text-based Elicitation   43
    3.1.4   Structured Methods   45
    3.1.5   Semi-structured Interviewing   49
    3.1.6   Shortcuts to CCM Data   55
    3.1.7   Automated Causal Mapping   57
3.2   Standardizing (Coding)   59
3.3   Comparison for Aggregation   66
    3.3.1   Interpretive-inductive Strategy   67
    3.3.2   Predefined Concept List or Pool Strategy   68

3.4 Trustworthiness—Validity 69
3.5 CCM Metrics: Counting the Countable 79
    3.5.1 *Modeling Real Systems* 81
    3.5.2 *Representing Mental Models and Belief Systems* 83
    3.5.3 *To Quantify or Not?* 87
3.6 Selecting a CCM Method 89

4 Computerizing CCM with CMAP3 **99**
4.1 CMAP3: An Overview 99
4.2 Installing and Starting CMAP3 102
4.3 Defining CMAP3 Projects 103

5 From Raw Data to Analyzable Output **107**
5.1 Preparing Raw Data 107
5.2 Keyboard Entry 111
5.3 Importing Data 116
5.4 Standard Term Vocabulary 124
    5.4.1 *Stage 1: Tentative Standardizing:*
    Provisional Standard Term Vocabulary 125
    5.4.2 *Stage 2: Inductive Construction of the*
    STV's First Approximation 127
    5.4.3 *Stage 3: Towards the Final STV and*
    Standardization Solution 128
5.5 Generating Output Data 132

6 Cause Map Analysis Tools in CMAP3 **137**
6.1 Standard Causal Units 137
6.2 Standard Node Terms 141
6.3 Focal and Domain Maps 143
6.4 Statistics Module 146
6.5 Visual Cause Maps 152

7 CCM Research in Practice **157**
7.1 Document-based CCM:
Mapping Chinese Foreign Policy Beliefs 157
    7.1.1 *DBCM Studies in IR* 158
    7.1.2 *Mapping Chinese Grand Strategic Beliefs* 160
    7.1.3 *Definition and Data Selection* 160
    7.1.4 *Coding the Speeches* 162
    7.1.5 *Data Importing and Map Generation* 166

	7.1.6	*Map Visualization and Analysis*	168
	7.1.7	*Working with DBCMs*	173
7.2	Causal Mapping Professionals' Mental Models		173
	7.2.1	*Background of the SBA Study*	174
	7.2.2	*Methodology*	175
	7.2.3	*Visual Analysis: NMF-Success/Failure*	182
	7.2.4	*The SBA Mindset*	184
7.3	Structured CCM: Comparing Methods		185
	7.3.1	*Research Process*	186
	7.3.2	*Individual Causal Maps*	192
	7.3.3	*Comparison at Aggregate Level*	195
	7.3.4	*Understanding the Differences*	199
	7.3.5	*Assessing Representativeness*	203
	7.3.6	*Methodological Lessons*	205

References 209
Index 229

List of Figures

1.1   A causal map:
        rural municipality directors' beliefs about the local economy   2
1.2   A causal map: aggregated belief patterns of factory supervisors   5
1.3   A datatable presentation of the causal map in Figure 1.2   6

2.1   Production of CCM data: a cognitive perspective   32

3.1   A schema of semi-structured interviewing (SIM)   50
3.2   CCM SIM interview notes sheet (INS) S01 CCM_Case1   54
3.3   Coding/standardizing in CCM:
        compacting and collapsing effect   64
3.4   CCM_Case1: S01-S09 hierarchical clusters (C/D index SCU)   85

4.1   CMAP3 opening interface—main menu (v.3.1.2)   102
4.2   CMAP3 Project Manager   104

5.1   Raw data sheet (RDS) for keyboard entry   108
5.2   Node Data & Standardizing (NLU) Module   112
5.3   Causal Links Data (NCU) Module   114
5.4   Concept pool/standard term vocabulary (STV) worksheet   119
5.5   Concept selection list (CSL) in project CCM_Case2   121
5.6   The PCM of S01 in project CCM_Case2   122
5.7   NLU/SNT matrix in a CCM project   130
5.8   NLU/STAG batch replacement tool   131
5.9   Generating cause map units module
        (before and after generation)   134

6.1   Standard Causal Unit (SCU) and
        Standard Node Term (SNT) browsing module   138
6.2   Reciprocal standard causal units (RSCU) in the SCU window   141
6.3   Focal Map (FM) browser   143
6.4   Domain Map (DM) browser   145
6.5   CMAP3 statistics & C/D index module   147
6.6   Calculating the correspondence/distance (C/D) index in CMAP3   150

6.7   A DM-F causal map (CCM_Case 1,
        focal concept O01 unit's output) created using
        CmapTools and CMAP3 cxl-export facility   153

7.1   Sample database for coding and standardization   163
7.2   Example of data importing   167
7.3   Example of NCU entry in CMAP3   168
7.4   The domain map (DMF) around China's utility (I02)   170
7.5   Domain map of China's strategic environment   170
7.6   Domain map—goal structure   172
7.7   Saturation of the SNT base (N = 123)   181
7.8   Causal map: SBAs' belief pattern of NMF-success/failure   183
7.9   Concept selection list (CSL) in the PCM/FDM comparison
        study (S01)   189
7.10   Pairwise comparison matrix worksheet (returned, S01)   191
7.11   S12's SIM cause map (N/SNT = 37, N/SCU = 72, N/RCU = 12)   193
7.12   S01's PCM cause map (N/SNT = 15, N/SCU = 103, N/RCU = 40)   193
7.13   S01's FDM cause map (N/SNT = 15, N/SCU = 22, N/RCU = 0)   194
7.14   PCM domain map around *NMF success/failure*
        (N/SNT = 11, N/SCU = 54, N/RSCU = 34)   197
7.15   FDM domain map around *NMF success/failure*
        (N/SNT = 15, N/SCU = 23, N/RSCU = 0)   198

List of Tables

7.1 Example of coding   163
7.2 Example of standardization   164
7.3 Standardizing (coding) in the SBA study: key standard node terms' NLU contents   177
7.4 Summary of SBA study's raw and standardized data   180
7.5 SIM, PCM and FDM comparison data   195
7.6 SBAs' feedback data (%) on SIM, PCM and FDM cause maps (N = 31)   204

About the Authors

Mauri Laukkanen is Professor Emeritus of the University of Eastern Finland, Department of Business, Kuopio Campus. He received his PhD (DBA) at the Helsinki School of Economics (now Aalto University School of Business) in 1989. He served at the HSE and the Universities of Vaasa and Jyväskylä before the University of Kuopio (now University of Eastern Finland), where he contributed to the founding of the present Department of Business, which he headed from 1995–2002. His research interests include managerial and organizational cognition, cognitive causal mapping methods and CMAP3 software (http://www.uef.fi/cmap3), entrepreneurship and local development. He has published a number of international papers in these fields, and several books in Finnish. Since retiring in 2004, he has concentrated on writing and cognitive mapping research and development projects. Mauri Laukkanen lives in Lahti, Finland, and Bergisch Gladbach, Germany. He can be reached at: mauri.laukkanen@uef.fi.

Mingde Wang is a Marie Curie Researcher in the PRIMO (Power and Regions in a Multipolar Order) Initial Training Network (ITN) funded by the European Commission, and a doctoral student at the Department of Politics and International Relations, University of Oxford. He received his Master's degree in International Relations and Diplomacy from Leiden University, and was a lecturer of East Asian international relations at the University of Erlangen-Nuremberg. His research interests include political psychology in international politics, security studies, and international relations theories.

Foreword

I first ran into Mauri Laukkanen a few years ago in the British Academy of Management at a time when he had been working on an earlier version of CMAP3. Although I had been familiar with CMAP from Mauri's earlier writings, it was a pleasure to meet him in person. He struck me as someone who is thoughtful, pleasant and intensely committed to his project. After the obligatory pleasantries, Mauri proceeded to give me a bird's eye view of the project. So later on, when I got a paper by 'anonymous authors' for review from a (peer reviewed) journal, I had to call the editor to disclose that I already knew who wrote the paper, so as to remain true to the spirit of the journal's practice of blind review. 'Causal mapping' community of scholars is small, although they are not closely knit—all of us have our own biases and stylistic preferences! I am gratified to note that the paper found a home in a revised form in the journal.

Ever since Axelrod developed causal mapping as a tool for policy research from several strands of behavioral, mathematical and applied mathematical disciplines, its use has been increasing in frequency for research in various disciplines. The essence of causal mapping is to capture patterns of human cognition from texts, either archival or interview generated, so that they can be examined for patterns or hypothesis testing. As I have noted elsewhere (Narayanan and Armstrong 2004), causal mapping has enabled a remarkable revolution underway in the organization sciences. Indeed, a new generation of management scholars is enthusiastically bringing the role of the human mind back into the study of organizations, after several decades' dominance of the deterministic school. This new breed of scholars takes inspiration from the works of Barnard, Simon and Weick, and focuses their attention on human cognitive processes. Their cognitive agenda is enabled by the availability of research tools such as causal mapping that have made possible the study of thought using 'normal science' approaches. Indeed, these tools have reached a level of maturity as underscored by their increasingly frequent use in papers published in major management journals (see Narayanan, Zane and Kemmerer 2011 for a recent review).[1]

---

1 Narayanan, V.K. Zane, Lee and Kemmerer, Benedict .The Cognitive Perspective in Strategy, *Journal of Management*. Vol. 37, No. 1, January 2011, pp. 305–51.

Large-scale works on cognition, especially those pertaining to 'strategic cognition,' are facilitated by software enabled causal mapping approaches. In this regard, Laukkanen and Wang's book fulfills three major functions: 1) to highlight for us the tradeoffs in the research designs that precede the use of causal mapping technique, 2) a detailed discussion of the technique useful for comparative purposes, and 3) a software that facilitates the tasks of the researcher. One remarkable characteristic of their exposition is the degree of specificity they have built into the characterization and elucidation of their approach. This is welcome news for PhD students who are newcomers to causal mapping, and yes, their advisors too, who can reasonably expect their advisees to pick up the technical details of the technique on their own. Even advanced readers will find some chapters of the book interesting. Unlike novices, Chapters 1 and 2 will serve as a refresher for them, reminding them of the ambiguity of mental models and process. However, they will find the discussion of selecting a comparative causal mapping method (especially the section 3.6) highly informative. Mauri and his colleague pick this theme up later in Chapter 7, where section 7.3 provides concrete evidence for the selection by highlighting the considerable outcome differences of a semi-structured approach (CMAP3) and a structured method. I especially found the three studies in Chapter 7 interesting, not merely because of the illustrations of CCM, but also because of fascinating stories they narrated. Who could resist learning what went on in the mind of Deng Xiaoping!!!

CMAP3 is a non-commercial application, which researchers or practitioners can download, test and use free of charge with support documentation. To *young* researchers this is perhaps not insignificant. They can get a tested versatile CCM-application without incurring any cost, other than the time for learning it. CMAP3 is an academic project of UEF, where the "value capture" has been based on (small) funding by a research foundation. The Project has required time and effort of the small team – I am told that since Fall 2004, there have been more than 100 different versions from the early prototypes to the present v. 3.1.2 – obviously not based on economic motives.

Laukkanen and Wang acknowledge that the type of data – archival, text based, templates or semi-structured – is a component of research design, although it is a deliberate decision made by a researcher, it is sometime dictated by the research context. Thus archival sources may be the only alternative in a historical context (as is illustrated by the case Deng Xiaoping), whereas interviews (sometimes long, sometimes short) that limit the size of the sample may not be of interest to researchers who want to engage in sophisticated statistical analysis.

Causal mapping methods share several of the same challenges as other social science methods, which must build upon human communications. First, it is pretty clear that different sources yield different 'information,' partly due to differences in intentional and unconscious distortions ranging from lack of awareness, selective disclosure and intentional misrepresentation by the interviewee. A second challenge is the selection of concepts by which the data is rendered meaningful for analysis and interpretation. Standardizing data around concepts (or 'natural language units') requires the assumption that for the respondent, the meaning of the concept has not changed over time (especially in historical analyses), and in comparative analyses, the individuals interviewed share the meanings. This assumes away the incommensurability in archival data, and cultural linguistic differences if causal maps are constructed from heterogeneous.

Finally, lest the technical sophistication of causal mapping should seduce us to uncritical acceptance, we have to acknowledge the ontological and epistemological underpinnings of the causal mapping process. Although causal mapping approaches may differ in terms of the specific technical details, almost all of them share the assumption that human beings process information in a causal fashion, and perhaps an additional, but implicit assumption that humans cannot hold contradictory worldviews, or even differing world views often invoked by different triggers. Of course, this implicit assumption is not quite consistent with the received literature on strategic cognition, which has alerted us to the possibility of switching among schemas, hypocrisy or the inconsistency between belief and action, and worse still our slavery to emotions. In this regard, I find it heartening to find Laukkanen and Wang underscoring that people often do have parallel contradictory worldviews and mental models. Moreover, the book has tried to elaborate on the rather volatile cognitive basis of CM/CCM which we all have to deal with. In social science research, there is no perfect world or methodology where these problems are totally absent, and researchers aspiring to utilize causal mapping methods should be mindful, but need not unduly ponder over the shortcomings that a given approach necessarily shares with other social science methods.

The *published* academic works on causal mapping focus on the content and structure of causal maps. Indeed, the case studies in Chapter 7 reveal the typical causal belief systems' contents to understand the cognitive basis of those actors and their "behavioral tendencies." I suspect though that CMAP3 is also useful for those researchers interested in the structural analysis. The authors, however, touch upon the problems with structural analysis, but that, as noted before is not unique to causal mapping.

Where else can causal mapping help us? I venture to suggest that for management researchers, just as in the case of Axelrod, the interest in causal mapping is partly utilitarian: Can it help facilitate strategic and managerial tasks? Thus, causal mapping is useful in intervention contexts; for one, it offers a means to predict the behavior of organizations using data collected from major actors. This is the most frequently observed set of works in this area. Indeed, there are now examples of intra-organizational level operational and organizational change interventions with the aid of causal mapping; the case studies in Chapter 7 illustrate this genre of works in causal mapping.

There are, however, fewer examples of application to strategic problems that deal with uncertain markets and competition. For 'strategic cognition' researchers, the predicting the implications of causal maps, what I have elsewhere labeled the 'behavior of causal maps,' offers research opportunities that have the potential to advance, if not transform, both the competitive dynamics and strategy formulation literatures. When Liam Fahey and I introduced Axelrod's causal mapping into strategy literature during the late seventies, our interest was provoked by the lack of systematic tools for understanding competitor's thought processes, however unreliable. Our hope was to enable the analysis of competitors, a problem that in the US legal context precluded on many occasions direct contact with competitors. For strategy scholars these kinds of problems remain the Holy Grail in research using causal mapping.

One way for this to happen is when we, the causal mapping community, build bridges to related epistemic communities, especially a) mathematics and operations research and b) scholars dealing with big data. First, some of the central assumptions behind causal mapping are also evident in the literature on logic, industrial dynamics, and influence diagrams. Pearl's celebrated work on causality (2000)[2] provide us with concepts that are particularly useful for the analysis of causal maps. Kosko (1994)[3] has reported success with coupling causal maps and neural networks. Although sometimes outside the range of interest of social scientists, these approaches appear worthwhile linking to the literature on causal mapping. Indeed, causal mapping procedure serve as *input* to these more formalized techniques. Similarly, the 'Big Data' movement may offer ways for generating input for causal mapping process. Although we are in early stages of this movement, the interested reader may want to listen the opening shot in this direction by Jelinek et al. (in press).[4]

---

2   Pearl, J. *Causality: Models, Reasoning and Inference.* Cambridge, UK: Cambridge University Press, 2000.
3   Kosko, B. *Fuzzy Thinking: The New Science of Fuzzy Logic.* Hyperion, 1994.
4   Jelinek, M., S. Barr, P. Mugge and R. Kouri. *The Big Data Lever for Strategic Alliances* (in press).

Bridges to other epistemic communities are also possibilities, prime among them being neural sciences. There is growing interest in neural technologies, and the field of neuro-economics—and attendant neuro-physiological tools such as fMRI or fNIRS—are attracting the attention of an increasing number of cognition researchers. Indeed, neuroscience theories are fast migrating to applications in marketing and economics, and organizational scholars have recently begun to articulate the utility of neuroscience to numerous domains of organizational research pertaining to cognition (Cunningham et al. 2013). Neuroscience tools may offer two related benefits to researchers exploring organizational phenomena. First, these tools allow the inclusion of physiological factors in explaining human behavior in organizations. Second, neural processes may lie at the heart of several puzzles researchers have uncovered in various areas of organizational research. In particular, the physiological data unearthed by the use of neuroscience tools can provide greater insight into complex cognitive processes that have been identified as relevant to organizational research (e.g., decision-making). During the past decade, functional Magnetic Resonance Imaging (fMRI) has been the predominantly used neuroscience research tool in business research. The immobile element of fMRI limits the accessible population, but recently, relatively inexpensive and portable alternatives, such as Electroencephalography (EEG) and functional Near-Infrared Spectroscopy (fNIRS) have been developed. Importantly, studies comparing these approaches against fMRI indicate these neuroimaging approaches can serve as an alternative measurement of brain activation. This is encouraging, and serves as a pointer to the opportunities for coupling neural science tools and causal mappings tools. Indeed the linkage between physiological and communicational elements may itself be a genre of works that can delight us. Tools such as CMAP3 can be fruitfully coupled with neural science tools to advance our understanding of human and strategic cognition.

A foreword has many purposes: to introduce the authors; to place their contribution in perspective; to signal the significance of the book; to signal the challenges ahead. I might add, there is fifth one: to celebrate the book. Yes, this book is another signal of the maturation of causal mapping as a method and the adolescence of the field of strategic cognition. Let us celebrate this occasion.

V.K. Narayanan,
Deloitte Touché Jones Stubbs Professor of Strategy & Entrepreneurship,
Associate Dean for Research, Le Bow College of Business, Drexel University

Preface

This book is an introduction to causal (cognitive) mapping, in particular comparative causal mapping (CCM), and to CMAP3, a PC software application for CCM studies. It is an expanded and revised follow-up of the first CCM-CMAP guide of 1998, and its update of 2008. A new book was necessary, first, because the new CMAP3 generation differs from its predecessors in several respects and offers new functions, which enable more and different research applications than before. They need to be explained. Second, a new book can address in more detail key concepts, research objectives and methodological issues in different types of causal mapping. In particular, computerized CCM practices can be discussed in more concrete terms.

The origins of CMAP3 go back to 1988 and the first author's doctoral research. The idea was to explore the formation of managers' "cognitive maps" and to try to understand why there are industry-typical thought and belief patterns, how they evolve and have some specific contents, which are widely shared in an industry but systematically different from those in related industries (Laukkanen 1994). The study's respondents were managers of two different but closely cooperating trading industries. The earlier structured and document-based methods were not applicable and a new approach, later called semi-structured CCM interviewing (SIM), had to be developed.

The new method did produce the required data, in fact, lots of it. This also created a problem: how to process voluminous natural data so that it would be possible to plausibly compare the respondents' domain-related causal thinking. This was a prerequisite of summarizing the data into aggregated causal maps, and of distilling the similarities and differences of belief patterns within and across the two industry manager groups. The solution was based on two insights, as usual, obvious in retrospect. The first was that cause maps, until then traditionally conceived of mainly as pictorial graphic entities, consist of and can therefore be decomposed into their constituent elements, individual nodes and node–node pairs. The second insight was that the node-node pairs can be computerized, analyzed and eventually put together again into a visual form by drawing the corresponding graphical causal map. The first computer solution was a set of database program modules to perform some CCM subtasks such as raw data entry and conversion of the original concepts into a standard vocabulary system. This elementary but effective stage was called CMAP1. A couple of years later the separate modules were compiled into an independent PC application, CMAP2, to be run in MS-DOS computers and later in Windows PCs using an MS-DOS window. The CMAP2 software and the SIM CCM approach were published and presented in MOC workshops organized by the EIASM and the Academy of Management. CMAP2 was also made available free and it found numerous users worldwide.

However, it became gradually obvious that a genuine Windows application is necessary to enable migrating the CMAP/CCM approach into the dominant Windows environment. This would make the application more accessible and above all enable advantages such as exchanging data with other Windows applications. Accordingly, a software development project was started and the first version (v. 0.9.2.) of the application, called CMAP3, was released in 2008. Eventually, several improved versions have followed and a CCM/CMAP3 webpage created for downloading the software and supporting documentation.

CMAP3 adheres to the original decomposing/composing logic in cause map data elicitation, processing and analysis, but adapted to the Windows environment. As before, it was originally designed for typical CCM studies, which are based on small or medium-size samples (N =< 50), and focus on eliciting, describing and analyzing the structure and contents of *several* actors' thought/belief patterns and their similarities, differences and changes. CMAP3 could also be used as a data processing and analysis platform in *composite* and *ideographic* causal mapping, which combine causal statement data from parallel sources such as documents, interviews, and so on. However, the latest versions of CMAP3 also support *structured* CCM approaches such as the concept pool method. As before, CMAP3 remains an academic, non-commercial application. Interested researchers can download the software package and support documents[1] without cost.

As emphasized at the outset, this book is an introduction to comparative (cognitive) causal mapping (CCM). It aims to discuss, in relatively uncomplicated terms, what CCM is about—as the authors have understood and experienced its different variants. Notably, CCM research too is underpinned and informed by different ontological and theoretic views and research purposes.

---

1   The CMAP3 for Windows application and support document can be downloaded (without cost) at: www.uef.fi/fi/cmap3. The current CMAP3 version is 3.1.2. The book's illustrations are based on this version and the two default CCM projects, which will be installed automatically when setting up the application.

This manifests itself in divergent methodological stances and approaches, which will be discussed, too. However, it is also quite possible that some of our ideas and views may not be entirely shared by all CCM researchers, in particular those leaning heavily towards more nomothetic and quantitative models and ideals of social research.

CCM methods and research can serve not only scientific, typically explorative objectives, but also pragmatic purposes such as problem-solving and decision support, systems planning and organizational interventions. Thus, CCM is potentially applicable in many fields such as management and organizational studies, political science, environmental sciences, ICT, health and social care, nursing, systems engineering, local economic development, organizational development, personnel training, and so on. Accordingly, readers who may find the book useful include advanced university students and PhD candidates and senior scholars interested in augmenting their methods toolbox, and also organization developers, specialists and managers in different organizations, social practitioners, educators and consultants.

Developing CMAP3 is a project of the Department of Business, University of Eastern Finland (UEF), Kuopio Campus. We would like to thank above all Mr. Marko Heikkilä for his programming skills, stamina and cooperation when developing CMAP3. We thank also Professor Päivi Eriksson, Department of Business, UEF, Kuopio Campus, and the IT Unit of the UEF, Kuopio Campus, for their cooperation and assistance; Professor V.K. Narayanan for writing the Foreword; and Professors Caroline Cassell, Gerard P. Hodgkinson and Daniela Stockmann for their kind words of endorsement. We are most grateful for the assistance and cooperation of our editors at Gower: Kristina Abbotts and Donna Shanks. We also thank Amanda Picken and Caroline Spender for editing the text into a grammatically correct and also more readable form. The Finnish *Foundation of Economic Education* (Liikesivistysrahasto) has generously supported the CMAP3 project.

Mauri Laukkanen

Mingde Wang

Abbreviations

ACM	aggregated causal map
AoM	Academy of Management
BAM	British Academy of Management
C	Cluster; a predefined group of Ss in a CMAP3 project
C/D	C/D index, a correspondence/distance measure
CAQDAS	Computer Assisted/Aided Qualitative Data Analysis Software
CCM	comparative causal (cognitive) mapping, also composite causal mapping
CMAP3	PC software application for CCM studies
CORE	a predefined minimum number of Ss using an NLU/NCU in a CMAP3 project
CSL	concept selection list, a worksheet used to import NLUs
CSTAG	identifier of a standard node term in a cause/antecedent position in standard causal map
CSTERM	standard term belonging to a CSTAG (using primary or secondary standard language)
DBCM	document-based causal map/mapping
DM	domain map: there are three types of DMs (DMF, DME, DMC)
EEG	electroencephalography

EIASM	European Institute for Advanced Studies in Management
ESTAG	identifier of a standard node term in an effect/consequence position in standard causal map
ESTERM	the standard term belonging to an ESTAG (using primary or secondary standard language)
FDM	freehand drawing method, also freehand drawn causal map
FEA	Finnish Entrepreneurship Agencies Assoc. (Suomen Uusyrityskeskukset ry)
FM	focal map, a simple cause map generated around a focal concept/phenomenon
fMRI	functional magnetic resonance imaging
FNTAG	NTAG of the "effect" NLU of an NCU
GTF	generating total frequency
Id	the number of causal links flowing into a causal map node/concept in a causal map/matrix
INS	interview note sheet
IR	international relations
LSE	large-scale enterprise
LTM	long-term memory
MOC	management and organization cognition
NCU	natural causal unit (NLU–NLU/node–node pair in an original causal map)
NLU	natural language unit (an original concept or set of associated words in the raw data)

NMF	nascent micro firm
NTAG	NLU identifier (for example, 010102)
Od	number of causal links flowing from a causal map node/concept in a causal map/matrix
PCM	pairwise comparison method, also pairwise comparison matrix
PNTAG	NTAG of the "cause" NLU of an NCU
RDS	raw data sheet
RDWS	raw data worksheet
REM	database field for comments about an NLU or STERM
RSCU	reciprocal or two-way SCU
S	a respondent or other data source such as a single document in a CCM CMAP3 project
SBA	small business advisor
SCU	standard causal unit (a standard language node-node pair in a generated cause map)
SIM	semi-structured interviewing method
SME	small and medium-size enterprise/firm
SNT	standard node term (a standard language concept/node in a generated cause map)
ST	standard term, contained in a CMAP3 project's standard term vocabulary (STV)
STAG	an identifier of a standard term (ST) in a CMAP3 project's standard term vocabulary

STENG   standard term expressed in the secondary standard
             terminology/language (optional)

STERM   standard term expressed in the primary standard
             terminology/language

STM   short-term (aka working) memory

STV   standard term vocabulary (STV) in a CMAP3 project; used
             in coding/standardizing the NLUs; contains STs, STERMs and
             (optionally) STENGs

TBCM   text-based causal map

Td   total degree, a sum of Id and Od

TF   (total frequency) (Td) in a causal map/matrix

UEF   University of Eastern Finland

VICS   verb in the context system: a coding scheme of Profiler Plus

W   weight indicator of NCUs (optional)

Chapter 1

Introduction

Causal mapping emerged as a social research method around the late 1970s, pioneered in particular by two landmark publications: one, the 1976 edited volume of Robert Axelrod: *Structure of Decision: The Cognitive Maps of Political Elites*, and two, the 1977 *ASQ* paper *Cognition in Organizations: An Analysis of the Utrecht Jazz Orchestra* by Michel Bougon, Karl Weick and Din Binkhorst. Since then, causal mapping methods have gradually become an established although specialized approach in several fields. To some extent, the development was fostered by the increasing popularity and acceptance of interpretive and qualitative methods in social research generally and in management and organization studies specifically (see Bluhm et al. 2011, Maxwell 2004b). Another factor was the growing interest in adopting a *cognitive* perspective (Miller 2003), salient also in management and organization studies and in political science. The new research agendas also created a demand for new methods and tools. Causal and/or cognitive mapping offered an innovative, intuitively plausible and relatively uncomplicated way to operationalize and empirically study the new, often nebulous cognitive target phenomena such as organizational knowledge and beliefs.

The cognitive movement has proved robust during the last decades. For instance, in the USA, the Academy of Management's Management and Organization Cognition (MOC) Division, at the outset a small academic interest group, has become one of its largest divisions. In addition to key volumes such as Sims and Gioia (1986), Huff (1990), Meindl et al. (1996), Eden and Spender (1998), Huff and Jenkins (2002), and Narayanan and Armstrong (2005), there has been a steady stream of published research papers. Many of these studies use causal mapping methods, showing their versatility. This applies not only to management and organization research in business contexts, but fields such as, for example, environmental risk research (Vári 2004), health and nursing (Wiginton 1997), economic development (Hine et al. 2005), engineering (Carbonara and Scozzi 2006), management of intellectual capital (Montemari and Nielsen 2013) and public policy (Eden and Ackermann 2004). Although often overtly different, they share an interest in social actors' and collectivities' knowledge, its formation and impact in organizational or social contexts.

Interestingly, in the originating field of political and IR studies, causal mapping methods have been dormant, but seem to be awakening again. In general, such a pendulum-like movement of research approaches is not unusual in social sciences. They mirror the evolving research agendas and resulting methodological needs, sometimes simply random changes in subjective likings and conceptions of what is customary—or perhaps trendy—in a given field.

1.1   What Are Causal Maps?

A general idea of causal maps (and mapping) can be obtained by examining a typical specimen such as the one in Figure 1.1. It consists of nodes (words, concepts), which refer to some phenomena and their attributes, and arrows, which represent the influence or causal relationships of the nodes, more accurately between the phenomena that the nodes stand for. This is roughly what causal maps usually look like, although they can be more or less complicated, that is, contain more nodes and links and additional information specifying some characteristics of the causal relationships, such as their direction of influence.

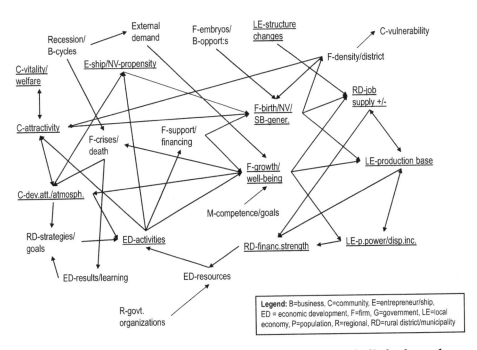

Figure 1.1   A causal map: rural municipality directors' beliefs about the local economy

Source: Laukkanen 2000.

This is perhaps an operational and practical answer to the question of what causal maps are. The more interesting issue, however, is what do they mean, represent or model? This is an ontological and methodological question, which has more than one conceivable answer. In general, there are two main alternative interpretations of causal maps and correspondingly different uses and purposes for them. Depending on the researcher's ontological stance, theoretical background, preferences and specific objectives, causal maps are usually defined as a model of either of the following two target phenomena:

1.   a single actor's or a collectivity's subjective phenomenological and causal knowledge (beliefs) patterns about a phenomenon, system or domain, or

2.   a physical, social or socio-technical system or mechanism, its structure and functional relationships.

In the former, *cognitive*, case, which is the dominant interpretation (in terms of published research), causal maps represent and operationalize some actors' cognitions, that is, their knowledge and/or beliefs about a given domain or issue. Notably, other terms such as mental model or cognitive map may be used to refer to the target phenomena in addition to knowledge or beliefs. Because of the key role that such essentially cognitive concepts have in causal mapping, we will discuss them in more detail in Chapter 2.

In the second, *system*, case, CCM studies' focus is not actors' cognitions or their knowledge patterns *per se*, but typically a social or socio-technical system such as an organizational process, a whole industry and its evolution, a local economy and its development drivers, and so on. Thus, the knowledge interest in such studies is the system itself, its entity structure and functioning, the research objective being, for example, to create a tentative model of the system to examine it or to influence or predict its behavior under different contingencies (Forrester 1971/1995, Roberts 1976). Further study goals could be designing a related ICT control system or to intervene in the processes by training people or by devising some system intervention. In the system case, cause maps have also been called influence diagrams or system models.

Which interpretation does the causal map in Figure 1.1 fit? Arguably, it could be both, depending on the researcher's viewpoint and purposes. Indeed, although often different in terms of *stated* objectives, the cognitive and systemic interpretations are not necessarily that far from each other conceptually or methodologically. First, a model or theory describing and explaining the structure and functioning of a system, for example a local economy, is usually or at least potentially something which the relevant persons in the context will probably share cognitively. It can be roughly defined as their typical way of conceptualizing and communicating about the system. Second, both cognitive and systemic causal mapping studies must often use similar research practices and methods. For example, in studies of the system modeling category, a typical starting point (and also the rationale) is that there is little or no previous knowledge about the target system at the outset, yet such knowledge is considered valuable, even critical, in pragmatic or research terms. Assuming such a situation, it makes obvious sense to go and ask people who should know the system well because of their long experience with it. They can be assumed to internalize the context and the system in order to cope with it or to control it. Furthermore, for a fuller and more accurate view, it is usually a good idea to approach several people and elicit their subjective concepts and causal beliefs and to explore what elements in the belief systems are shared or how the more idiosyncratic notions can be understood.

Comparative causal mapping (CCM) is a logical and efficient method for studies like those above. Why? CCM enables *aggregating* several respondents' views for a summarizing representation or model of the target system on the one hand. On the other hand we can pinpoint and examine the idiosyncratic, that is, less shared, elements in the belief patterns. When the research object is a real system, the data for the respective cause maps is typically acquired using a case-study-type saturation or engineering logic, which tries to maximize valid information yet watches carefully the marginal value added of additional packets of information. Therefore, in cases where some previous knowledge, at least at a general level, exists, the data can and probably must come from different parallel sources in addition to key actors in the context, such as textbooks, domain documents, field observations and interviewing of scientific experts. The objective is usually to obtain a tentative but empirically plausible model of the system so as to grasp and to conceptualize its key elements and underlying causal mechanisms. Depending on the system and the case, further research, for example laboratory tests or field surveys, may be used to deepen and validate the tentative model.

1.2 Visual vs. Non-Visual Presentation

While it is traditional to think of a causal "map" in visual terms, a causal map (more precisely, its information content) can and, depending on the purposes of research, indeed must often take also a non-visual form, either simultaneously or exclusively. To show this in practice, let us begin with a simple cause map such as the one depicted in Figure 1.2.

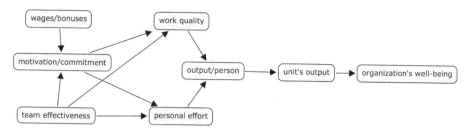

Figure 1.2   A causal map: aggregated belief patterns of factory supervisors

The first and most obvious non-visual alternative to the map is of course *text*. The causal map's contents in Figure 1.2 can be expressed in an informatively roughly equivalent text form as something like this:

> *This group of supervisors believes that their unit's output is important to the firm's overall success, and sees the output as a sum of what each employee in the unit produces. For them, the unit members' output depends on their personal effort and the quality of their outputs. These in turn depend, first, on the person's motivation and commitment, and, second, on the team's guiding and motivating impact. These supervisors are aware of the role of money, but see it as less important. Furthermore, they downplay the disciplinary functions, which are characteristic of their colleagues, who represent the more traditional role perception.*

In typical CCM studies, the sequence is reversed: they begin with textual data such as interview transcripts or documents, and end up with extracted visual causal maps. However, there are cases where it is important for additional analytical reasons to use other formats of representation than the two. Before addressing the other alternatives, it is useful to observe that the basic building block of a causal map is a pair or dyad of linked nodes. Even though it is customary to think of causal maps primarily in graphical terms, they cannot directly begin in a visual form. Instead, a researcher (or a practitioner) must first acquire the building blocks in some separate process. Only then can they process the data further and assemble it into a visual form by drawing by hand or using graphics software. For example, when someone uses a tool such as computerized concept or mind mapping, the node pairs could exist either in the mind mapper's working memory or they are extracted from a document. After this they can be converted into independent building blocks, which the researcher combines, piece by piece, into a graphic map form for further analysis or treatment. It follows that the visual form or dimension is not necessarily analytically the initial or primary one in causal mapping. Rather, it is the contents and meanings of the causal propositions understood as a holistic system. The overt format is generally a technical and secondary issue, which depends on the specific needs of the study and presentation.

A traditional non-visual way of presenting the key information of a causal map is a *square (adjacency) matrix* (Axelrod 1976, Bougon et al. 1977, Weick and Bougon 1986). In this case, the nodes of a map correspond to the rows ("causes") and columns ("effects") of a matrix. The existence of causal relation is denoted by "1" and the non-existence by "0". Matrices were common in early causal mapping studies in political science and organizational research. They enabled matrix mathematical operations on the basis of digraph theory, and to calculate influence paths, their lengths (in terms of phenomena in the causal chain), and different outcomes. Thereby, it was usually posited that the mapped system and its mechanisms actually exist and operate, as modeled, in the context (Axelrod 1976, pp. 349ff). This may or may not be the case, implying a risk that the matrix and path exercises can be carried too far if the actors' beliefs are accorded an unwarranted reified status of real systems. In typical CCM studies, which are largely about subjective cognitive phenomena, such mathematical operations are usually more or less pointless.

A third format of presentation is the *database table*, which explicitly displays the individual building blocks of node-node dyads. This is the format CMAP3 uses, which makes it particularly relevant here. In a database table (Figure 1.3), the individual causal pairs of concepts, of which the causal map in Figure 1.2 consists, are presented as datatable rows. The set displayed in Figure 1.3 corresponds to what the browsing module of CMAP3 shows. It could also exist in the form of *worksheet*, for example, as created by exporting CMAP3's corresponding file to MS Excel. The technical details will be discussed in Section 6.2.

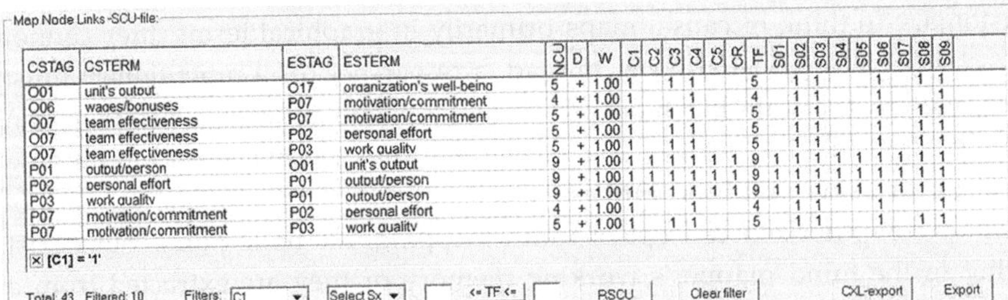

Map Node Links -SCU-file:

CSTAG	CSTERM	ESTAG	ESTERM	NCU	D	W	C1	C2	C3	C4	C5	CR	TF	S01	S02	S03	S04	S05	S06	S07	S08	S09
O01	unit's output	O17	organization's well-being	5	+	1.00	1	1					5	1	1				1		1	1
O06	wages/bonuses	P07	motivation/commitment	4	+	1.00		1					4	1	1				1			
O07	team effectiveness	P07	motivation/commitment	5	+	1.00	1	1	1				5	1	1				1		1	1
O07	team effectiveness	P02	personal effort	5	+	1.00	1	1					5	1	1				1		1	1
O07	team effectiveness	P03	work quality	5	+	1.00	1	1	1				5	1	1				1		1	1
P01	output/person	O01	unit's output	9	+	1.00	1	1	1	1	1	9	1	1	1	1	1	1	1	1	1
P02	personal effort	P01	output/person	9	+	1.00	1	1	1	1	1	9	1	1	1	1	1	1	1	1	1
P03	work quality	P01	output/person	9	+	1.00	1	1	1	1	1	9	1	1	1	1	1	1	1	1	1
P07	motivation/commitment	P02	personal effort	4	+	1.00	1						4	1	1				1			
P07	motivation/commitment	P03	work quality	5	+	1.00	1	1					5	1	1				1	1	1

⊠ [C1] = '1'

Total: 43   Filtered: 10   Filters: [C1 ▼]   [Select Sx ▼] [ ] <= TF <= [ ]   RSCU   Clear filter   CXL-export   Export

Figure 1.3   **A datatable presentation of the causal map in Figure 1.2**

In conclusion, it may be added that, compared with formats such as text or datatable, visual causal maps do have advantages, which is why using them at least in parallel with other formats can be useful. First, researchers, practitioners and readers may have different cognitive styles and preferences. Some prefer holistic visual information, imagery, some propositional text form and some numbers. Moreover, even for someone who routinely uses non-visual data, visual maps can provide a transparent, *systemic* and more communicable view of the target and thus facilitate a holistic comprehension and, above all, a mental simulation of the domain or system. This aspect probably underlies the use of causal mapping for heuristic and decision-support purposes (Bryson et al. 2004, Eden 1992, Eden and Ackermann 1998). In scientific reporting, in particular the differences or longitudinal changes in the target system or the respondents' thought patterns can be made more salient by visual causal maps. Sometimes they can suggest the reader details and implications, which the researcher did not mention, note or even think about.

1.3 Why Causal Maps?

In everyday communication, using a rather unconventional formalism like a causal map would probably not foster but rather complicate the processes of understanding. What then is the added value of causal maps and mapping compared with, say, using oral communication or texts for knowing or reporting about someone's beliefs? A brief answer is that causal maps are suited for certain types of communication and research tasks and may be clearly superior to conventional ways of communication, presentation and analysis. However, to use or not to use causal maps and some specific format is a case-by-case decision and depends on one's objectives. Some of the grounds for using causal maps include the following:

The first and probably most intuitive point is that (visual) causal maps provide a *holistic* view of the studied knowledge structure or system, its constitutive elements and the causal mechanisms, which are pertinent to the focal issue or domain. This form of presentation facilitates a *systemic, dynamic comprehension* of the issue or domain of interest, although that usually assumes an adequate pre-existing knowledge of the target phenomenon. In contrast, a text or oral discourse in daily communication, media and scientific publishing follow a *linear* sequence of transmission, conveying ideas one after another. The recipient must also receive the messages sequentially and process them to comprehend the meanings intended by the sender. This kind of transmission is often slow and inefficient in oral conversation. Using printed media or corresponding electronic media is more effective because it may be possible to return to the text when necessary.

Second, compared with an oral or textual description, a causal map can provide a compact, *parsimonious* way of representing complex causal beliefs patterns, especially for analytical purposes. It focuses on causal concepts (nodes) and their logical linkages and interactions. These are typically the most relevant elements and aspects in research and from the viewpoint of scholars and practitioners in fields related to public or business decision-making. Furthermore, as a mode of communication, this is often also more *reliable*, and less prone to selective biases in interpretation. This is an important dimension of empirical analysis when a causal map is derived from data elicited from diverse sources.

Third, a corollary of the above advantages is that a causal map can be superior to traditional presentation modes, when the task requires (mentally) *simulating* the behavior of a phenomenon or system for further understanding and prediction. Indeed, in the early causal mapping studies the typical research objective was to further understanding of decision-making cognitions and behavior as a quasi-rational process. The causal mapping method was argued to provide "a new and explicit way of conducting Weberian *verstehen-analyses*" (Bougon 1983, p. 182). A modern manifestation of this is the so-called *counterfactual* inference, which sometimes underlies this type of analysis (Byrne 2002, Tetlock 2001). For example, in the field of foreign policy analysis, political scientists typically ask *what-if* questions (Axelrod 1976). Using the information of actors' elicited belief systems presented as a causal map, they extrapolate the apparently underlying decision-making norms, and hypothesize what would happen in terms of decision outcomes if the belief systems change. A causal-map-based simulation is possible even for the idiosyncratic beliefs of a single actor, which normally stay covert in linear, interactive communications. An example is Cossette's (2002) study of Frederick Taylor's belief systems, extracted from Taylor's publications. However, this kind of simulation must be *qualitative*. Causal maps cannot simulate the dynamics of a system quantitatively, for example to predict the magnitude of causal effects of a factor or mechanism change. Simulations of this kind, for example in econometric modeling, can be undertaken by specialized software and computer systems. Nevertheless, causal maps that are properly derived from expert surveys can provide a useful starting point for constructing such dynamic, quantified models.

Fourth, a key reason for using causal maps—in fact, the point of departure of this book—is the need to *aggregate* and *comparatively* analyze the knowledge and belief patterns of several individual actors and collectivities. Aggregation and comparison are essential tasks in typical organizational cognitive studies for descriptive or explanatory purposes. In this context, CCM methods have unique advantages over traditional text-based analysis methods. This is easy to see by imagining a study which must distill and summarize the shared causal ideas of, say, 30 interviewees (possibly speaking different languages) regarding an issue. To a limited extent this can be done by manual methods and somewhat better by qualitative data analysis software (CAQDAS) (Levins and Silver 2007), which are designed for processing, coding and thematically analyzing rich qualitative data like narratives. It is, however, difficult to use such techniques for aggregating causal beliefs from several data sources (documents or interviewees), comparing belief patterns, calculating numerical indicators and presenting formal results. CCM methods and software like CMAP3 provide an intuitive and efficient way for such functions.

1.4 Plan of the Book

This book has four parts. The first consists of Chapter 2, which addresses some of the cognitive concepts and theoretical foundations that underlie causal mapping research, such as mental models and cognitive maps and the formation, stability and impact of knowledge. We believe this is useful for planning CCM research and for understanding the methodological preconditions of causal mapping in general and the applicability of different CCM methods.

The book's second part consists of Chapter 3. It describes the typical research approaches in comparative causal mapping, especially methods of data acquisition. It also examines methodological issues in CCM such as coding, aggregation, validity and quantifying causal maps. We also discuss selecting CCM methods.

The third part consists of Chapters 4 to 6. They deal with the technical how-to issues in CCM research when using CMAP3. They cover installing the software, preparing and entry of data, techniques of coding, generation of causal maps and their analysis. We recommend downloading and installing the CMAP3 software and testing the different functions by running the two default demo projects. This is a good way to get familiar with CMAP3 but also for understanding CCM in general. The three chapters provide a hands-on guide for CCM CMAP3 techniques for all users, but may be particularly interesting for someone who is just contemplating entering the CCM field.

The last part, Chapter 7, presents three study cases with the purpose of demonstrating CMAP3-based CCM research in practice. We believe that augmenting the previous chapters' more general discussion of cognitive concepts and different CCM methods and techniques with a more tangible description of real study examples is useful. This can highlight the main CCM approaches' methodological characteristics, resource requirements and technical alternatives to enable better informed research design and method selection decisions.

Chapter 2
Concepts in Comparative Causal Mapping

This chapter focuses on the target phenomena in causal mapping. In other words, what are causal maps supposed to represent? Are there perhaps divergent assumptions and interpretations? And if so, what are the implications? Admittedly, questions like these might seem an invitation for trouble and an unnecessary burden. Indeed, it is not unusual to see them bypassed in CCM literature by simply stating at the outset that one proposes to examine a plausible-sounding entity like cognitive maps, defining them tautologically in terms of other abstract notions like knowledge structures or mental models. However, an idea of notions such as mental representations and knowledge, their formation and impact, is necessary to appreciate the nature and complexity of the different cognitive factors and processes which are unavoidably involved in CCM. This is useful also for developing research questions and for understanding what is and what is not methodologically feasible and plausible in CCM research.

For the sake of discussion, let us begin with a thought experiment and assume a CCM study of a group of professionals such as small business advisors (SBAs). They could (as they were, see 7.2) be interviewed, among other things, about what they believe are the causes and consequences of nascent firms', their clients', growth. As responses we might hear, for instance, that growth (and smallness) depends on factors such as the entrepreneur's personality and competence, their goals, the kind of business, market demand factors, available financing, and so on. Furthermore, we would probably hear that growth creates things like more jobs and personal and societal wealth, but also has a flipside: more personal and financial risks, more work, and less independence and time for the family. This suggests some questions. Where and how do such responses (interview data) originate? In what forms do they exist in the persons' minds? What sources or generative mechanisms are there? Why are there causal statements that A causes B or B leads to C, and so on, that we hear from the respondents? Why just those and not something else? And finally, why is it that we hear similar things from persons in similar positions such as the SBAs and systematically different things from persons with different backgrounds?

In a broad sense, the answers and therefore also much of cognitive research and methods, including cognitive or causal mapping, can be traced back to some self-evident observations: First, social actors' knowledge and beliefs, which enable, if not a perfect, at least a sufficiently accurate cognitive grip of their everyday or professional contexts, are essential for action and performance, even for survival. Our knowledge and beliefs influence what we observe or ignore, what inferences we draw of the perceived information, how we solve problems, plan and decide, and finally, as a result, what courses of action, including non-action, we choose or recommend. This has consequences for us individually and organizations we manage and control. Second, no person can know and comprehend everything. Everyone must abstract and select, not necessarily mindfully, those aspects of the world one heeds to and those that will be ignored. Moreover, it is not sufficient to know or carve out only which things, factors and events exist. We must also understand how the world *works*, that is, why and how something happens and what could result from an event or a specific course of action, if chosen.

2.1   Models in the Mind

The basic idea of internal, cognitive representation and modeling, which also underlies causal mapping, is not a recent one. In a documented form it can be traced back to early Greek philosophers' treatises about perception and mental imagery. Their more recent followers include philosophers such as Kant, Peirce and Wittgenstein (see Johnson-Laird 2004b). Since the 1970s particularly, the notion of modeling has become increasingly prominent in many research fields and contexts. For instance, Forrester (1971/1995) emphasized the omnipresence of models and modeling when explaining the new field of "system dynamics" to the doubting Thomases of his time.

In cognitive psychology, the idea of a mental model or "simulacrum", in the literal sense of analogous representation, was apparently first proposed by Kenneth Craik, a pioneering UK cognitive psychologist, in the 1940s. Unfortunately, he died young. Developing Craik's ideas further, P.N. Johnson-Laird, a leading UK researcher of human reasoning, has explained the underpinnings of mental models as follows:

Understanding ... depends on knowledge and belief. If you know what causes a phenomenon, what results from it, how to influence, control, initiate, or prevent it, how it relates to other states of affairs or how it resembles them, how to predict its onset and course, what its internal or underlying 'structure' is, then to some extent you understand it. The psychological core of understanding ... consists in your having a 'working model' of the phenomenon in your mind. If you understand inflation, a mathematical proof, the way a computer works, DNA or a divorce, then you have a mental representation that serves as a model of an entity in much the same way as, say, a clock functions as a model of the earth's rotation. (Johnson-Laird 1983, p. 2)

As to the term *cognitive map*, it was probably first used by Edward Tolman, a US psychologist (Tolman 1948), to refer to the hypothesized *spatial* representations of animals (white rats navigating in mazes), that is, to their internal representations of two- or three-dimensional information of space. Of course, Tolman really assumed that something similar is going on in the human brain, too. Notably, in those days, mainstream psychological thinking was dominated by stimulus-response behaviorism, making it unorthodox to even propose that unobservable intervening elements such as "cognitive maps" could have explanatory powers. Because such things cannot be directly observed, only inferred, they were problematic for the "scientific" psychology of that era (for an interesting discussion of Tolman's experiments and his paradigmatic context, see Goldstein 2011, pp. 11ff). Perhaps ironically, the cognitivist perspective has since become more or less dominant and current psychology is very much occupied with issues of mental representation (mental models, schemata, cognitive maps, and so on), how they are computed, and how they influence reasoning and behavior.

Today, cognitive psychology and applied fields like cognitive geography have usually retained the original, Tolmanian, spatial interpretation of the term cognitive map (Kitchin 2001, Pick 2001). However, it is occasionally extended to also include other than physical environments (Kearney and Kaplan 1997), that is, used roughly in the same general sense as the mental model. For clarity and benefit of keeping the two different kinds of referents separate, however, it might be preferable to reserve the term "mental model" for this more general, and more frequent, conceptual meaning, and use the term "cognitive map" for the spatial sense. In this book, a "mental model" refers to the internal representations and knowledge structures of individuals and collectivities. Occasionally, terms like knowledge or belief system will be used. Thus, the term "causal/cause map" can be reserved for their visual or other overt descriptions.

In passing, it may be useful to note that the terms cognitive map and causal map too have been used in varying meanings in causal mapping literature. For instance, in the influential volume of Axelrod (1976) and thereafter (see, for example, Budhwar and Sparrow 2002, Carley 1997, Chaney 2010, Clarkson and Hodgkinson 2005, Doyle and Ford 1998, Tyler and Gnyawali 2009), cognitive maps often refer to *overt representations* of (for example, political) actors' knowledge/belief systems, that is, to the operationalizing devices like causal (cause) maps. In this view, a cognitive map is a *map of cognition*, that is, a model of somebody's (causal) knowledge and beliefs (mental models) in the same sense that a street map is a representation of a city. In the case of Eden et al. (1992, see also Ambrosini and Bowman 2002), a cognitive map is even less than that, understood only as a *visual tool* that can be heuristically useful for explicating somebody's ideas for heuristic and pragmatic purposes without making any claims of actually representing the actors' thoughts, let alone their thinking processes. Interestingly, for example, Bougon et al. (1977) used the term cause map to refer to organization members' internal notions and representations, that is, to their mental models in our present meaning. In their case this was understandable; the field and the focal phenomena were new and established terms did not exist. However, terminological innovativeness and inconsistency is not entirely unknown in later causal mapping literature. As already shown by Walsh (1995), especially MOC studies are often characterized by a wish to introduce new idiosyncratic terms instead of using established ones. More confusing is that the terms *cognitive map* and *causal map* may be used to refer to the internal knowledge structures *and* their operationalizing devices, occasionally to both even in the same paper.

As to *mental models* (or cognitive maps in the general sense), in cognitive psychology, they refer to a person's internal representations that are assumed to support understanding, reasoning and prediction about a domain, situation or logical task. Thus, the notion also conceptualizes how knowledge is assumed to be created, stored and used by an adult person (see, for example, Fiske and Taylor 2013, Johnson-Laird 2004a, 2005, Jones et al. 2011, Markman and Dietrich 2000, Markman and Gentner 2001). Mental models can be understood as systems of mental *symbols or tokens*, which represent, that is, are considered at least roughly *isomorphic* or *analogous (iconic)*, with some relevant aspects of the environment or some entity (Evans 1988, Fiske and Taylor 2013, Gallistel 2002, Gentner 2004, Gordon 1992, Gruber 2004, Pinker 2008, Sloman and Hagmayer 2006). Cognitive psychology and related fields like cognitive anthropology also have other terms, which too denote model-like representational and sense-making structures. For example, the term *schema*, which refers to *general* belief structures, is sometimes used instead of mental models (or cognitive maps).

Scripts are a special type of schema, which represent event sequences in a linear temporal order. *Frames* or frames of reference (Fiske and Taylor 2013, LeBoeuf and Shafir 2005, Pinker 1997) also have parallels with mental models. They define those aspects of a situation that are heeded to and in which terms it will approached, Finally, *naive* or *folk theories* (Gelman and Legare 2011) are also models but usually denote wider systems of beliefs about larger domains such as environmental trends, fiscal policies or biology. In particular, theories like this and mental models overlap, though the latter are typically more specific in their application than theories (Markman and Gentner 2001, p. 230).

To complicate matters slightly, there are two main approaches to the study of mental models in cognitive psychology (Markman and Gentner 2001, pp. 228–9). The first, represented by Johnson-Laird, Byrne and their colleagues,[1] sees mental models as *transitory* working memory constructs that support logical reasoning tasks (Johnson-Laird 1983, 2005, 2008). These Markman and Gentner (2001) call *logical* mental models. In the second view, mental models are interrelated systems of causal knowledge and beliefs, which support understanding and reasoning in knowledge-rich domains. These are called *causal* mental models. By necessity, they too are built in the working memory, but they are assumed to also draw on knowledge, which is retained as long-term memory structures (Markman and Gentner 2001, p. 229). The causal mental model view is the dominant, although sometimes implicit, interpretation in causal mapping and MOC studies and literature. It is also the one we use in this book.

To sum up, mental models can refer narrowly to transitory cognitive devices, which are constructed ad hoc in the short-term working memory (STM) for logical (syllogistic) reasoning from premises (Gentner 2004, Johnson-Laird 2004a, 2005, 2008, Jones et al. 2011). In the present wider meaning, (causal) mental models are cognitive representations, knowledge structures and "runnable" situational models for mental simulation in the mind's eye in the conscious working memory. Depending on the case, mental models can be created ad hoc, but also recalled from memory for different situational needs of comprehension, explanation and projection (Frederiksen 2004, Fiske and Taylor 2013). Often they will be a combination of both. Indeed, when engaged in cognitive tasks like problem-solving or decision-making, a person can be assumed to use not only the immediately perceived information or premises, but also retained knowledge, which is searched and eventually recalled from the long-term memory (LTM). Depending on the specific task, overall

---

1   See http://mentalmodels.princeton.edu/.

situation and personal factors, the triggered and recalled materials can include analogous, iconic elements like experienced events, entities or processes, and propositional knowledge, which vary in abstractness and generality versus domain specificity.

That people tend to process information in such a "theory-driven" manner is currently widely accepted among scholars of cognition and decision-making. On the one hand, mental models influence what and how information is available and can be retrieved. On the other hand, new incoming information in STM tends to be assimilated into pre-existing structures of knowledge (Aronson et al. 2012, Conover and Feldman 1984, Larson 1994). It can be seen that the notion of mental models implies a complex of different cognitive contents and processes, which can be involved in creating, storing and using knowledge, depending on the case. For example, when building ad hoc a situational model for comprehending a given real situation, a person may first try to recall and use their repertoire of general, abstract models. These can include broad metaphors and analogies (Gavetti and Rivkin 2005, Ghyczy 2003) and something like naïve or folk theories (Gelman and Legare 2011). Such an initial framework, cognitive scaffolding, needs to be adapted, updated and coordinated in terms of local information about the immediate context. However, the new data and information will be sought, perceived and interpreted (or blocked) using *previous* beliefs and models as filtering "lenses". An example of this might be how a physician works with someone having a heart problem. As a trained person, they would begin with a general idea of how a heart normally functions. Using various diagnostic methods they can test different hypotheses, eliminate some causes and mechanisms, and eventually arrive at a situational model, called a diagnosis, which seems to explain that particular patient's problem and suggests a treatment. However, different physicians can have and arrive at different models which influence what hypotheses they generate and, eventually, the efficacy of the selected treatment.

To complicate matters, there are also *tacit* processes in play, called, for example, imagination or creativity. Even in everyday situations, when engaged in a mental simulation of a recalled iconic or abstract conceptual model, a person can, in the mind's eye, go quite far from the initial image and situational premises and create widely different explanations and potential future event scenarios. In scientific research this is normal. Well-known examples are deducing testable hypotheses from existing theories, using Einsteinian thought experiments for theory generation, the induction of patterns and new concepts in case research (Eisenhardt and Graebner 2007), counterfactual analysis (Byrne 2002) and, of course, the sudden enlightenment and insight which often comes after a long gestation period preceded by gathering of data and trials and errors.

The above notions have some presently relevant implications. Most evidently, mental models do not refer to any general cognitive dimension such as aptitude or intelligence, nor should we assume that someone could have a single mental model which resides somewhere in the LTM, waiting to be recalled one-to-one in a problem-solving situation, or, for that matter, in a CCM interview. Instead, there are many and different things in people's minds: retained models and a huge amount of propositional and iconic knowledge items and structures, varying in abstractness and generality. That such cognitive contents cannot constitute a single entity, recallable (or mappable) as such, is evident considering the size and complexity of the knowledge of a normal adult, let alone an experienced, educated professional (Chi and Ohlsson 2005, Evans 1988). It can usually be assumed that adult people possess large repertoires of general and domain-specific knowledge and models (Hirschfeld and Gelman 1994, Markman and Gentner 2001) at different levels of abstraction, generality and accuracy. These necessarily reside in the long-term memory and are therefore variably accessible.

An important special case is *expertise* (Evans 1988, Gruber 2004, Hirschfeld and Gelman 1994). One of its defining elements is, first, knowledge that goes way beyond lay ideas in terms of domain coverage, detail and accuracy. It is also often based on formal verification like scientific research and systematic diffusion of working knowledge within a community of practice (see below). By definition, professionals gather and possess advanced knowledge, which is characteristic of their fields of expertise or life domains. However, whilst knowledgeable and skillful in a special field, in other domains professionals are cognitively in the same position as any layperson. Moreover, they, as other people, can also possess mutually conflicting models, even for the same domain (Gentner 2004). Many beliefs and models are seldom tested against each other or against some quasi-objective reality simply because there is no pressing need to do so.

Conceptually, the relation between notions of knowledge and mental models is a complex one. First, mental models, especially retained, can be considered *knowledge*, one form of it. For instance, we can "know" how a technical device like a vacuum cleaner or a socio-technical system such as a macro economy is built, what its components are and, roughly, how it works. Second, mental models enable *generating* new knowledge through reasoning based on propositional causal knowledge and situational information.

Examples are the prediction and knowing that if A happens, so will B, or when someone infers that because C exists, A and B must have occurred, too. Third, causal propositional knowledge triggers and enables *creating* mental models and thus new knowledge. For an example, a typical small business advisor knows that unemployment is a major burden on public resources. Consequently, it is likely that many SBAs would conclude that increasing self-employment will reduce unemployment and free public resources and increase welfare. Such causal knowledge can become a part of their mental models about the consequences of creating new firms.

What makes the notion of mental models so relevant in causal mapping, perhaps vice versa, too? On the one hand, this follows from the target phenomena, that is, causal mental models, and what causal maps can do as a representation device on the other hand. First, models (other than the logical ones) are essentially *causal* and consist predominantly of propositional causal knowledge. The causality aspect is particularly salient when mental models are created, recalled or exchanged and developed in social communication to enable an individual or collective "mind's eye" experimentation and simulation to explain or predict events or to evaluate and choose action alternatives. For such pragmatic purposes, mental models *have* to contain or generate causal propositions or simulated images of processes. These can be verbally expressed in causal terms (Markman and Dietrich 2000, Markman and Gentner 2001, Pinker 2008, Sloman and Hagmayer 2006).

Thus, there is a correspondence or equivalence in terms of content. By definition, causal propositions imply two types of knowledge about the focal domain's entities and mechanisms: (a) *phenomenological* beliefs (that certain things, characteristics, events and factors A, B, and so on, exist or that B is/ has C, and so on) and (b) *causal* beliefs (including correlational and temporal knowledge that A leads to or precedes B, C follows from/after B, or D is an outcome of C, and so on). In addition, of course, active mental models may well contain more and different types of knowledge such as procedural and iconic knowledge (images) about entities and their behaviors. They can also include conceptions about the relative importance and specific characteristics of the entities or their causal relationships. From a causal mapping perspective, however, the main point is that to the extent mental models contain causal propositions they can be usefully operationalized as causal maps.

Finally, there is also a broad equivalence of knowledge type or level. The propositional knowledge about causal relationships, which people have and can cognitively process as mental models in the working memory, is mainly *linear, qualitative* and *ordinal* (Gentner 2004). Whilst thus necessarily often fuzzy and informatively weaker than quantitative and evidence-based relationships, this level of knowledge is, in addition to being cognitively feasible, usually sufficient for those pragmatic purposes people have. Importantly, this is also the level or type of information that causal maps can capture and represent.

2.2   Formation of Causal Ideas

In typical causal mapping studies, the research task is usually *descriptive*, focused on *what is* type questions such as which specific causal belief systems (mental models) certain actors have relative to a given domain or issue. However, causal mapping studies can also address *explanatory* and/or *predictive* questions. They are involved, for example, when trying to understand why and how some actors have adopted just some specific beliefs and not something else or what practical consequences that could have. Therefore, the formation of causal beliefs/knowledge and the general routes and mechanisms involved are relevant issues. There are often two further aspects. One is to explain the *specific* knowledge contents that have been adopted; the other concerns the *permanence* (volatility) of knowledge and beliefs. Thereby, we use the terms knowledge and belief as synonyms to refer to propositions about the world that a person or a collectivity uses and holds (consciously) to be true, or at least does not question seriously (Good 2001).

In Western and in particular Anglo-Saxon tradition it has been and is common to emphasize individual-level experiential and vicarious learning as the main source of knowledge/beliefs. Obviously, this is one key mechanism in everyday and professional contexts. Related processes include perception, inference and reasoning about possible causes when explaining events and phenomena. Thus, several cognitive factors and processes are involved. In particular the adoption of causal beliefs has been described as a process of backward reasoning, which begins when something different, unexpected or problematic is noticed (Einhorn and Hogarth 1987). The next stage is attribution: a search for potential causal factors that could explain the perceived anomaly or event. If/when found, causal candidates will be examined and tested, whereby the main cognitive task is to detect a connection path or mechanism that can plausibly link the event and the cause and thus provide an explanation and understanding of the former. In these processes, people are known to pay attention to logical aspects like covariation, temporal proximity and sequential order of occurrence. Moreover, sometimes people may intuitively expect that a potential causal candidate should have some overt similarity with the explained thing or event. For example, a small, let alone normally invisible, thing (microbe such as a virus) was not earlier and may still not be an intuitively plausible explanation of a major consequence (disease, epidemic) for many lay persons.

There are several factors that influence causal reasoning and make the outcome difficult to predict. First, as noted, people's *retained beliefs and models* influence which aspects and factors of the situation are perceived or ignored. In particular, although the basic logic of explaining and understanding remains, in professional and organizational contexts the explanatory chains and mechanisms are often established and readily available. A typical example of this is ICT systems, which are used to monitor and control organizational processes and alert actors about anomalies. By definition, organizations have—consist of—established practical knowledge about how things are "known" to work or should be done. This enables faster and more reliable and predictable reactions, but implies also risks of mindless action and slow adaptation. Second, there are generic biases or tendencies that can influence attribution processes (see, for example, Bazerman and Moore 2008, Fiske and Taylor 2013, Kahneman 2011). For example, the so-called *availability bias* means that salient, easily observed factors and events in the situation will be more likely considered as initial explanatory causal candidates. A special case of this is the so-called *fundamental attribution error*, whereby overweight is given to visible actors in the situation, their disposition and characteristics, for example, the entrepreneur or top management as the main explanation of the success or demise of a firm (see, for example, Fiske and Taylor 2013, p. 169). A further common phenomenon is the *confirmation bias*: people have a tendency to notice and prefer, even to actively seek, evidence which supports their prior beliefs or initial explanatory hypotheses. A consequence is that divergent observations will be resisted, with harmful consequences for learning and new ideas. This is contrary to what, for example, scientists are trained and expected (in principle) to do: to deliberately and systematically seek *disconfirming* evidence (Markman and Gentner 2001).

Although difficult to measure (Chi and Ohlsson 2005), it is obvious that the knowledge base of a normal adult, let alone an educated professional, is huge. However, experiential learning is not the main mechanism behind this. In developed societies and professional contexts, knowledge and beliefs are predominantly acquired through social interaction and diffusion (Bandura 1986, 2001, Fiske and Taylor 2013, Pinker 1997). Such life-long processes and arenas include the early growth environment, different cultural milieus and later formal education and participation in organizational and professional environments. How do we acquire notions such as virus, radiation, motivation, organization, management, culture, strategy, manager, fiscal deficit, unemployment, age pyramid, global warming and many many others? We do not observe and conceptualize such things ourselves. Instead, we are told or educated about them directly or more often by reading or hearing about them. When this occurs repeatedly and the learned notions appear necessary and relevant professionally or for personal well-being, intellectual curiosity or social status, they will be gradually internalized. We begin to consider them as our own knowledge and use them more or less automatically when thinking and communicating about the respective phenomena.

It may be noted in passing that the very idea of causation and thus much of the basis of causal knowledge and beliefs, which cause mapping is about, is not at all obvious. Causality has been formally controversial at least since the late 1700s when Hume argued that causal relations cannot be observed and thus empirically shown (Byrne 2002, Gadenne 2001, Pinker 2008). They can be only inferred, based on *spatial* or *temporal contiguity* of observed phenomena, that is, on weak *correlational* evidence. Paradoxically, to some a corollary is that research and methods, which *study* causal beliefs, must also be controversial. This, however, confuses two things: one, what can be formally shown about a given state of affairs and its causal mechanisms, and two, what some people subjectively consider true and believe about it. Both aspects are obviously important and thus legitimate topics of research. It may be added that especially in social sciences the above traditional *regularity view* of causality is being increasingly contested and replaced by a *process view*. The so-called realist position (Maxwell 2004b) in philosophy of science does not regard causality necessarily as consisting of regularities but of real and potentially observable causal mechanisms and processes, which can (but must not) manifest themselves as regularities. Interestingly, CCM research is usually about exploring just such mechanisms and processes, or more often, about how some real actors seem to conceptualize them.

Controversial or not, causality has proved robust as an everyday and scientific notion and premise of action. This also has compelling grounds, largely based on the functional role of causal thinking. For one thing, as is often pointed out, it is difficult to even imagine a "non-causal" world, functioning without the assumption of causal knowledge or beliefs, however problematic formally (Axelrod 1976, Buehner and Cheng 2005, Pinker 2008, Rouse and Morris 1986, Sloman and Hagmayer 2006). Purposive behavior requires *symbolic* thinking, that is, internalizing what phenomena exist in the environment, explaining and understanding why something happens, and predicting what will *follow* of external events or one's own actions. This is perhaps one reason why causal and/or stable temporal relations are usually taken for granted in everyday thinking. Mental models and relevant knowledge also facilitate seeing what is important or irrelevant and thus where attention and efforts should be focused. For problem-solving and decision-making, they indicate alternatives and enable evaluating them in terms of immediate objectives and more distant goals. Such functions and outcomes are important pragmatically. It is therefore not difficult to see why causal beliefs are emphasized in discussions of policy and organizational decision-making (Forrester 1971/1995, Hodgkinson and Healey 2008, Holsti 1976, Huntington 2002).

In addition, there are *psychological* and *social* factors. For example, people's knowledge and beliefs and mental models often mirror *shared* patterns of thinking largely because of their social origins. Importantly, sharedness enables social and professional cohesion, communication and organized cooperation. In addition, a person's knowledge and mental models, even those that are perhaps objectively dubious, can give a personal feeling of comprehension and provide a *sense of cognitive control* and *security* (Einhorn and Hogarth 1987). In social contexts, they sustain at least an appearance of comprehension and cognitive control. For these purposes, even inaccurate and illusory models may suffice. As noted, we can also have those, which follows partly from the fact many everyday beliefs and "folk theories" are never really tested in practice against evidence or against each other's implications logically. Thus laypersons and experts alike can possess accurate knowledge but also conflicting and mistaken conceptions about what exists and how things work.

The learning processes, however, do not explain the *contents*: what *specific* knowledge and beliefs will be learned and why. One obvious explanation of this is *functional*: people can be assumed to adopt contents which are necessary and useful in terms of their social background, organizational position and recurring tasks. At a societal level, the same processes are manifested in the slowly evolving division of labor and established professions in modern societies. Paralleling social specialization, there are bodies of knowledge which are considered standard in a specific field and will thus define the related professions and fields in knowledge terms at a given time. Moreover, societies have educational systems which mirror and reproduce the specialized structures. They transfer each field's standard knowledge and belief systems and often also inculcate specific value systems and behavioral patterns. As a result, important parts of modern knowledge are not adopted piecemeal but rather as whole packages belonging to a given field or line of education and profession. This, however, is not all. Practitioners in different fields, industries and specific organizations and professions must and will develop specific knowledge and ways of thinking which reflect and are adapted to their particular needs. Driven by shared tasks and supported by field- or industry-typical transfer mechanisms and arenas, the participants' knowledge and belief patterns will become more or less unified, at least a common core of mental models will gradually emerge (Laukkanen 1994, Porac et al. 1989).

Important manifestations of the above functional logic and social diffusion are so-called *epistemic communities* (Haas 2001) and *communities of practice* (Brown and Duguid 2001, Thompson 2005, Wenger and Snyder 2000, Wenger 2001). Their members have shared practices, evidenced in common resources like experiences, stories, tools and ways of addressing recurring problems. Especially in research and business organizations, a key driver of communities of practice is the members' need to repeatedly solve similar tasks. This and the arena-specific methods of communication tend to homogenize the participants' problem-solving approaches, knowledge bases and belief patterns. This will be manifested in the broad similarity of concepts, terms and underlying belief patterns (Carley 1997, Hutchins 2001). An example of a community of practice is the small business advisors (SBAs) who participated in the CCM study discussed in Section 7.2.

2.3   Stability and Change of Thinking

In causal mapping research, the stability of beliefs is a significant issue. Should the mental models underlying actors' reasoning and decision-making be volatile and unpredictable, it would be both difficult and even pointless to study them. Fortunately, this is not the main case. Whilst the mental models accessed and generated in situational communication are necessarily transitory short-term memory contents, the *underlying* models, knowledge and beliefs residing in long-term memory and also people's reasoning tendencies seem relatively stable.

The permanence has several grounds. Perhaps the most important is that significant parts of organizational and professional knowledge and beliefs—which are also the typical targets of causal mapping studies—are functional and instrumental. They are intimately linked to professions and specific work domains and serve recurring tasks in organizational contexts. They are often critical for organizational and individual performance. A corollary is that as long as the task environment itself does not or does not seem to change, there are fewer grounds and less pressure to change the existing patterns of beliefs and to introduce new ideas. Another permanence factor is that many of the beliefs, which underlie organizational and social behaviors, are deep-seated and culturally sanctioned. Thus, even if someone might wish to reject them, they may find that difficult. This is reinforced by the fact that work-related and professional knowledge-in-use is specialized and distributed organizationally, that is, has its own division of labor. This too is stabilizing because organizational changes involve many people. Adopting new ideas and changing previous ideas demands rejecting old ones and often structural changes, too. All that can be found asymmetrically needless and risky, if the changes' value and validity have not been unequivocally demonstrated or immediately obvious.

In addition, there are stabilizing factors at individual level. One is the earlier noted epistemological problem. Verifying new ideas' utility or invalidating old notions, especially those concerning social and psychological phenomena, can be difficult, if not impossible, at least expensive. As a consequence, if/when unequivocal evidence of the accuracy or validity of knowledge is not available (or the actors do not wish to seek it as a result of biases or social pressure), the standard and cognitively more convenient solution is to employ proxy evidence such as the field's or organization authorities' opinions or so-called "common sense" instead of specific experimental data. The overall outcome is that previous ideas, which *seem* to work (again partly a subjective assessment), are not easily abandoned. A further important stability factor is that the acquisition of new knowledge, and its common byproduct of having to unlearn old beliefs, implies costs and cognitive work, sometimes cognitive stress and cognitive dissonance. It is well known that people are, as a rule, cognitive "misers" or economizers, who would rather minimize thinking when possible (see, for example, Fiske and Taylor 2013). People prone to the confirmation bias, for example, tend to accept evidence that supports their pre-existing beliefs or the first plausible-appearing explanations that have come to mind.

However, although the tendency of pre-existing beliefs may be to persist, knowledge and belief systems do change, but the scale and pace of this vary by individuals and organizations. First, a person can change their beliefs, even rapidly, assuming the absence of the external conditions discussed above. However, most changes take place at the periphery of belief systems. For someone to change their most central beliefs usually requires very strong emotional experiences or highly salient evidence, which unambiguously shows the previous beliefs' inaccuracy and/or the new ideas' higher utility. In addition, change usually needs social examples, sometimes pressure from one's peers or accepted authorities. Importantly, conditions like that can exist in an appropriate culture, for example, a research community. Sometimes they are created through deliberate managerial action, which encourages acceptance of erring and of searching and testing of new ideas, instilling a "learning culture" into the organization.

Second, in particular organizational and professional knowledge and mental models cannot stay unchanged for ever. They have to evolve. This, however, happens mainly gradually, too, by unnoticed processes of forgetting and attrition, largely driven by constant addition of new knowledge. Following the functional logic, the new knowledge and models usually reflect the individual's or the organization's responses to changes in the task environment, organizational structures and goal-setting, sometimes also the exit and entry of people in the social system. The adoption of the new knowledge is thereby often fostered by the fact that it is perceived as new and non-competing and thus cognitively and socially less problematic. Because of the general slowness in organizational learning processes, studying the evolution and changes of knowledge can be challenging. It may take years of longitudinal study. That changes do happen and, moreover, follow the logic of preserving a working isomorphism between the operative knowledge and the strategic and operating context is, however, clear. For example, in a CCM study of the mental models of a Finnish CEO (Laukkanen 2001), the span of time covered eight years. During that period, the Finnish economy experienced a severe depression and the firm's strategic and operative environment shifted dramatically as a result of external changes, such as the introduction of new product categories, adoption of ICT technologies and the emergence of new "lean" business practices. In the CEO's new causal maps, collected using the same method as earlier, the evolution was clearly visible in a number of new concepts and causal mechanisms as well as in the disappearance of several earlier notions.

2.4   Impact of Knowledge

Underpinning most theorizing and research about notions such as knowledge or mental models is the implicit premise that what people know, believe and how they reason is important, sometimes even critical. In everyday contexts this is usually unquestioned, as based on daily evidence. For instance, people customarily consult knowledgeable experts, not random persons on the street, about important medical or legal matters. Moreover, everybody has occasionally experienced not knowing something vital or interesting and had momentary difficulties in recalling or comprehending something. More dramatic evidence of cognitions' impact is brain damage caused by an accident or a disease like Alzheimer's, which cause a temporary or an irrevocable loss of the cognitive foundations of intelligent behavior. Thus, cognitions obviously matter. However, for research purposes, just observing that is not sufficient. We also need an idea about how knowledge and mental models function and are mediated or translated into decisions, action and outcomes and which characteristics and aspects of knowledge are relevant from an action viewpoint.

One line of MOC and political sciences research on knowledge impact has focused on *cognitive complexity*, which refers to how far actors' beliefs are differentiated and integrated as manifested in the relative number (richness) of concepts and their interconnections in the belief system or mental model about an issue domain (see, for example, Tetlock 2005, Walsh 1995). The complexity idea is salient in many causal mapping and related studies (Carley 1997, Clarkson and Hodgkinson 2005, Eden et al. 1992, Mohammed et al. 2000, Nadkarni and Narayanan 2005, Walsh 1995). A possible reason is that cause maps provide a handy device for operationalizing people's conceptual differentiation and integration. Moreover, they facilitate convenient quantitative measures of complexity, as will be shown later.

Why should cognitive complexity matter? The reasoning is that complexity is related to an actor's ability to view things from different perspectives, to understand the issues more deeply and thus to see and devise more and better alternative solutions for cognitively tackling the different problems (Bartunek et al. 1983). In his landmark study of over 284 foreign policy experts, the political psychologist Philip Tetlock finds that "foxes"—who are predisposed to a complex, skeptical cognitive style—perform better at short-term forecasting than their "hedgehog" counterparts, analysts who "know one big thing" and "aggressively extend the explanatory reach of that one big thing into new domains" (Tetlock 2005, pp. 73–5). The worst performers tend to be "hedgehogs", who embark on tasks of long-term prediction with considerable confidence (Stein 2013). Thus, complexity should influence and correlate positively with cognitive performance. However, in typical MOC studies, the complexity argument is usually taken to a higher level of analysis. It is suggested, for example, that a CEO's or top management team's cognitive complexity also positively affects the respective organization's performance. Whilst this is intuitively appealing, there are some issues.

First, what is plausible at individual level cannot necessarily be projected to higher levels, arguing, for example, that cognitively complex managers' firms perform well, whereas unsophisticated managers' firms do not. One problem is that the mediating paths from what, for example, a CEO thinks, communicates and does to the level of the organization's measurable cumulative performance are often long and complicated. In addition, external factors can influence what happens in or to an organization, often dramatically. However, this does not mean that there are no linkages between managerial cognitions and firm performance or that they are too weak to be relevant and worth studying. It is well known that erroneous managerial beliefs sometimes generate decisions which put the organization in a vulnerable position and may create a crisis.

However, if it is argued that policy-makers' complexity or some specific beliefs influence their organizations' performance, a plausible path or mechanism must be shown through which this is realized. The classic CCM study of Hall (1976) described such a case: rise and fall of the old *Saturday Evening Post*. A general difficulty is that the mediating processes, especially in large multi-layered organizations like LSEs, are complex and slow. In contrast, in small owner-managed firms, the leading figure's impact is usually more direct, rapid and transparent and the mediation processes thus more traceable (Laukkanen 1997). It follows that cognitive research in organizations may have to choose between two strategies. If one simply must study large organizations, one may have to focus on more concrete, intermediate forms of key actors' beliefs' impact, de-emphasizing cumulative and long-term performance perhaps excepting major crises. The other route is to study small organizations such as SMEs or micro firms and their more transparent processes. This would mimic natural sciences' typical use of prototypes, simple organisms and laboratory tests.

Second, and perhaps more importantly, it can be argued that, as a dimension of knowledge, complexity is a *derivative* and thus secondary aspect, whilst the real issue is how pertinent and valid (isomorphic) the actor's or collectivity's knowledge is relative to the operating tasks, context and systems. This decides the quality of the *cognitive grip* of the task situation the actors can/will have, and thus the extent to which they can adapt to it or control it, as far as that is feasible in each case. It is possible that a solid grip manifests itself in more complexity, but this is not necessary. The key question is the *isomorphism* of the knowledge relative to the situation and its demands. In this respect, at least two interrelated dimensions can be differentiated.

The first is the *coverage* of knowledge or mental models, that is, the isomorphism and correspondence of, say, a management team's aggregate knowledge on the one hand, and the strategic and operative domain's key elements and their characteristics. To use a metaphor, one should have a map of the terrain where one moves, not of some other terrain. Moreover, the detail level or grain of the map should be appropriate for the task at hand. The second aspect, *accuracy* or *validity*, means that the discerned phenomena and entities and the causal beliefs held or formed and accessed are essentially correct or true. In practice this means that if someone believes (and acts accordingly) that

A influences B, A and B must both exist and there must also be present a stable causal or quasi-causal (for example, a tight temporal) relationship between them.

Obviously, coverage and validity are relative matters. As noted above, a major difficulty in managerial and political decision-making is that the relevant knowledge and models concern *social* phenomena, where there are seldom, if ever, *invariant*, evidence-based causal relationships such as those (assumed) in natural sciences. Instead, typical knowledge is largely probabilistic, about propensities and likelihoods that things *often* behave in a certain way, but sometimes not. Moreover, especially in strategic decision-making, the level of knowledge is often even lower than this, yet decisions must be made. This is usually realized by resorting to inferences, logic, projection from parallel cases and metaphors, and sometimes simply hunches and intelligent guesses. In ambiguous and fuzzy situations the prudent manager's solution is a stepwise, testing approach. Resources will be committed only gradually, based on intelligent feedback and accumulating evidence which confirms or helps adjust the underlying initial models and beliefs (Collins and Hansen 2011).

There is also empirical evidence supporting the isomorphism argument. In MOC, an early tradition focused on the *pathological* aspects of organizational beliefs such as missing or plainly erroneous knowledge, and its consequences and problems. It was argued that key managers' beliefs determine the strategies the firm adopts, which explains the firm's performance, in particular its decline and crises (Bettis and Prahalad 1995, Hall 1976, 1984, McNamara et al. 2002, Nystrom and Starbuck 1984, Prahalad and Bettis 1986, Starbuck et al. 1978). Studying collapsed firms, that is, ultimate crises, is partly explained simply by a better access to data. Whilst plausible and pragmatically relevant (Walsh 1995), this research tradition may, however, overemphasize the role of managerial cognitions, especially if it is assumed that there always exists some compact set of managerial beliefs with exceptional leverage, which can be found out in a brief interview or documentary data. Such a "small error-big consequences" hypothesis usually oversimplifies managerial thinking and its impact. Second, whilst focusing on organizational crises often produces fascinating reading and findings, crises are not necessarily symmetrical with normal situations.

Although intuitively obvious, the notion of isomorphism and cognitive grip presents a methodological problem: how to define and show that something *specific* and important is missing or inaccurate in some actors' belief systems. Obviously, a researcher cannot usually know this *a priori* nor decide that themselves. For example, the above crisis studies were done *ex post* as a kind of a post mortem using data of the focal firm and actors. However, there also had to be some evidence that other competing firms, which prospered, thought and did something essentially differently. A similar situation arises when the research task is to locate ideal knowledge patterns and mental models in a profession or an ongoing organization's domain. That requires a design that systematically compares well and weakly performing actors' belief patterns. This is one type of MOC research where CCM methods can be used (Laukkanen 1997).

2.5 Towards Eliciting Knowledge and Mental Models

This section forms a bridge to the next chapters' discussion of CCM methods by discussing the notions of mental models and causal knowledge from an empirical data acquisition viewpoint. Essentially, the question is how entities like knowledge/beliefs or mental models are known and what implications the underlying cognitive processes have in terms of CCM data and findings.

To recapitulate, (causal) mental models or cognitive maps in the general (causal) sense are *theoretical constructs* which refer to an individual actor's or a collectivity's interrelated sets of causal knowledge and beliefs about an issue or domain. Some causal models and knowledge are *retained* in the long-term memory and recalled to the conscious short-term (working) memory for further processing. Some will be *created* by ad hoc reasoning, problem-solving and imagination processes, also in the working memory. It follows that we are dealing with internal representations and memory contents and ad hoc products, that is, *covert* phenomena, which cannot be observed independently of their owner. As such, there is nothing unusual about this. Social research studies have many notions such as ideal types or attitudes, values or different types of intelligence, which are also theoretical constructs (Fiske and Taylor 2013, Sternberg and Sternberg 2012). They refer to individual characteristics, traits or cognitive capacities and serve typically as hypothesized mediating variables in explanatory models. They too are not observable but must be inferred and operationalized based on *overt* responses to stimuli such as questionnaires or standard tests.

The situation in *cognitive psychology* and neighboring applied fields like studies of expertise or artificial intelligence (AI) is similar. To elicit people's knowledge and constructs like mental models they must use direct or indirect methods based on what people say or do (Ericsson et al. 2006, Evans 1988, Gentner 2004, Hoffman and Lintern 2006, Klein and Hoffman 2008, Rouse and Morris 1986). The *direct* methods include interviews and questionnaires, which explicitly inquire about the participants' beliefs. A slightly different, partly indirect method are so-called think-aloud protocols, collected when participants verbally describe the flow of their reasoning during a problem-solving task. In addition, cognitive psychologists use *indirect* methods, because some types of knowledge like tacit ideas or procedural knowledge about how something is done cannot always be fully articulated. Indirect methods include analyzing participants' answers and in particular systematic errors when answering model-based questions, their response times, or clinical studies of eye movements when respondents select concepts. Indirect methods may be used to validate those mental models which have been first inferred of direct method data such as interviewing (Gentner 2004).

In recent years, *neuroscientific* methods such as electroencephalography (EEG) and functional magnetic resonance imaging (fMRI) have become salient (Fiske and Taylor 2013, Sternberg and Sternberg 2012). These tools have been used in a limited way in marketing studies (Morin 2011) and there is some discussion of applying them eventually in MOC research as well (Cunningham et al. 2013). Whilst the vision of a direct *independent* look into people's minds may be intriguing, even alluring, it does not seem a realistic one in the *foreseeable* future. Scanning can provide data of how the central nervous system functions, in particular about the brain areas that a person activates in response to different stimuli. However, this does not tell anything about the memory *contents*, that is, exactly what that person knows or thinks about something. Thus, the collected data is of a different and less relevant kind for the purposes in comparative causal mapping or similar approaches.

However, the interest in indirect clinical methods and, more recently, neuroscientific techniques, is in itself perhaps noteworthy. It suggests that, to some researchers in a field like MOC, only what neuroscience or cognitive psychology does is real and proper. In contrast, our own efforts are somehow feeble and not far from unlicensed dabbling in areas which are really more or less out of bounds for us. This is a misunderstanding. The knowledge interests of organizational and political cognitive studies in general and in CCM specifically are fundamentally different from those of cognitive psychology and related fields. We are not studying *generic* cognitive processes or contents for findings which are generalizable, say, to all normal adults. Instead, we are typically interested in capturing and describing some *specific* actors' beliefs about *specific* issues, often to explain those beliefs or to predict their implications. In other words, for example, CCM is not cognitive research pure at a general and individual level, but organizational or political research from a *cognitive perspective* using some cognitive concepts and assumptions.

From an empirical viewpoint, however, the conditions and constraints at individual level in CCM are more or less similar to those in cognitive psychology. Comparative causal mapping, too, is dependent on eliciting data about people's mental models and knowledge and beliefs but, as cognitive psychology and related fields, it too has no *direct* access to people's minds. In practice, CCM data can be acquired only by either of *two* main strategies or by using some combination of them:

1. The respondents can be induced to inform (communicate) about their causal ideas. This could take place orally in an interview setting *in situ*, by responding by writing an essay, or by answering a questionnaire in paper or electronic form.

2. Relevant actors' causal beliefs may be available and can be located in their *existing* communications. These can be written documents such as memoranda, position papers and books or traced in electronic communications like emails or blogs.

In principle, there is a third approach of systematic *observation* of people's overt behaviors when performing a task. As in indirect methods of cognitive psychology, the resulting data would be used to *infer* what the observed actors *probably* know or assume or heed to (or ignore) in the context of the focal task and/or what mental models they may have. Whilst observation makes obvious sense as a validation method in cognitive psychology, in CCM studies, which by definition involve several respondents and usually focus on eliciting, comparing and aggregating often rather complex entities of practical knowledge, observation does not seem a realistic primary strategy. However, it can be useful for corroborating specific belief findings of a CCM study based on either of the two main approaches.

Thus, for practical purposes, CCM data about a person's knowledge/ beliefs or mental models will be based on their *overt communications* in one form or another. An important question is what are the productive cognitive mechanisms and origins of the causal concepts and ideas that will be elicited in an interview or located in a document such as a position paper or a CEO's letter to shareholders. To examine this, Figure 2.1 outlines the factors and processes which can be usually assumed to be involved in a normal discourse or when someone communicates their knowledge in an administered situation such as acquisition of primary CCM data.

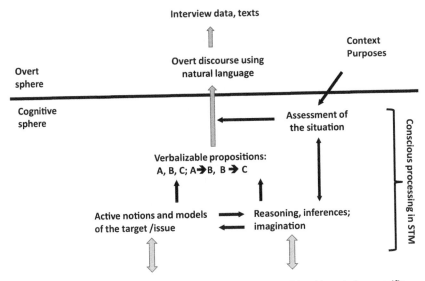

Figure 2.1   Production of CCM data: a cognitive perspective

The model has two spheres: a *cognitive* one, which refers to entities and processes that are assumed to exist and go on covertly in the respondent's mind, and the *context*, where the actual overt production, for example, for data acquisition takes place. The model's cognitive sphere is a rough replica of the currently accepted model of the basic cognitive machinery and architecture (for an overview, see, for example, Sternberg and Sternberg 2012, Frederiksen 2004). It comprises, first, the notion of a long-term storage function, memory (LTM). How knowledge/beliefs will be stored and how the association-based retrieval functions is less relevant now. It suffices to note that the LTM is assumed to contain different kinds and levels of knowledge. As noted, these include *propositional knowledge* (that A, B, and so on exist, that A is X, that A causes B, and so on), which is retained at varying levels of abstraction, including levels which are too abstract to be expressed in symbols such as words, in so-called mentalese (Sternberg and Sternberg 2012). Another type of knowledge consists of (causal) *mental models*. They too exist at varying levels of specificity or concreteness, iconicity, and will therefore often overlap with images of entities and evolving events. A third category called *procedural knowledge* is about how things happen or are done temporally in typical or specific cases. Importantly, a person can have parallel knowledge about the same referents, which is retained in different forms such as analogous models and conceptual propositions about some aspects of them.

Second, a capacity for processing different kinds of knowledge is necessary, too. This is usually called the working or short-term memory (STM). One of its functions is to initiate retrieval of knowledge from LTM when triggered by a perceived need. Working memory is also the place where the manipulation of retrieved knowledge, models or propositions takes place. This involves simple retrieval and subsequent formulation of the materials into verbalizable propositions. There will also be reasoning, deduction and induction based on the retrieved knowledge or on locally observed interpreted materials. In addition, something like imagination is often necessary to simulate the retrieved models and to test hypotheses and inferences, for example, in a search for possible causal chains in the mind's eye. Usually, more than one retained knowledge component and process will be involved. The implication is that the production of communicated knowledge/beliefs is seldom a *retrieval* issue only. In many cases it will be also a *generative* process.

In research practice, however, the processes and factors underlying overt communication cannot be understood in individual cognitive terms only. Not only everyday discourse and written communications, but also administered data elicitation such as in CCM will always take place in some context. This means that there are things like stated or hidden objectives and purposes, anticipated consequences, participants of different social status, a given environment, different attitudes and states of vigilance, time frames, cultural habits, and so on For example, do the participants know that their communications will be used as primary data for research purposes? If yes, what could that mean? This is often difficult to know. To some respondents it may call for carefulness and mindful filtering whilst some feel obligated to sincerely tell all what they think or remember. Some wish to impress the interviewer, and may invent and fabricate things. As noted, it is often argued that secondary documentary data is not contaminated by such speculations or hindsight. This may be so, but when documentary data is or was produced, there are usually other purposes and criteria, such as influencing a specific audience or presenting something or oneself in a favorable light. Here, the point is only that specifically in primary data elicitation, the participants must be assumed to make different subjective assessments of the situation along the above dimensions, perhaps starting with an implicit one and updating it later. To some extent, such assessments and their outcome can be influenced by instructions, legitimizing information, assurances of anonymity, choice of time and place, and so on. However, *some* subjective interpretation of the situation occurs and influences what and in which form the person or respondent will communicate. These factors will manifest themselves as data's dependability, traditionally assessed in terms of data *validity* and *reliability*, discussed in more detail in Section 3.4.

Considering exclusively the *cognitive* preconditions, it is obviously, as a main rule, possible to elicit and thus "know" about people's causal knowledge and beliefs and mental models. Moreover, for reasons discussed earlier, it can be usually assumed that especially the more instrumental knowledge and the core of people's belief systems are relatively stable. However, there are some cognition-related factors that will influence elicitation in addition to the subjective situational assessment.

First, most people, especially knowledgeable, vigilant and motivated persons, can, if they so wish and are allowed, let alone encouraged, generate lots of data in the form of verbalized causal proposals. For example, in an interview, the probes and recalled events, instances and models and proposals will trigger an associative recall of more notions. They can also prompt the person to generate new ideas, inferences and tentative conclusions which they, however, may not necessarily seriously mean nor would use in practice. The problem is that the researcher cannot know this, and, because there are no grounds to assume otherwise, what is heard or read can thus end up as valid data. It would seem that there is no absolute remedy to this beyond obvious counter methods such as instructions and sticking to uniform time frames. Fortunately, in CCM studies it can often be assumed that such creative processes are random and will therefore produce *idiosyncratic* results, which usually cancel themselves out and thus have less impact at the *aggregate* level.

Second, in contrast to the above "volume" issue, there is the problem of abstract and in particular of tacit knowledge. As noted, some knowledge and models will be stored by unconscious processing in *abstract* declarative form, using concepts, that is, words and word combinations (propositions). This kind of knowledge is normally accessible for data elicitation. However, the abstraction can go further. Parts of especially experienced laypersons' and experts' complex knowledge will be gradually and automatically converted into a *tacit* form, which enables knowing without consciously knowing and "without knowing why" (Claxton 1998) and thus using one's knowledge *intuitively* in problem-solving and decision-making (see, for example, Ambrosini and Bowman 2002, Hodgkinson et al. 2009, Prietula and Simon 1989, Simon 1987, Spender 1998, Wassink et al. 2003). However, tacit knowledge is, by definition, less or not at all communicable in everyday contexts or by verbal or written reports and interviewing (Evans 1988). The incidence, extent and significance of non-accessed knowledge are difficult to assess. However, it seems reasonable to assume that knowledge and causal mental models, which are in frequent use, will be retained *also* in an explicit form and thus more accessible because they are regularly needed in professional and organizational communication. Furthermore, tacitness is not an either/or issue: people, especially experts, can, by conscious effort although not always quickly, reconvert parts of their tacit knowledge into an explicit, communicable form. Whether and how far this is feasible and valid in each case will vary and requires corroborating evidence in a research case.

One of the consequences of the above is that it is difficult to know from which sources the elicited causal knowledge and beliefs will be retrieved and which models, imagination, reasoning and situational assessment actually contributed into the data production process. The causal proposition data, elicited as primary data or located in documents in a typical causal mapping study and eventually presented as causal maps, can represent respondents' knowledge/beliefs and mental models as they are or were momentarily recalled from long-term memory, but also products of their ad hoc inference, reasoning and imagination processes, all tempered by a situational assessment. The resulting paradox is that it is difficult to argue, let alone show, that one is accessing specifically a "mental model" or a "cognitive map", indeed that there are some such stable measurement targets. In view of the operationalizing difficulties and inherent diffuseness and volatility of the underlying cognitive phenomena, it may therefore be better to avoid a rigid, dogmatic stance about what cognitive target phenomena one maps or "measures" at least in MOC, political science, or other non-psychological fields. When common terms like mental models or cognitive maps must be used, they should perhaps be understood and defined in a general *metaphorical* meaning. A terminological alternative is to use concepts like "belief system", "thought pattern" or "explanatory tendency", a practice common in cognitive political science and in many MOC studies. This would neutralize some of the potential ontological and epistemological questions that could be raised about studies using a cognitive perspective.

Chapter 3
Comparative Causal Mapping

This chapter discusses the methods and practices of data acquisition and analysis and the related methodological issues in comparative causal mapping (CCM) research. The first section describes different types of CCM data and main method approaches to acquiring CCM data. The next two sections discuss the CCM-specific and methodologically critical questions of coding, comparison and aggregation. The fourth section addresses the problem of dependability of trustworthiness—in conventional terms, validity and reliability. The fifth section discusses quantifying aspects of causal maps in terms of numerical indicators. The final section addresses some design issues and discusses selecting between different CCM approaches.

3.1   Data Acquisition

In everyday interaction, knowing or at least conjecturing about what other people think is usually based on two resources. On the one hand, people have general knowledge about their own thought processes and beliefs and those of others and about the ways they and people in general usually react in different situations. This rudimentary ability to "mind read" is often called the theory of mind (see, for example, Leslie 2001). On the other hand, there is overt situated communication and observation of others' decisions and behavior, including the so-called body language, which updates and confirms what is initially presumed. In research contexts this kind of lay observation can be present, too. For example, whilst even experienced interviewers cannot read thoughts, they often have at least a rough idea about whether an interviewee is sincere or intentionally holding back something.

Lay methods, however, are different from systematic observation of actors' overt behaviors for grounded inferences about what beliefs and perceptions (or lack of them) could be guiding them and, accordingly, what they seem to assume, know, prioritize, heed to or ignore. First, as discussed in Chapter 2, cognitive psychologists use indirect methods to validate the mental models inferred from directly derived data. Second, in organizational research, systematic indirect, observation-based methods include, for example, *critical incident analysis* (Chell 2004) and in particular *shadowing* (McDonald 2005, McDonald and Simpson 2014). In addition to providing data for organizational analysis, these methods can furnish clues about underlying beliefs, assumptions and perceptions, including errors and omissions. Third, on a higher level of analysis, MOC researchers can use *narratives* of for instance entrepreneurs' behaviors and examine their firms' behaviors, such as competitive moves (Porac et al. 2002). Such methods enable inferences about what belief systems or "dominant logic" might have guided the firm's managers (Huff and Jenkins 2002). In this case, causal maps and mapping may be used for visually representing and analyzing the inferred belief systems.

A difficulty of observational methods is that the inferences must be influenced by the researcher's preconceptions, *a priori* models and theory-based hypotheses. This, as such, is unavoidable and does not render such methods dubious, but it means that additional and independent evidence is required to corroborate (or refute) the inferences. There are also research circumstances and situations where the applicability of observational and indirect methods is limited. Most importantly here, they would not provide the kind of causal proposition data which CCM ideally requires. Thus, lacking the third way, that is, an independent access to a person's mind and propositional or other knowledge and mental models, causal mapping data has to be acquired using *direct methods* entirely or additionally. The *phenomenological* and *causal propositions* on which causal mapping builds—that A, B, C and so on exist and that A influences B or C follows B, and so on—must exist at the outset or they have to be elicited and made available in a communicated overt form. The first methodological problem in CCM research is thus how to acquire this kind of propositional data.

There are two obvious approaches. First, we can use already available relevant documentary or similar *secondary* sources. This data is called secondary because it is usually originally created for other purposes, not as data for a specific research use. Second, depending on the research task or non-availability of secondary data, we can elicit *primary* CCM data using an appropriate method which differs in particular in how open or *a priori* constrained, that is, more or less structured, the data acquisition is. This influences the techniques and tools that can be used. In this chapter we will first discuss using documentary and similar secondary data and move after that on to other major methods of data acquisition.

3.1.1 DOCUMENTARY DATA

Using documentary data has a long history in causal mapping studies. Typical such data include textbooks, personal memoirs, diaries, meeting minutes, diplomatic and intelligence archives, published speeches, political parties' manifestos and organizational papers such as internal memoranda and CEOs' letters to shareholders or similar formal statements. Increasingly, such data is in electronic form, such as emails or blogs. This book has a special discussion (Section 7.1) about the principles and techniques of using documentary materials in causal mapping studies and specifically how CMAP3 can serve in such contexts. The present section focuses mainly on some more general aspects of using such data.

The use of documentary data in CCM can be traced back to Axelrod's seminal volume *Structure of Decision: The cognitive maps of political elites* (1976). The idea guiding Axelrod and his colleagues was that causal mapping offers an innovative method for operationalizing (political) actors' beliefs and assumptions, which are posited to underpin their decision-making behavior. The resulting descriptions, using extracted visual causal maps, enable researchers to have a holistic understanding (*Verstehen*) of the actors' cognitions and thus creating hypotheses about why they behaved the way they did. This approach also facilitates *normative* studies of political decision-making and *counterfactual reasoning* (Tetlock 2001), that is, a *what if* analysis of what might have happened had the political actors thought or known otherwise. The practices of coding the individual causal statements, a prerequisite of comparison and distilling of collective views from the documents into a causal map form, were explained in detail by Wrightson (1976). The methodological chapters in the Axelrod volume and in specialized content analysis texts (for example, Krippendorff 2004) are still key reading when planning CCM research of this genre.

There are many significant pros and cons in using documentary materials as CCM data. As to the advantages, first, the actors usually express their ideas for personal or organizational purposes, perhaps using pen and paper, today more likely a computer. This means that the persons themselves were not explicitly probed for research purposes. Thus, compared with interviewing, questionnaires or other proactive ways of data acquisition, documentary methods are basically non-invasive and non-reactive. This can minimize but does not abolish the reconstruction biases and memorizing problems which may be present when a person is asked about past events and earlier ideas. Second, documents reflect thought patterns and beliefs which prevailed at an earlier time point, obviously assuming no intentional biasing or weighting or that the researcher can detect them and neutralize their impact. In positive cases, documents can therefore be sincere and accurate, and thus more or less ideal data. A third advantage is that documents enable studies that focus on events and issues which happened in the past and/or focus on actors who are no longer accessible. For this reason, documentary data can be particularly useful in political science, which often involves actors whom researchers can reach only with difficulty or not at all any longer. Finally, documentary data enables accessing not only agential beliefs, but also cultural norms, values and doctrines, which influence individual beliefs. Because of the relative stability of cultural values (Inglehart and Welzel 2005), studies of cultural beliefs by documents are relevant to research of long-term implications on policy-making.

Documentary data also has limitations and issues. Their severity depends partly on the research purposes at hand. The first concerns the documents' validity and ability to represent somebody's beliefs and mental models. It is sometimes difficult to locate the exact authors of the documents and to know the specific purposes for which the documents were originally created. For instance, CEOs' letters to shareholders or other organizational statements do not necessarily reflect the ideas and beliefs of the person in whose name they are released. They can reflect anything from the top management's consensus opinion and modish industry views to the creative ideas of a PR agency. This problem tends to become increasingly severe along the ladder of social hierarchy. In a vast bureaucracy like the Chinese state, for example, even a single policy speech by a national leader cannot avoid taking inputs from multiple factions and various personnel in the party's Central Committee and the central government (Wu 1995). Indeed, many organizational and political documents are *deliberately* created and biased to serve a specific objective, such as influencing the general public or investor opinion or the self-defense and "shield-polishing" of a retired politician or CEO. This, however, must not necessarily be fatal, if the origins and the purposes are known and/or they or the uncertain background can be identified and factored in the conclusions. Moreover, a bias at a private level can be irrelevant if the research question focuses on beliefs at a collective level. Historical textbooks created for nationalist myth-making, for instance, may not actually mirror their creators' understanding of history. Yet, they can be highly accurate samples of the historical memories that have been institutionalized in a society.

Second, documentary materials are problematic, even useless, if the research is dependent on valid *representativeness* and *comparability* of *several* social actors' belief patterns. This is the case in typical CCM studies. The problems follow from the above circumstance that typical documents are not created for the purpose of comparison but to serve different, often pragmatic or political goals. Therefore, they may contain statements that are irrelevant for the research task, but which the actors themselves considered germane from their particular viewpoint at that specific time. Other notions and causal beliefs, which the actor/s may well also possess, but which were not considered relevant enough to publish, will not be revealed and therefore do not enter the raw database and analysis. Consequently, secondary documentary data is in particular relevant and useful in *composite cause mapping* which seeks to capture the essence of the belief systems of a significant collective or single actor. The edited volume by Axelrod (1976) has several examples of the former type. A good specimen of the latter type is the study of Cossette (2002), which summarizes and analyzes the thinking of F.W. Taylor, commonly known as the father of scientific management.

Third, a problem can be the limited and even diminishing availability of useful documents. This, however, depends on the field. For example, many states like the US, the UK and Japan have institutionalized the declassification of diplomatic archives, so that the flow of useable sources for certain types of study may be actually increasing. The situation in MOC studies, however, seems different. Increasingly, some organizations, such as small and medium-size firms (SME), are relying mainly on verbal communications and minimize or shun documenting discussions in decision-making groups and seldom use internal memoranda. Consequently, ideal materials such as the verbatim minutes of the British Eastern Committee in 1918 (Axelrod 1976, p. 77) or transcripts of parliamentary debates (Maoz and Shayer 1987) may never even exist in such organizations. Unfortunately, the accelerating pace of organizational life and the growing dominance of verbal and short-term, short-lived electronic communications such as email means that less and less archived material will be produced. Moreover, the materials which are archived are increasingly in electronic, not printed and public form, and thus often less accessible to outsiders. Developments such as these can be assumed to increase the significance of personal access and of classic direct methods such as interviewing for acquiring primary data. At the same time, new methods based on Internet telephony, electronic questionnaires and available contents in electronic and Internet-based materials such as emails and blogs will probably be increasingly important in CM/CCM studies.

Finally, processing and analyzing secondary documentary data can be technically demanding. This is typically caused mainly by the sheer amount and redundancy of documentary data. It often has the character of "polished" speech. In addition, documentary data may require considerable interpretation, filtering and coding by the researcher and consequently an independent validation, for example, by external reviewers. These steps, however, are integral parts of this genre of causal mapping research and must be observed and taken care of (see Section 7.1). Appropriate software tools such as CMAP3 and, with limitations, standard CAQDAS applications can be necessary for performing the tasks of organizing and analyzing the rich natural data.

3.1.2   LOW-STRUCTURED INTERVIEWING

As once observed by March and Simon (1958, p. 192), "for many purposes, the simplest and most accurate way to discover what a person does is to ask him," whereby "doing" refers not only to overt behaviors but also to covert processes like thinking and knowing. Interviewing is a systematic form of asking and collecting data in social research, quantitative or qualitative. A quick web search reveals a huge number of texts and specialized guides which describe the principles and techniques and different variants of interviewing.

Interviewing methods in CCM studies differ mainly in the degree of *structuration*. Low-structured interviewing usually takes place in a face-to-face situation, *in situ*. The interviewer asks relatively open-ended questions or other types of probing, which obviously focus on research-relevant topics of interest or themes. Examples of such approaches in the CCM context are Bougon's *Self-Q interview* (Bitonti 1993, Bougon et al. 1990, Wassink et al. 2003) and the *social construction* approach, which was compared with the Self-Q approach by Nicolini (1999). The general idea in low-structured elicitation is to induce the respondents to express, in their own words, their perceptions of the focal topic, describing and explaining what things and phenomena they perceive as existing and go on in the domain or that kind of work or organization. In terms of CCM data, the researchers will hear/learn, in the first place, which *phenomena* the respondents seem to discern or heed to in the context, and the semantics of expressions, original vernacular, which they employ when referring to the phenomena. Second, by listening to and specifically using questions such as how, why and what if about the perceived phenomena, that is, about the subjective purposes and objectives, explanations and predictions, their underlying *causal* and mechanism beliefs of the respondents can be revealed.

The immediate outcome of low-structured interviewing is rich raw data, which initially exists in the form of researcher notes and usually voice recordings. They must be *transcribed* into a text form and then processed further, that is, coded and analyzed. As above, for controlled processing of rich textual data, qualitative researchers increasingly use so-called CAQDAS tools, discussed briefly below. This makes the processing and analytic tasks easier, more rigorous and at the same time more transparent.

Assuming a normal interviewing situation without significant distorting factors, low-structured interviews can be assumed to elicit original and valid (sincere) natural statements as raw data. The data quality and richness are important advantages but they come at a price. First, low-structured methods trigger normal oral communication and have an inherent tendency to elicit "rich" data, in practice large numbers of verbal statements and expressions and subjective personal ruminations. In terms of typical CCM research, a considerable part of this richness can be more or less redundant. However, what is relevant (or redundant) can be known only by processing all data. This takes time and contains risks of errors such as unintentional omissions and thus of less validity and reliability.

Second, by definition, low structuring means that the researcher has less control of the communication process, its focus, and thus over what the elicited contents and data will be. This can be a serious problem, particularly in comparative causal mapping, which is dependent on *comparable* data elicited systematically from several respondents.

Finally, as documentary data, low-structured data usually also requires coding. This introduces an element of researcher interpretation and subjectivity to the analytical process and influences the analysis and findings. To counter this problem requires appropriate measures, such as eliciting peer opinion and organizing an external review of the coding scheme and individual coding decisions. However, in this respect low-structured CCM does not differ from other research methods such as content analysis, which also use rich qualitative data (Krippendorff 2004, Maxwell 2012, Merriam 2009).

3.1.3 TEXT-BASED ELICITATION

A close parallel to low-structured interviewing in CCM is to use relatively open text-writing tasks focused on a research-relevant topic. For instance, Nadkarni and Narayanan (2005) used standardized writing tasks (open-ended questions and a two-page report) to elicit what they call *text-based causal maps* (TBCM). In their case, a group of MBA students was asked to diagnose the same strategic management case and to make recommendations and explain/defend them. As a consequence, the respondents had to tell, in a relatively comparable manner, about their views about the case using those concepts and causal ideas they had, including those internalized (hopefully) in class when taking the respective course. The texts were coded, the coding reviewed and converted into causal map form for numerical analysis.

In general, text-based acquisition of primary CCM data can be versatile. For example, assuming a relatively narrow, specific topic or domain, it could enable an efficient elicitation of CCM data of even large samples. However, TBCM is not a panacea and should be seen in a reasonable perspective, as all CCM methods. For example, Nadkarni and Narayanan (2005) argue, quoting Axelrod (1976), that TBCMs are non-invasive and non-reactive, trigger less recall biases, and thus reduce the risk of changing the cognitions of the participants as interviewing might do. They also maintain that documentary materials enable examining the contents and evolution of belief systems over longer periods and to study individuals no longer available. Finally, they are claimed more economical and require less time and effort, both of the researchers and the participants.

Whilst the points of Nadkarni and Narayanan are certainly often valid, they perhaps equate two unequal things: one, text-writing for *primary* CCM data, and two, distilling causal data of *secondary* sources data such as existing documents, as discussed above. In the latter case of prior documents, the arguments of non-invasiveness and data longevity may hold. However, when text-based methods (TBCM) are used for eliciting *primary* CCM data, as in the above case, there is arguably no essential difference compared with, for example, interviewing. For the MBAs the writing task was a test, which, by definition, is invasive and is assumed to launch not only memory recall but also several "cognitive changes" when responding. The student can both recall the learned materials and employ their ad hoc reasoning and imagining. The test and the produced texts can therefore be assumed to reflect different cognitive sources.

The argument that TBCM methods save time and effort is also not convincing as a rule. It is technically possible to limit the texts produced per participant, for example, to two pages as in the Nadkarni and Narayanan study. This will save time, but even mundane factors such as personal differences in handwriting/typing (or natural fluency) make simple limits such as fixed pages (or interview time) doubtful. Furthermore, any limiting is problematic, possibly counterproductive, if the objective is to compare and to examine the depth of knowledge and the understanding of a topic, even if one wishes to measure a characteristic like cognitive complexity as Nadkarni and Narayanan. Limiting seems justified if the topic is relatively narrow and *a priori* clearly definable, or if administrative ease has absolute priority. However, when no output limits will or can be set, TBCM methods behave more or less as low-structured interviewing, producing voluminous, rich and thus also redundant data. Thus, the researcher faces the same problems of processing, coding and interpretive analysis as in low-structured interviewing. This is one more example of the methodological trade-offs not uncommon in CCM research.

3.1.4   STRUCTURED METHODS

In contrast to text-based and low-structured CCM methods, structured elicitation uses a *template approach*. It is based on a set of concepts which are predefined by the researcher and are the same for all respondents. Thus, instead of acquiring *original* language data, structured approaches emulate psychometric methods that are built around a measurement instrument. There are different ways of structured elicitation of the raw data, that is, the concepts and the causal relationship information.

The earliest, still relevant structured CCM approach was the *fixed-list method*. The respondents are administered a predefined set of concepts, ranging typically from 10 to 15 (for example, Bougon et al. 1977, Clarkson and Hodgkinson 2006, Ford and Hegarty 1984, Hodgkinson et al. 2004, Tyler and Gnyawali 2009). Their only task is to indicate the causal links they perceive as existing between the list's concepts. Thus, all variance differentiating the respondents will be based exclusively on the variation in the causal relationships, in some cases possibly also on the differences in how the respondents specify the relationships (see below).

To widen the scope for variance in the comparison and thus the measurement base, the so-called concept pool method was developed by Markóczy and Goldberg (1995). The new feature in this approach is that the participants are first presented with a larger predefined concept set, consisting typically of 40 to 60 concepts. Their first task is to select, from the pool, a smaller "personal" set (n = 10–15) of concepts. A typical instruction is to pick concepts which the participant considers most important from their viewpoint or by the criteria specified in the instructions. In terms of emerging concepts, this approach can lead to more variance, but still within the predefined concept pool. In the second stage, the participants indicate their perceived causal relationships among the selected concept set and often also *specify* the identified causal links (see below). The pool approach has also been called the *hybrid* method, as it is argued to combine the characteristics of the low-structured methods and the highly structured fixed-list method. Clarkson and Hodgkinson (2005) describe an advanced software-based version of the hybrid method.

It is evident that the critical component in structured CCM methods is the predefined concept list or the pool. It creates a measuring instrument which determines the quality and relevance of the elicited data from the viewpoint of valid representation of the participants' cognitions and usefulness in terms of the research questions. Researchers have used different techniques for deriving the concepts. Bougon et al. (1977, p. 608), for example, obtained their fixed list of 17, finally 14, "variables" from the organization members through "naturalistic observation, discussion and interviews". In the Ford and Hegarty (1984, p. 274) study, the fixed list of eight concepts was derived by the researchers from current organization literature. In general, for example, Markóczy and Goldberg (1995, pp. 309–10) note that the pool's constructs could be derived by interviewing people in similar positions as in the final sample. They also suggest augmenting these concepts with items from relevant literature and to test the pool using a pilot sample. In a more recent case (Clarkson and Hodgkinson 2005), the 55 constructs in the pool were selected from different literature sources, some from the studied organizations (call centers) and related research, some represented more theoretical and empirical work in the MOC or "adjacent literatures". The constructs were finally "refined and translated into an appropriate language form during the pilot phase" (Clarkson and Hodgkinson 2005, p. 324). Finally, it is possible to offer the participants the option of adding some personally important concepts to the pool (see Section 7.3). Whilst this may adapt the concepts locally and improve representativeness, it also introduces an element of idiosyncrasy and thus problems of comparability and the need of coding, all weakening the structured approach's unique advantages.

The recommended number of constructs in the fixed list or the selected set in the pool method is usually somewhere between 7 and 15 concepts. The selection of such a number of concepts from the concept pool is usually not a problem, assuming the pool is not too large, the concepts somehow familiar and the selection criteria subjectively meaningful. The bottleneck is in the next stages. If the predefined list or the selected subset grows, it quickly makes the respondent's job more difficult and increasingly tedious, endangering reliable acquisition. This concerns especially studies where the selected concepts must be compared in both directions and where the causal links will also be specified, as discussed below. The difficulty is obvious considering the respondent's task when identifying the causal links by a pairwise comparison. The number of all theoretically possible links among n concepts is $N = n*(n–1)$. For instance, for $n = 7$ there will be $N = 42$ comparisons ($N = 6*7 = 42$). For $n = 15$, $N = 210$, a major difference.

The second stage (the only one in the predefined list approach) in the pool method is to elicit the respondents' beliefs about causal relationships. This uses typically a *pairwise comparison* of all concepts in the list or selected subset. The respondents first indicate whether they perceive a causal relationship between each pair of concepts (A→B) in both directions or only one. In addition, they may specify the identified relationships (the arrows in the cause maps) usually in terms of two dimensions. The first typically concerns the causal relationship's type as direct (+) or inverse (-), meaning that an increase of A is perceived as leading either to an increase (+) or a decrease (-) in B. The second dimension can be, for example, the perceived weight or importance of the relationship (as defined in the instructions) using a three-point scale (for example, 1 = weak, 2 = moderate, 3 = strong). In that case, the links would have values such as -3, -1, + 2, +3, and so on. Conceivably, there could be other dimensions such as subjective certainty of the relationship, its personal influencability, temporal versus causal character, linear versus concave, reversible versus irreversible, eventual threshold or triggering or contingency factors or clauses, and so on.

More generally, the significance of specifying the causal links' dimensions, indeed whether it makes sense at all, must be judged in view of research objectives and common sense. On the one hand, the higher the number of elicited concepts and relationships and the more detailed the specification, the more accurate and covering are the emerging causal maps relative to the target issue or cognitions. On the other hand, more detail requires more data, time and concentrated effort. At some point, however, things turn counterproductive. Each added list or pool concept and specification dimension complicates the task and makes it more tedious. This increases risks of unreliability and of dubious data, especially if the probing takes place without an administrator, for example, electronically. To some extent such problems may be alleviated, although the number of concepts can never grow much, perhaps to somewhere between 15 and 20, depending on the target domain. One way is to elicit causal links data in one direction only (that is, assuming no significant direct reciprocal influences and/or to avoid or simplify the specification of the causal relationships). A third option could be to limit the number of links a participant can select. For example, in the study of Tyler and Gnyawali (2009, p. 106) this was set to n = 3. However, it must be ensured that such constraints will not significantly bias the data and the conclusions.

Structured CCM methods can use different techniques which involve different roles of respondents, interviewers and/or researchers. For example, the concept selection in the pool method and the eliciting of the causal links and their specifying can be administered *in situ* by face-to-face interviewing using, for example, sets of concept cards and notation forms for the selection and causal link data (Budhwar 2000, Hine et al. 2005, Markóczy and Goldberg 1995). A second approach is to use sets of *mailed cards and adjacency matrices* (Tyler and Gnyawali 2009). Third, in the *free-hand drawing* method the researcher or the respondent arrange the predefined or selected concepts on a piece of paper (or use a computer application's interface) and the respondents draw arrows connecting those concepts, between which they perceive a causal link, eventually also specifying the relationships (Hodgkinson et al. 2004). The result can be mailed or sent electronically to the administrator. Fourth, the acquisition and selection processes can be partly or wholly computerized. This could be done by using the hybrid method specific software application, *Cognizer*™[1] (Clarkson and Hodgkinson 2005), or the stagewise process based on CMAP3 and Excel tables and their email transfer (see Sections 5.2 and 7.3). Undoubtedly, further variants of structured CCM methods can be developed.

Notably, the different variants of structured CCM methods are not necessarily psychometrically equivalent and thus not substitutable. For example, Hodgkinson et al. (2004) found that the *paired comparison* of concepts (using a questionnaire) elicited roughly five times more causal links than when the respondents linked the same concept set using *freehand drawing*. In other words, the former produced much denser cause maps. This was also the case in the comparison study examined in Section 7.3, where the conceivable technical and psychological grounds will be discussed. Here, it is important to note that differences of this magnitude can make the comparison and aggregation over respondents and metrics such as complexity measures problematic, not only across studies but also within a given study.

In general, structured CCM methods have especially technical advantages. They use the same concept list or pool for all participants and separate the elicitation of concepts and causal links, enabling an administratively clear process. They reduce the volumes of elicited data to a minimum, especially compared with low-structured interviewing or using TBCM and secondary documents. Furthermore, the common concept list/pool sets up a shared meaning space, within which all participants must stay. This eliminates the need of *ex post* coding. Such factors imply less labor and potentially more reliability and allow, at least in principle, studies with higher Ns and thus nomothetic, generalizing CCM studies (Hodgkinson and Clarkson 2005). In addition, there may be some more subjective benefits. Assuming the participants' cooperation, a structured CCM study can be expected to "work" in the tangible sense of

---

1   For product and purchasing information about Cognizer™: http://www.mandrake.myzen.co.uk/.

producing analyzable data, cause maps and indicator-based quantitative results, that is, some empirical results to report. In addition, structured CCM emulates psychometric methods, which to some may convey a reassuring aura of quantitative rigor and being more "scientific".

However, structured CCM methods also have critical downsides which cannot be ignored. The main issues are perhaps potentially problematic data validity and the ability to cover only small cognitive domains. These are consequences of the methods' inherent characteristics. First, the acquired data is strictly taken, not original but based on predefined concepts. Second, the number of selected and evaluated concepts must be very limited. In addition, the unintended demand characteristics could lead to biased data. We will discuss the implications of these issues more below in the section about the selection of CCM methods.

3.1.5 SEMI-STRUCTURED INTERVIEWING

The methods discussed above have advantages but also potential problems. In the low-structured and TBCM CCM approaches, the issue is more practical and related to the fact that they tend to generate rich data which will be partly redundant in research terms. In structured CCM methods, the problem is methodological and therefore more serious. Because of the predefined instrument (concept list or pool), they do not necessarily elicit original, natural concepts, that is, notions which are actually known to be used by the respondents. In addition, there are problems related to the small numbers of concepts and the potential demand characteristic. The semi-structured interviewing method (SIM) tries to combine the advantages of the other methods and to reduce their inherent problems (Laukkanen 1994, 1998).

The idea of the SIM method is described in Figure 3.1. In an SIM interview, the participant is probed *in situ* about and around *anchor topics*, inquiring about the *antecedent* factors, which they think influence (cause, precede) the anchor phenomenon and about the *consequences* (effects, outcomes) that are perceived to follow from it. The same format is (usually) repeated to elicit a *second data layer* by using the elicited first layer concepts as new anchors. The second layer can mimic the first layer probing, as shown in Figure 3.1, or it can be limited to inquiring only about "the antecedents of the antecedents" and "the consequences of consequences" of the initial anchor phenomenon. In principle, it is obviously possible to elicit a third or even more data layers, but this lengthens the session and is seldom necessary in order to achieve an adequate view of the participant's typical belief patterns (mental model) about the focal target/anchor phenomenon.

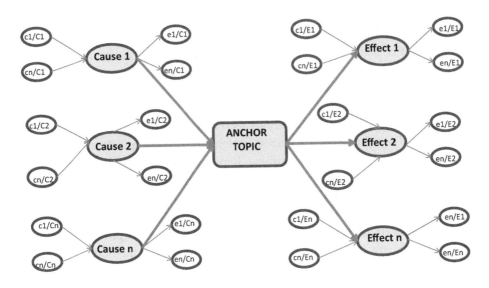

Figure 3.1   A schema of semi-structured interviewing (SIM)

The SIM focuses, by definition, on specific domains or issues, which are represented by the initial anchor concept/s. Thus, it emulates the general *domain-specific* nature of human knowledge and reasoning. Because of the interview format, the acquired data consists predominantly of *causal statements*, that is, A → B, C, and so on, and D, E and so on → A, containing little redundant data. Moreover, the data equals the respondents' *natural* expressions and concepts and is thus known to originate from the participants in their own vernacular. A typical SIM interview takes about 1.5–2 hours assuming a probing of two to four anchor topics and the second data layer (see Section 7.2). The duration depends on the themes, respondents and the overall context. In this section we examine the original form of the SIM approach, how it can be varied and related techniques.

The first critical SIM component is the anchor terms, around which the first layer of original concept and links data is elicited. The anchor topics can be thought of as labels that signify and refer to those phenomena and factors in the domain which its typical actors discern and consider important. As phenomena, they are operatively or strategically essential for action and performance in the context and can thus be assumed to require the actors' continuing attention, problem-solving and control. For a valid comparison, aggregation and subsequent analysis, the anchor issues must obviously be shared and relevant for all respondents. The problem in especially explorative studies is that we may not know at the outset which phenomena and factors of the domain are significant and therefore potential anchor topics. In this case, a preliminary interview may be used to provide contextual knowledge and a broad view of the focal business, its operations and issues, as the respondents themselves see them. This must be conducted without *a priori* structuring so that the respondents will describe the context and its issues in their own terms, telling what they think goes on there and is critical. This can usually be achieved by asking general questions such as what do success and failure mean in the business, which factors influence them, what are the key elements in the environment, what is their impact, and so on. These discussions are often best conducted in a neutral sense, framed as what *typical* similar actors in the context *generally* think and heed to. Only later should one inquire how far this reflects the respondent's own views or where their ideas perhaps differ from those of typical others. In addition to getting a good idea of the main issues and phenomena in the context, the initial session can be used to collect background data about the respondents and their organizations, and so on. This data is easily recalled and demands less vigilance of the respondent. One way is to use forms which the respondents complete at the end of the interview.

Notably, a preparatory interview is not always necessary. In some SIM cases, the anchor topics are self-evident or reliably identifiable at the outset. For instance, the focal issue/s may have been recently discussed in the context or public media or it is known that the respondents have strong views about the issues, for example, they have participated in public or organizational debates about it. This was the case in a recent study of municipality directors' views about local development of entrepreneurship (Laukkanen and Niittykangas 2010) and in a study of faculty views of academic entrepreneurship (Laukkanen 2003). In the former, salient issues such as "birth and entry of new firms" and "creation of jobs" were obvious anchor topics; in the latter, the controversial notions of "entrepreneurship of faculty members" and "university cooperation with external firms".

The number of anchor topics and anchor-based interviews are interconnected and depend on some obvious factors. First, the scope and complexity of the focal domain or issues and the research objectives determine how much detail versus how broad a view of the participants' related thought patterns should the data cover. For instance, in the original SIM CCM study (Laukkanen 1994), the idea was to elicit detailed data of the managers' belief systems for distilling their dominant thought patterns about the operative and strategic key domains in two industries. Therefore, several anchor topics and two interview sessions (in addition to the preparatory one) were conducted. However, in the more recent studies, such as the one described in Section 7.2, only one interview session and two anchor topics were used. Thus, the SIM does not have to follow the original format but can be varied within relatively wide boundaries as required.

There are also practical constraints on how many interviews and how much access time is realistic. Usually, a reasonable compromise can be found between data needs and the always limited available time. Moreover, typical SIM respondents seem genuinely intrigued and motivated by this kind of "think aloud" task. They find it an unusual and positive opportunity to examine their own beliefs and ideas. Therefore, a typical experience is that, without external disturbances, most respondents are, if necessary, prepared and willing to go on until a normal vigilance begins to taper off, typically sometime after 2.5 hours. However, whilst it is difficult to predict what happens in each case, a preparatory session usually gives the researcher a good idea of how the anchor-based interviews will proceed with each respondent. Even in this case, however, it is prudent to plan the interviews so that the core themes will be covered certainly and one has a clear idea about which additional anchor topics to address and in which order if that becomes possible.

In addition to the basic format of the anchor-based interviews, there are some general principles to observe. Some follow from the earlier discussed notions about cognitive processing underlying overt communication (Section 2.5). First, when describing the research and interview process, the researcher should emphasize that the respondent can/should concentrate on what they personally consider most relevant and significant in the domain, for example, in terms of good performance in the business and that the researcher is interested in hearing about exactly those things, including notions that seem mundane to the respondent, but which an outsider cannot know. It may even be useful to stress that there is no need to "impress" by special inventiveness or by relating some modish or academic concepts.

The interview should also follow a consistent routine. The order and manner of presenting the probes should be uniform and use the same terminology and inquire about the cause-and-effect sides similarly with all respondents. It is a good idea to use additional probing questions (What else does it influence? Do you see something else influencing it?), but they should be uniform and their number limited (for example, to two). However, people's memory recall and processing speed, communication style, vigilance, and so on, vary. It is reasonable to allow for this by giving some individual flexibility to respond to each subtopic. As a rule of thumb, the subinterviews around the first layer of the anchor topics typically take about 30 minutes per topic (+/- 10 minutes).

The second-layer concepts/causal links usually need less time, mainly because the issue/topic has become cognitively activated.

Because human memory functioning is based on associations, it is advisable to change the approach and repeat the questions using a different viewpoint when probing around anchor topics. Changing the perspective emulates what typically happens in real-life problem-solving and will thus foster memory access. One way is to ask about the anchor phenomenon's (for example firm's liquidity, customer traffic) antecedents and consequences in different states or situations, for example, when it is good or bad or has high or low values. A parallel technique is to vary the ways causal ideas are expressed when inquiring about them (follows from A, precedes B, comes next, and so on).

Fourth, needless to add, good interview practice is to create, as far as possible, a trusting, non-threatening and normal conversation-like situation. At the outset, this requires explaining the research objectives and methods, how the data will be used, that no sensitive issues or data will be inquired, and so on. It is often good to inform the respondent that they can add things if something important comes to mind later. Highly important for a productive interview, as well as for time-saving, is to conduct it as far as possible without disturbances. This often requires not only turning off mobile devices, but ideally also an isolated place and/or time outside office hours.

In SIM interviews, it is important to ensure that the researcher or interviewer has correctly understood the meanings of the respondents' expressions. It is not unusual for people to interpret concepts and expressions differently, particularly when they use terms that have been migrated from academic sources to managerial jargon. Examples are notions such as culture, strategy, commitment, organization, innovation or motivation. Although it is neither necessary nor possible to clarify every concept, the most salient and critical notions, which usually are the most frequently occurring, should be clarified uniformly with all respondents. This is important for coding and comparing data later.

Finally, all interviewing needs appropriate techniques of note-taking and recording. As far as possible, they should be inconspicuous, neutral and avoid distracting the flow of conversation. An obligatory tool is an interview notes sheet. Because SIM interviews elicit mainly causal propositions, a simple form for quick written notes is sufficient. For example, an *interview note sheet* (INS), which has proved practical, has a cell in the middle for the anchor topic and a grid of rows and columns, that is, empty cells, around it (Figure 3.2).

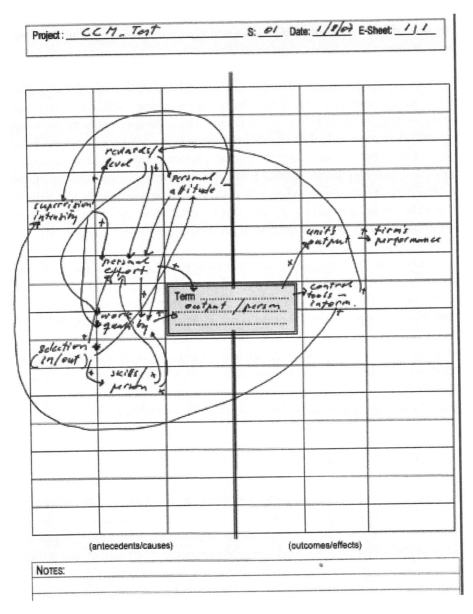

Figure 3.2   CCM SIM interview notes sheet (INS) S01 CCM_Case1

The forms for each anchor theme can be printed earlier and contain also
rows for remarks and guidelines for the interviewer. The same technique
can sometimes also be applied for collecting CCM data from documentary
sources. Another highly recommended tool in interviews is a reliable

voice-activated digital recorder, used of course with the respondent's permission. It backs up the written notes but can be very valuable when the interviewee is too verbose or fast and when there are difficulties in interpreting the hastily written notes later. Data transcription and entry techniques for CMAP3 will be discussed more in Chapter 5.

3.1.6   SHORTCUTS TO CCM DATA

The methods discussed above represent the so far typical ways to acquire CCM data. Although different in the type of raw data and techniques of elicitation and subsequent processing, the methods have a common core. All collect sets of causal propositions which are assumed to represent the phenomenological and causal beliefs of the studied actors or collectivities. It does not, however, take much imagination to see that there can be further ways to collect causal proposition data. Perhaps particularly interesting are simpler and thus faster elicitation techniques, which, in spite of that, provide satisfactory data, for example, in pragmatic CCM cases. The above and later (Section 7.3) discussed structured free-hand drawing method based on a predefined concept list is an example of such a highly efficient approach. For instance, in the CCM comparison study discussed in Section 7.3, the average duration of the FDM task (15 concepts, no specification) was M = 18.5 minutes (SD 12.5). Further conceivable methods could include the following:

Cause map template

In this method, the respondents are probed using a cause map template, which is similar to the SIM interview schema in Figure 3.1. It could contain one or two predefined anchor concepts in addition to several empty text boxes (perhaps N = 10–20). The template could be arranged in logical and labeled groups, corresponding to the normal categories of means, ends and givens relative to the focal issue. The respondents' task is to fill the boxes with their own concepts as they see fit. The template/form could be administered *in situ*, by surface mail using simple paper and pencil methods, or electronically using a PC/notebook and MS PowerPoint or by an email-attached MS PowerPoint slide. In terms of raw data entry, the filled-out templates/forms correspond to the INS forms (Figure 3.2). The data can be transcribed using an intermediate form (RDS or RDWS) for keyboard entry or CSL import (Section 5.1, 5.3).

Combining concept selection and causal links elicitation

A variant of the structured method is to present the concept pool in the form of sticky notes. The participant first selects the relevant ones and arranges and affixes them on piece of paper or cardboard and then draws the connecting arrows as they see fit, perhaps specifying them too. The process could be administered *in situ* by an interviewer or by using surface mail. The data could be entered using the manual or spreadsheet import-based techniques described below.

Combined electronic elicitation

A variation of the above technique is to use electronic elicitation built upon a widespread application like MS PowerPoint. In this case, the concept pool could be displayed as text boxes, perhaps grouped as above, on one slide, from which the respondent copies the selected ones to a second sheet and arranges them into a cause map form for drawing the connecting arrows. A small number of concepts could be placed on the same slide and simply selected, moved and then combined. This too could be administered *in situ* as above or, in favorable conditions, electronically using attached email files.

Combining Delphi methods and CCM

A further option combines some of the above CCM approaches with so-called Delphi methods, where typically a group of experts is interviewed about future developments in a domain. The results of the first round are fed back to the group to elicit new insights and ideas, this time triggered by knowing what others in the group have suggested (Linstone and Turoff 2002). In the present case, the aggregated causal map emerging of the first elicitation round would be sent back to the same respondents for amendments and additions in a second and possibly a third elicitation round. Thus, the previous stage provides probes and stimuli for the next second round and also validates the cumulative findings. The causal maps' function in this case is to provide a common platform and focusing instrument. It appears that some researchers have applied CCM and Delphi approaches using different techniques (Sheetz et al. 1993).

Needless to say, the critical issue for any shortcut elicitation methods is not their technical realizability but applicability, that is, when and where they make methodological sense. This depends, once again, on the research task and situation, including the characteristics of the participants. Some of the contingencies are probably the same as those in structured methods (Section 3.6). In general, shortcut tools seem applicable especially for preliminary and explorative elicitation tasks which concern narrow cognitive domains or compact issues and models, but must, at the same time, reflect the respondents' original views and thus be based on *primary* data. In addition, it would be beneficial if the participants are cooperative, knowledgeable, computer-savvy and view the study as important, fully understanding the explorative nature of the elicitation.

3.1.7 AUTOMATED CAUSAL MAPPING

Document data-based causal mapping requires data refinement and coding, which can be extensive. To support these tasks, content analysis software such as *AutoMap*, *Profiler Plus* and *WorldView*[2] have been developed. They enable extracting, from texts, interrelated causal propositions to represent and analyze mental models; in other words, ideally "automated" causal mapping, where a computer takes over most of the work (text reading included) which normally requires human labor (Carley 1997, Diesner and Carley 2004, Young 1996). However, there are significant preconditions and trade-offs to observe.

The main contribution of automated causal mapping software is the simplification of the data extracting and coding processes. However, they can only operate together with an in-built dictionary (tokenizer) and sets of instructions rendered by a pre-programmed coding scheme. An example of this is *Profiler Plus*, which is a general purpose system of natural language processing developed by Social Science Automation. For representing the mental models (causal maps) embedded in a given text, *Profiler Plus* must first break the text into sentences, recognizing the tokens in each sentence. This is followed by the creation of a data structure and assignment of a part of speech for each token. Next, the application observes the rules specified in the coding scheme in order to manipulate the tokens and, in causal mapping, to generate the final data of causal relations (Stone and Young 2009). This data can be imported to *WorldView*, which is a causal map analysis platform for displaying the data in visual form (Young 1996). *WorldView* can identify compound concepts, synonyms, shared or high salience beliefs, and perform inter-map comparison. In principle, when combined, these two applications could perform most of the CCM data processing tasks discussed above, especially extracting causal beliefs from secondary documents and writing samples of individual subjects.

---

2   For AutoMap, please visit: http://www.casos.cs.cmu.edu/projects/automap/. Profiler Plus can be accessed upon request: http://socialscience.net/tech/ProfilerPlus.aspx.

Thus, ideally, the amount of labor is considerably reduced and the researcher's role confined to only selecting the texts for analysis and rendering them in formats compatible to *Profiler Plus*.

In reality, however, automated content analysis tools are not the cure-all solution for text-based causal mapping research which they may appear to be at first glance. First, although they can ideally reduce labor, their usability and the results' validity depend critically on the quality of the underlying tokenization and the coding scheme. When either of them is unavailable for the target texts, a lot of time and energy is needed to develop the tokenizer and the coding scheme before any operations can commence. A situation like this is very common. It is difficult to find a tokenizer for most languages outside English. For instance, the current version of *Profiler Plus* has tokenizers for only four other languages: Arabic, Spanish, Chinese and Russian. Existing coding schemes that are sufficiently mature for empirical analysis are usually ill-suited to applications beyond their specific theoretical background. A researcher who wishes to develop their own tokenizer and/or coding scheme will soon find that these tasks require considerable and usually unavailable expertise in linguistics, computer programming and cognitive science. This perhaps explains why using automated causal mapping is not common, but instead usually field-specific and clustered around a few sophisticated coding schemes.

A second major issue with automated causal mapping is the incurred loss of contextual richness of the acquired data. This can be particularly severe in open-ended analysis of texts involving vocabularies and grammatical structures that the tokenizer and coding scheme do not recognize. For example, the *VICS* (*Verb in the Context System*), a coding scheme of *Profiler Plus*, can identify the directionality (+ cooperative or - conflictual), the intensity (+3 reward to -3 punish) and the attribution of verbs (self or other) in a causal statement (Walker et al. 1998). However, when used in automated content analysis, there is a risk of overlooking, first, significant causal relations signified by adjectives and, second, many verb expressions that emerge from, say, rapidly changing lexicons such as new words on the Internet. Furthermore, automated content analysis has problems in capturing most contextually embedded relational structures. When dealing with textual analysis, for instance, human coders must frequently infer causal relations from the use of pronouns and the logical sequence of sentences (Wrightson 1976). So far, such "content analysis" has been technically too complicated to be realized in professional software.

To conclude, while technical developments in content analysis have made some new automated tools and methods available to researchers, their application in causal mapping tasks is not yet unproblematic, especially in innovative projects which require theory-specific manipulation of rich data. At least in the foreseeable future, the more realistic and accessible route is the combination of human coding and computer-supported data processing and analysis.

3.2 Standardizing (Coding)

The need and functions of coding in comparative causal mapping can be demonstrated by a thought experiment. Let us assume a hypothetical CCM study, where the respondents represent three different nationalities and use respective native languages, and that the research is about discovering their typical causal belief patterns by interviewing. To extract the shared notions of the elicited data, it is necessary to compare what the interviewees have said. To do so, the original statements must be translated into a common meaning space, *standard* language, which could be one of the three original ones or a fourth one. Assuming correct translation, adopting a standard language enables detecting statements which appear similar and can be assumed to refer to similar meanings and underlying beliefs.

In this book, coding is called *standardizing*. The basic logic, however, is more or less the same regardless of the method: to map the original expressions and concepts used by the respondents or text sources into a common meaning space, a standard terminology or language. In some cases, the first-level standard expressions will be converted further into a different, usually a higher-level, second concept system. Technically, standardizing means simply that the natural concepts (in CMAP3 terms, NLUs (natural language units)), of which the original causal statements in the data consist, will be interpreted as mutually same-denoting and belonging to the same homogeneous concept category or meaning basket. When using CMAP3, these categories are labeled using a descriptive *standard concept* (SNT (standard node term)). They are stored in the project's standard term vocabulary (STV) database.

In CCM studies, standardization is implemented in different forms. Sometimes, it involves a simple word-to-word dictionary-based conversion. In other cases, researchers need to introduce inductive, sometimes deductive, reasoning, theoretical insight, even creativity. There are at least six typical situations that require standardization:

1.   The data contains *synonyms*, that is, the respondents or documents use different expressions/terms to refer to essentially the same targets or referents (for example, cash flow, liquidity, bank balance, and so on). The difficulty is that the sameness is sometimes an issue of definition and is relative and also ambiguous. In practice, this must be solved considering which meanings are apparent, how the terms are linked to other terms, and which interpretation seems logical and makes most sense in the context. In addition, the level of analysis and description must be observed.

2.   Another case, which is often more difficult to detect and solve, is the use of *homonyms*, that is, overtly same concepts/terms which, however, refer to different things. For example, the word "organization" can, to some, mean a social unit, a bureaucratic rule system or just orderly practices of management and team functioning. As above, the intended meaning or referent can usually be understood or detected by examining the term's usage in the context. In the case of critical concepts, the idiosyncratic meanings should, when possible, be clarified with the respondents.

3.   An important typical goal of coding/standardizing is to *compress* data and/or to remove elements that are irrelevant or redundant, unnecessary or even distracting from the research point of view. Such a data "oversupply" is normal in everyday discourse but also in open interviews and documentary sources and manifests itself as verbosity, background information, frequent use of synonyms, double attributes and polar states (good/bad liquidity versus horribly weak cash flow, and so on). Typical (but not all) CCM studies are, however, interested in the phenomena or factors (variables) to which the original expressions refer. That those phenomena may vary and have different values or states is usually implicitly obvious and does not need to be specifically noted using different terms for such states. However, there may be studies where such differentiating *is* important, for example, between low and high values. The different states may also have different causes and/or consequences and causal mechanisms which may be interesting in that specific case. Research objectives and the researcher's theoretical insight and common sense usually tell what is important.

4. A self-evident case for standardization are CCM studies where multiple languages are involved, as noted at the outset. When the research is published internationally, the standard language into which the original expressions using different languages are coded is today usually English.

5. In the above cases coding is essentially about interpreting and inductive *distilling* of the original statements into a more general, shared meaning system. Some CCM studies need to do exactly the opposite. Their objective is to explore the diffusion or *incidence* of an *a priori* causal model or general notions in a given social context. This requires comparing the elicited expressions against a predefined concept system, a template. This could be derived of, for example, theories of macroeconomics, management or entrepeneurship, the study's idea being to find out how far they have been adopted among laypersons.

6. Finally, there are inductive and explorative CCM studies where the goal is to distill and evoke *new concepts* and to develop theories/ models. This is also the situation when the researcher wants to devise a system of higher-level standard concepts/categories which compress and summarize the lower-level standard concepts into a more general concept system to highlight the basic underlying mechanisms. In such cases, creating new constructs requires theoretic insight and imagination, but also systematic and usually iterative analysis of the original data and first-level concept systems. This is similar to what takes place in so-called grounded theory or inductive research as discussed in methodological literature (for example, Corbin and Strauss 2008, Eisenhardt and Graebner 2007, Eriksson and Kovalainen 2008, Merriam 2009, Silverman 2006).

In general, what is relevant and appropriate in coding in each case depends on the research needs and available data. For instance, a participant-centered "emic" CCM study would emphasize the idiosyncratic differences in actors' causal patterns. Therefore, they are likely to use and preserve details such as qualifying attributes and polar states of variables. The standard terminology must mirror this and will therefore contain mainly "near-natural" standard terms/nodes, differentiating, for example, between positive and negative states, attitudes, and so on. However, in other and probably the more typical CCM cases, the original rich detail may be irrelevant, even counterproductive, because such studies emphasize extracting the underlying and *shared core* elements in the causal belief patterns. In addition, there are usually different pragmatic trade-offs to consider. For instance, the more detailed the elicited raw data, the fewer distinct phenomena or issues and less cognitive domains can be covered in the interviews, nearly always constrained in terms of access and available time. The different objectives and contingencies mean that coding/standardization will have to apply different degrees of compression. In practice, three rough levels of coding can be defined:

Level 0

In this case the standard term system corresponds closely to the elicited (original) expressions (NLUs). By definition, this is so in a structured CCM approach such as the concept pool method because all respondents use concepts from a predetermined pool—of course with the critical difference that the expressions are not necessarily original. Level 0 standardizing may also be sufficient in other cases such as when creating composite (idiosyncratic) causal maps. There the raw data comes from several informants or documentary sources and will be combined into a composite cause map representing the beliefs about the issue or domain. Because of the relative homogeneity of such raw data, there may be little need to standardize it and the standard term vocabulary can be a more or less "tidied-up" version of the natural expressions in the raw data. Another example is a dictionary-based translation of natural expressions into a standard language.

Level 1

This is perhaps the typical coding situation in low- and semi-structured CCM or document-based studies. In this case the standard language will also be close to the original, but is mainly about neutralizing some of the inherent problems in natural language data (items 1–3 above). At this level, standardizing has two main objectives. First, it removes those original language elements (for example, attributes, polar states) that are considered irrelevant for the research task at hand. Second, it adopts a set of common terms to replace synonyms and to differentiate homonyms. The general idea is to define homogeneous concept categories, to which original terms, interpreted as having similar meanings and/ or referents, will be assigned. Thus, standardization at Level 1 will involve a degree of researcher-based interpretation and compression of original meanings.

Level 2

The highest level corresponds to item 6 above and involves the inductive creation and interpretive use of new, higher-level standard categories with appropriate standard terms as labels. Depending on the case, the standard term vocabulary (STV) can be created iteratively directly from the original natural statement data and/or by combining Level 1 STV/STERMs into more encompassing standard concepts. In general, Level 2 standard categories will necessarily contain expressions and terms which refer to more than one different phenomenon or factor contained in original data and cannot therefore be internally homogeneous in a normal sense. Instead, there must be a common core or more general referent which makes the categories/standard terms relevant and plausibly homogeneous. For example, in the original CCM/CMAP study (Laukkanen 1994), the higher-level concept system combined several Level 1 standard terms, which referred to a small firm's different profit components or those concerning personnel, organization, and so on, into single overarching standard terms.

Thus, in essence, coding/standardizing is about assigning the original notions to standard baskets of similar meanings. In *inductive* coding, the baskets typically emerge through an iterative process. As will be discussed in more detail later (Section 5.4), it usually begins by setting up broad, tentative categories which are then successively partitioned into smaller categories with a common meaning or referent phenomenon. Notably, sometimes coding is *deductive*, mainly about assessing the correspondence of the elicited natural concepts and those in an *a priori* coding scheme or template. The coding scheme and researcher's individual standardizing decisions can be validated through different methods such as respondent feedback, peer or expert review and expert panels, as discussed more below. More advice can be found in general texts on coding and content analysis (for example, Krippendorff 2004). Practical and useful discussions about coding are also Levins and Silver (2007) in the context of qualitative studies and CAQDAS software and Wrightson (1976) for document-based composite causal mapping.

The differentiated three levels imply a rising degree of inductive generalization and thus a heavier *compression* of the original data. This has important consequences for the coded outcome data, analysis and the conclusions. Other things being equal, the higher the level of generality and compression, the higher will be the *collapsing effect* and the emerging *commonality* of the active standard node terms (SNT) and standard causal units (SCUs) among the respondents. This follows simply from the fact that coding assigns the original concepts (NLUs) into the corresponding standard term categories, which also will collapse the NLUs' original causal links into the respective standard causal units. What happens as a result of standardization is shown schematically in Figure 3.3. In general, the compression effect and thus the emerging sharedness of standard terms and causal links will

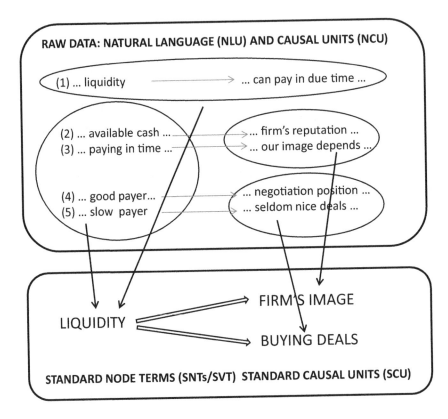

Figure 3.3   Coding/standardizing in CCM: compacting and collapsing effect

increase the more general and encompassing the standard term vocabulary is, merely because more original concepts will be interpreted as belonging to fewer standard term categories. Respectively, the "artificial" sharedness will *decrease* when the compression effect is reduced and the applied standard term vocabulary approaches the above Levels 0 or 1.

In view of the critical impact of coding/standardizing, what is done in a given CCM study should be understood clearly not only by the researcher but also made comprehensible and transparent to the reviewers and the eventual audience. A simple, often adequate solution to this is to provide an idea of the coding using, for example, an appendix or a table like Table 7.3, which displays the original concept contents (NLUs) of at least the more shared standard node term categories (SNTs).

In practice, coding must usually be an *iterative* process (Section 5.4). This needs appropriate techniques in particular when operating with a large volume of original data from multiple sources. Therefore, it makes sense to use software tools such as CMAP3. First, this provides for an efficient, controlled and transparent handling of the data through the whole process, from data entry to coding to output and analysis. Second, computerizing makes the iteration work towards the final standardizing solution much easier because computerizing enables the researcher to test and evaluate the impact of using different, higher- or lower-level, standard vocabulary. Third, computerizing also supports the review procedures for checking the validity and reliability of the coding scheme (standard term vocabulary) and the individual coding decisions.

In causal mapping literature coding is occasionally presented as somehow difficult and problematic. In particular, it is argued that it is messy and cumbersome and involves too much researcher subjectivity (Armstrong 2005, Clarkson and Hodgkinson 2005). As a consequence, coding-based causal mapping and documentary or interview methods in general can, probably unintentionally, acquire a problematic, even dubious, aura in particular compared with structured CCM approaches which do not require *ex post* coding. However, this line of argumentation is not entirely tenable or useful.

First, focusing on an overt and derivative issue such as alleged workload or subjectivity arguably misses the point. The need and appropriateness of a coding-based strategy depend on the research tasks and objectives at hand and the context. Therefore, to code or not to code is not an isolated issue, to be decided *a priori* at the outset. Rather, it is a methodological corollary of the researcher's objectives and research questions. Second, coding can be difficult if the researcher does not have a clear theoretical base and perspective, meaningful research questions and does not understand the studied domain and issues. If such preconditions are missing, the collected data cannot "speak" to the researcher but appears an undifferentiated, fuzzy mass. The undertaking will become truly arduous, indeed "messy", if the researcher in addition does not use computerized techniques but tries to manage with manual paper methods.

As for researcher subjectivity, it is first important to note that subjectivity can *never* be eliminated entirely, only understood and ideally accounted for when designing a study and evaluating its results (Maxwell 2012). This concerns not only CCM but all research, whether natural or social science, qualitative or quantitative. In causal mapping specifically, it is sometimes implied that, by eliminating *ex post* coding, structured CCM methods will be more "objective" (Clarkson and Hodgkinson 2005, see below). However, as noted earlier, this overlooks that considerable subjectivity remains, for example, in the construction of the concept pool/lists. More generally, it is inaccurate to say that coding in CCM *always* implies a lot of subjectivity. As noted above, standardizing can mean very different things depending on the necessary level of generality. The different levels require varying amounts of inductive or deductive insight and subjective interpretation. In most (but not all) CCM studies coding is mainly about removing redundancy and compacting of data, which involves usually self-evident, "harmless" decisions at Levels 0 or 1, as shown, for example, in the study case in Section 7.2. It also means less need and room for interpretation and hence for mistakes, in particular frequent, systematic errors.

However, there is of course CCM research, perhaps the most unique and interesting studies, which specifically do need and aim at interpretive and inductive generation of new theoretic or general concepts. Possibly someone could fundamentally object even to this, rejecting *any* construction of new concepts and all deviation from ("manipulation") the original communications. However, such a nihilistic stance would preclude, for example, much of mainstream qualitative research, which has the objective of meaningful *theoretic* generalization and understanding, *verstehen*, of social units' and systems' behaviors, and, in the case of CCM, of actors' belief patterns and action tendencies. As inductive studies generally, CCM research too often must look behind the overt surface of respondents' original expressions, conceptualizing the underlying phenomena, attributes and relationships using inductive "synthetic" constructs which can occasionally be distant and different from the original vernacular. The positive side is new knowledge and innovative constructs, often key conditions for important, interesting and relevant research (see Bartunek et al. 2006). However, to counter the potential negative impact of errors and unthinking judgment, appropriate validation methods and transparent reporting of findings and the path leading to them are necessary.

3.3   Comparison for Aggregation

A key task in comparative causal mapping is to determine the similarity or dissimilarity of the causal statements acquired from multiple sources, in particular of the *phenomenological* components (A, B, C, and so on) in terms of their meanings or referents. This is necessary, first, to *aggregate* individual causal maps into *collective* causal maps, which represent the typical thought patterns shared by all respondents or their subset. Second, comparison is needed when creating *composite* causal maps by extracting and combining causal statement data from documentary sources. Third, the calculation of the descriptive and comparative numerical metrics and their analysis also assumes that the similarity or difference of individual statements and their meanings and referents has been validly determined.

There are two main strategies for determining the similarity (dissimilarity) of cross-source notions and causal assertions. They are closely linked to the specific methods of CCM data acquisition and will necessarily overlap with the issues and different approaches in coding/standardizing.

3.3.1 INTERPRETIVE-INDUCTIVE STRATEGY

This approach is characteristic of those CCM methods which use data from interviews or documents. As noted, they include low- and semi-structured interviewing and text and secondary document-based approaches. In these cases, comparability is created in two stages. The first, more or less implicit, stage is the *acquisition* of raw data itself. It should be designed and realized so that the elicited data will be as focused, relevant and comparatively useful as reasonably possible for the research objectives. Ideally, this means that the data will consist predominantly of representative and valid causal statements that are task relevant and pertain to the focal issues, not to something else.

How such requirements are manifested in practice depends first on the type of data the study needs. When secondary data is used, it is obviously crucial to locate first the data sources which are relevant to the research question, such as minutes of meetings, official statements, personal memoirs, blogs, and so on. Sometimes the process is reversed, when interesting data becomes available, for example, previously classified documents are released and thus initiate their study. In low-structured interviewing and text-based elicitation of primary data, the selection of respondents and probes such as the addressed topics are the key issue and should therefore be carefully selected. In semi-structured interviewing, the selection and formulation of the initial anchor topics, around which the first data layers will emerge, will influence the likelihood of eliciting further representative, non-redundant causal statements. In addition, in interviewing it is important to ascertain the meanings the respondents attach to especially uncommon and apparently pivotal or frequent notions, particularly if the terms are clearly used in different meanings by different respondents.

The second stage in the interpretive-inductive strategy overlaps with the standardization process, discussed above. Essentially, this means examining the elicited concepts in terms of the similarity (dissimilarity) of their meanings or referents. This is often an uncomplicated detection and recognition task when the coder and the respondents have the same language base and the coder is familiar with the different expressions' normal meanings. Sometimes there is prior knowledge of the respondents' local jargon and vernacular. As emphasized, a clarification of idiosyncratic meanings and referents may be necessary in particular in the case of synonyms and homonyms. Sometimes the meanings of original expressions have to be inferred by examining their notions' links and usage by comparing data from different respondents or located in other documents of the same source. Especially in the case of salient and frequently occurring notions, such a validation may be necessary even if the original concepts in documents or interviews appear obvious and commonplace expressions in a culture.

3.3.2   PREDEFINED CONCEPT LIST OR POOL STRATEGY

This is how comparison and aggregation basis is created in structured CCM methods. As described above (Section 3.1.4), the key feature of them is a short fixed list or a larger pool of standard concepts, which are predefined by the researcher/s. The consequence is that the predefined concepts establish a common meaning space, a template and a measuring instrument which is the same for all participants. It also precludes the emergence of idiosyncratic concepts, excepting the special case that the participants can add some concepts of their own. The obvious result is that there is in most cases no need for *ex post* coding. In the prefixed list or the pool method's short list of concepts, what the participants select from the pool will be metaphorically "self-coded" for comparison and aggregation.

In general, in terms of potential validity, the interpretive-inductive strategy is more powerful and less sensitive than the structured, template-based approach (see 3.4). This, however, is not automatic. It assumes, first, that the data elicitation has provided the preconditions of valid and useful primary data and often also additional interpretation information. Next, the subsequent data and coding must build upon the preconditions and extract the meanings and referents in particular for the most critical and salient original expression. In addition, adequate steps may be needed to assess and improve the validity and reliability of first-level coding. Thus, in general, low- and semi-structured and text-based CCM require more resources and researcher input. In contrast, a structured approach such as the pool method requires relatively more resources and researcher effort in the preliminary stages, in particular to ensure the relevance and validity of the critical instrument, the concept pool.

Thus, there are always some trade-offs and no approach can be argued to be absolutely superior to the other. Like standardizing/coding, comparison too is an integral component of the specific method.

3.4 Trustworthiness—Validity

Trustworthiness of data and findings is a key objective and also an assessment criterion in social research. Traditionally this is discussed in terms of *validity*—in everyday terms, a method's ability to "measure what it is supposed to measure"—and *reliability*—the measurement's consistency and stability in repeated tests.

The conventional and also lay notion of validity is based on the ontological assumption that there is an external reality which can be known and faithfully mirrored by empirical methods and data. To proponents of qualitative research and methods, however, such an assumption is problematic. They emphasize the socially constructed basis of what is experienced and considered as "the" reality (Maxwell 2004a, 2012). Consequently, qualitative criteria of a study's trustworthiness or dependability are different. First, they observe and evaluate the overall plausibility of research practices and findings, focusing on what other researchers could corroborate in similar or different conditions. Second, they emphasize the role of the researcher's judgment and the consensus opinion of informed peers and audiences. Thus, validity in a qualitative sense is more a matter of *credibility* and *transferability* of results, whereas reliability is related to the study's *confirmability* (Maxwell 2012, pp. 122–3, Merriam 2009). More specifically, validity, that is, credibility and transferability, refers to the design and overall plausibility (face validity) of the study and to the applicability of its findings to other contexts, whereas reliability/confirmability is mainly a function of the (relative) appropriateness of the study's methods and operations and of how feasible it would be for interested researchers to repeat the study and/or in other ways to corroborate its claims.

Which interpretation of data and research quality is relevant specifically in CCM research is not immediately obvious. For one thing, CCM researchers also have their different, often implicit, ontological and epistemological positions, which are manifested in their methodological preferences and views about the relative merits of different types or traditions of research and methods. For instance, there are CCM scholars whose ideal and methodological model is *nomothetic* research and methods. In CCM this implies studies which emulate psychometric methods but are based on large samples and therefore primarily on a quantitative analysis of data (Hodgkinson and Healey 2008). This position is one driving factor behind the structured CCM approaches. On the other hand, there are CCM researchers (including the authors of this book) who have some reservations about the general feasibility and relevance of large-scale nomothetic and quantitative approaches in CCM. As grounds, they refer to the above discussed theoretical diffuseness and volatility of the cognitive target phenomena and the ensuing methodological issues which can render quantitative measurement (and findings) problematic. In concrete terms, moreover, most CCM studies so far are "qualitative" and "explorative". They are based on relatively small samples and, even in the case of a predominantly quantitative approach, depend significantly on researcher and peer judgment and interpretation. For such reasons, the qualitative notion and criteria of trustworthiness seem now more relevant than the traditional validity/ reliability view. In research terms, this is usually also the more operational interpretation, as will be seen below. This does not mean, however, abolishing established terms such as validity and reliability, only changing the way they are interpreted.

In causal mapping literature, trustworthiness in CCM studies is often framed mainly as an issue of coding—in practice, the semantic and face validity and internal consistency of the coding scheme and operations. This would make trustworthiness an issue which concerns only document, text-based and low- and semi-structured CCM methods, whereas structured template approaches, which do not need *ex post* coding, would, by definition, be more or less free of such problems ("inherently valid"). This would obviously much oversimplify a complex, multifaceted issue. In particular, it puts too much emphasis on *ex post* assessment and downplays what must happen before and the efforts to ensure and improve validity and reliability.

To begin with, perhaps needless to repeat, the preconditions of a scientifically interesting or pragmatically useful and trustworthy study will be created (or removed) and largely finally settled in the early stages of research planning and design. These are broad issues which are examined extensively in general and specialized methodology texts. A wider discussion of them is beyond the present scope, but there are some practical points which seem sometimes ignored in CCM studies. They both follow from the common-sense rule that one should promise only what is realistic but also do what one has promised to do.

The first point is that, when contemplating a CCM research project at the outset, one should avoid, if possible, being locked into preconceived ideas about a method approach or which data or which specific respondents and context one is going to study. Instead of such *a priori* fixed points, it may be better to keep an open mind until there is a balanced combination which makes sense and seems workable and meaningful to oneself and, preferably, to one's peers and mentors, too. Moreover, it is important to ascertain by preliminary research that preconditions such as access to informants and thus satisfactory data will be there.

A further antecedent condition of validity/credibility is a correspondence between the research task and the applied method approach. To take an extreme example, if somebody proposes to do a CCM study of an organization or social group to capture their belief patterns *in toto*, that would indicate an unrealistic and weak theoretic understanding of social cognition and that the target phenomenon, as defined, and the proposed methodology are not matched. Should the study moreover aim to use a structured CCM approach, there would be even less agreement with the stated objectives and research design.

Task-method correspondence is mainly a function of common sense and theoretical and methodological knowledge. However, the acceptance and *a priori* plausibility of research depend also on the scientific community's attitudes, knowledge and judgment, which are not entirely objective or logical phenomena. As to CCM research and methods in particular, it would be ideal if we could assume that peers and reviewers are familiar with them and accept them. This is not always the case, which can make the playing field not as level as when using conventional methods. For the researcher this means building scientific contacts or a network of knowledgeable and respected mentors in the field. It is also important to be aware of which journals are potential publication forums. Obviously, one must do one's homework properly and, for example, note carefully relevant extant studies and methodological authorities. It is also important to explain the study's theoretical underpinnings and methods and in particular to ensure the transparency of all critical aspects such as coding and its reviewing. Such things foster *a priori* credibility, which is a precondition of dependability and eventual confirmability.

The second condition of trustworthiness in CCM studies is *data quality*: a bottleneck issue in all research which relies on human communication-based data in one form or another. In CCM literature in particular, one occasionally gets an impression that CCM data in documents or elicited by interviewing is always inherently suspicious. Underlying this may be an implicit, possibly culture-specific, premise that informants will never reveal what they really think or know but instead purposely try to hide their "true" beliefs. In addition, it is assumed that proactive data acquisition such as interviewing always alters and biases the participants' cognitions and communications (Nadkarni and Narayanan 2005, p. 10). Whilst such misgivings are not entirely unfounded, it is also obvious that the prevalence and methodological implications of such problems should not be exaggerated and generalized either. For one thing, eventual tendencies to conceal one's thoughts or to be actively "economical with the truth" can be assumed to vary across national, local and organizational cultures. In addition, they reflect unique individual experiences, which sometimes can support concealing, but also the opposite—openness and frankness. Thus, there are both inherently problematic and normal, unproblematic elicitation contexts and resulting data. It must be assumed that the researcher and the scientific community of practice are familiar with the local contingencies and can factor them into the research operations and analysis. Secondly, it is important whether the eventual biasing or concealing tendencies produce mainly random or systematic effects such as fabrication of data or omissions. As noted, a useful aspect of CCM studies is a degree of self-correction; the impact of random factors and biases can be assumed to cancel themselves out at *aggregate* level. This is because they use data from *several* data sources and extract *shared* causal belief patterns. The detection of systematic biases and omissions can be more difficult but not impossible, but that will usually require additional, independent evidence.

In practical terms, *data's quality* and validity in CCM studies can be assessed in terms of three aspects: authenticity, sincerity and accuracy or truthfulness (Axelrod 1976, pp. 6, 252ff, Merriam 2009). We will begin with the first two issues, which are usually the most relevant aspects in the present context. In typical CCM research *authenticity* is seldom a problem, given that the data is usually in an easily accessible and verifiable form, such as documents or interview transcriptions and perhaps voice recordings. However, this can be an issue if authenticity requires a demonstrated connection with a document or similar and a given actor or collectivity—in other words, showing who said or wrote this or that. Therefore, knowing and being able to show the origins and creation context of such data can be highly important.

Sincerity is a different problem and more difficult to assess. It is about whether the informants, like interview respondents, express what they really know and believe. In plain terms, do the respondents say (or in the case of the pool method, select) what they think and know and do they really mean what they say? In general, a basic sincerity can be expected. However, this assumes that there are no *systematic factors or motives* for the respondents to conceal or bias their thoughts. As observed above, there may be, for example, contexts and cultures where (or scholars for whom) concealing or even deviousness is the assumed norm, but also cultures and situations where contrary rules apply.

However, in interview- and text-based CCM primary data acquisition about normal, non-sensitive issues, a basic sincerity usually seems more probable. This has common-sense reasons. First, considering typical acquisition situations, it is reasonable to assume that it is primarily the retained and frequently used knowledge and mental models that will be tapped. This is because it would be cognitively parsimonious and thus more logical and practical from the perspective of the respondent. Indeed, assuming appropriate and clear instructions, a normal level of trust and/or a low issue or situational sensitivity, why would a rational, busy person take the trouble to fabricate something when the relevant inquired stuff is readily available in their memory? Fabricating seems even more unlikely with experienced and/or professional persons and when the studied issue, task or domain is professionally important to them. However, the elicitation situation will become more volatile and less predictable when the respondents are asked about novel, unfamiliar issues. In this case it is both cognitively necessary and thus also more likely that the respondents must (see Section 2.5) revert to ad hoc inference and imagination, possibly building on recalled parallel cases, metaphors or naïve folk theories (Fiske and Taylor 2013, p. 151). This, however, does not render the data *intentionally* insincere. The data still reflects the respondent's retained knowledge, mental models and reasoning tendencies. However, it is probable that such data will contain more random and volatile elements and thus show less similarity across the participants.

Instead of intentional insincerity, perhaps the more relevant issues in CCM interviewing practice are how *much* data will be produced and how *useful* it will be. In practice, problems can arise from two asymmetries. First, as noted above, a participant could indeed decide to *conceal* some of their beliefs. Sometimes, this reflects a negative attitude towards research in general, sometimes towards the interview (or interviewer). In any case, the participant can be assumed to do a subjective assessment of the situation (Section 2.5). This includes dimensions such as the sensitivity of the topic, initial trust, organizational or other social positive or negative consequences of participating or not participating, time pressures, personal state of vigilance, and so on (Nicolini 1999). This may introduce an unpredictable element into the acquisition process, which can either systematically or randomly influence elicited data's volume and validity. In practice, researchers can use different methods to neutralize an initial negativity or specific doubts. These include formal legitimation of the study and the researcher, appropriate information and a consistent and transparent overall behavior. Ideally, in interviewing and text-based data elicitation, the respondents should have a feeling of trust and confidentiality and that the research process and the addressed topics are not sensitive or risky (Maxwell 2012, Merriam 2009, Nicolini 1999). However, as in interpersonal relationships in general, the development of an ideal or at least a neutral elicitation setting may take some time. In practice this can mean things such as using preliminary interviews and/or avoiding tackling too complex and especially potentially personally sensitive issues—or at least postponing them—until a feeling of mutual trust and rapport has been achieved.

The second asymmetry problem, especially when interviewing well-informed, talkative and vigilant respondents, is that they could, if willing and allowed, produce *apparently* valid data almost endlessly (see Section 2.5). In this case, the responses consist not only of the participant's typically used and recalled causal and phenomenological knowledge, but also of products of ad hoc imagination and reasoning. The latter would be based on simulating and projecting from the probe-evoked causal paths and phenomena to new, perhaps completely fabricated ones (Mohammed et al. 2000, Morgan et al. 2001, p. 25). In our experience, fabrication is rather infrequent for practical reasons such as time constraints. It can become harmful if the interview's purpose is misunderstood because of unclear instructions or if the interviewer is careless or too timid to stick to the protocol, uniform topics, probing formats and time frames. Should the interviewer feel that something like this is happening, it is important to bring the discussion back to the main track quickly but cautiously so as not to disturb the climate and the motivation. This can usually be accomplished by restating the purpose of the interview and type of data sought, sometimes by asking the respondent to comment and explain a response which the interviewer finds problematic.

As to *secondary data* such as printed documents or similar, sincerity (or its lack) can be a major factor affecting data quality, too. It is well known that such data, for example, political or company statements, is sometimes intentionally biased to serve a pragmatic purpose such as influencing investors or voters. It may be necessary to check the data's origins case by case: the probed issues, the production situation, overall objectives and social context from the participants' viewpoint and their relative qualifications (Nicolini 1999). Sometimes it is necessary to acquire parallel data such as other simultaneous documents or even to conduct interviews in order to be able to assess the original causal beliefs' sincerity and representativeness.

Finally, data quality issues should also be placed in a wider perspective. It is useful to recall that the very idea of CCM studies is usually to locate actors' or collectivities' *typical* belief patterns by collecting voluminous data from multiple sources and using inductive and interpretive methods to extract the shared and/or systemic patterns. Such data will contain, in addition to the dominant shared notions, a number of *idiosyncratic* ideas of single or a small number of respondents. In terms of the shared elements, they are not errors but rather *outliers*, that is, unusual and untypical notions. Furthermore, the processing and interpreting and coding of large amounts of qualitative data will introduce some unintentional errors, too. These and the idiosyncratic elements, "noise", however, are usually *random* occurrences. It is reasonable to assume that such errors and outliers do not usually *significantly* distort the emerging shared patterns of beliefs at *aggregate* level (Spender 1998). In CCM practice, such animpact willbe usually eliminated when the original data is converted into analyzable standardized data.

The third aspect of data quality, *accuracy*, is different from authenticity and sincerity. The issue now is the *factual correctness* of the elicited knowledge and causal statements. In plain words: if a collective or a person says that A $\rightarrow$ B, can we take it that A indeed influences B in the sense of causing certain changes in the phenomenon to which B refers? For example, all small business advisors studied in the SBA study discussed in Section 7.2 say that successful founding of new firms (A) will reduce local unemployment (B). The subjective evidence for this causal link they find in their daily experience when previously unemployed small entrepreneurs employ themselves and perhaps one or two other persons. What could be clearer than that? It is, however, possible that the new firms replace old firms and their jobs, sometimes leading to a net reduction, not net increase, of employment. What is the message of this example for practical purposes?

First, as noted earlier, a considerable part of the kind of knowledge/ beliefs that will be elicited and analyzed in typical CCM studies concern *social* phenomena, where the causal relationships are, at best, varying probabilistic tendencies, not law-like invariances assumed to prevail in the physical world. In many cases the expressed causal ideas do not have even this level of empirical grounding. Thus, the accuracy or correctness is usually a relative and volatile matter even in the best of cases. The corollary question is, does this matter? This depends obviously, once again, on the purposes of the CCM study. For example, in studies of political actors, the objective may be just to extract and analyze their phenomenological and causal beliefs and to observe what the actors or a collectivity *seem* to hold as true and accurate, irrespective of whether that is so in some objective sense. However, if the research were about a *what if* analysis predicting the real-life consequences of the elicited belief patterns, or a CCM study of the structure and mechanisms of an important socio-technical system, the accuracy or truthfulness of the causal statements could become critical. In such cases there would certainly be additional, corroborating studies, as discussed below.

Depending on the specific CCM approach, there are also more concrete things and conditions that influence the study's validity and dependability. First, as discussed in Section 3.1.4, a key task in *structured CCM* is to validate the study's concept list or concept pool, that is, to ensure their *representativeness* and *relevance* in terms of the participants and the research task. In the literature, the attitude about this task appears somewhat casual, leaning asymmetrically to ensuring the concept pool's completeness rather than its relevance. For example, Markóczy and Goldberg (1995, p. 310) recommend testing the pool on a pilot sample and asking the respondents whether anything important is *missing*. This reflects the implicit assumption that whatever the respondents later select from the pool and connect in a concept list is, by definition, valid and representative of their belief systems. This is problematic as a general premise. First, the fact that a respondent selects a given subset of concepts from the pool can, but does not necessarily, mean evidence that they really understand or know those concepts and, more importantly, actually use them in real-life so that the selected data could be considered valid and representative of their belief patterns. Concept selection can also be based on other, even trivial and random grounds. Second, the fact that the same standard concept is selected by two or more persons is not evidence that they also have identical interpretations of them, that is, similar meanings or referents in mind. Indeed, it is not at all unusual that the idiosyncratic subjective meanings and interpretations differ, even widely. This can be expected especially when the concepts are unfamiliar, concern general issues, or when they refer to inherently ambiguous notions and aspects such as those of organizational and social contexts. This can be critical in terms of valid comparison and everything that depends on it, such as valid aggregation or quantitative indicators. The obvious counterstrategy is that structured methods should be used in appropriate research tasks. Some of the selection criteria will be discussed below and in Section 7.3, which compares a structured and a semi-structured CCM study.

The corresponding issues in CCM studies which rely on *ex post* coding were already discussed above. The key task is to ensure that the study's category system (standard term vocabulary) and coding decisions are satisfactory and relevant in view of the research task and objectives. The coding scheme and individual decisions must produce aggregated cause maps which are valid representations of the studied actors' relevant belief patterns or theoretically and/or pragmatically useful models of the target real system. How can we know this?

In low- and semi-structured CCM studies, the usually recommended validation strategy is participants' *self-evaluation* (Huff 1990, Nelson et al. 2000). In practice, they can and would assess mainly whether their own notions and concepts were correctly interpreted and assigned into the more general standard categories. It is less plausible that they could validly evaluate how well the other participants' expressions were coded, perhaps excluding obvious mistakes. Thus, participants' feedback-based assessment can function at the lower levels of standardization (Level 0 or Level 1). Moreover, the feedback strategy needs some further preconditions. First, the assessment task must be feasible considering the participants' knowledge and judgment. Second, it must make practical sense and not ask too difficult, but also not trivial, questions such as interpretations of common synonyms. Third, the participants should be motivated and well informed. They need adequate instructions and explanatory materials in addition to task materials. For example, a thesaurus explaining how natural concepts have been interpreted and categorized could be useful (see Table 7.3). There are different ways of organizing the feedback depending on method of data processing.

However, a feedback strategy obviously cannot always make sense. For example, it can hardly work in an international study, where the participants could not assess whether their expressions were correctly converted into a standard language which is foreign to them. In general, asking feedback becomes increasingly irrelevant the more distant the standard terminology (to which the original expressions must be compared) is from the participants' natural language and original conceptualizing of the domain or the issue. This means the higher levels of standardizing, which were referred to above as Level 2. Unfortunately, the more interesting and important CCM studies tend to represent just this category. Therefore, other validation strategies are needed. There are mainly two additional, potentially parallel approaches. First, it is usually possible to replicate or at least pre/review what the researcher has done or proposes. Second, we can use an evidence-based approach, seeking other, corroborating or logically contrasting findings or data about the same phenomena.

The first approach means in practice usually informal peer assessment and feedback or a systematic review of what the researcher (coder) has done.

In important research both should be used. First, assessing the logic and relevance (content validity) of a new higher-level concept system is ideally a two-way street and provides iteratively constructive feedback and suggestions from well-informed colleagues and peers who clearly understand what the researcher wants to do. This enables a meaningful evaluation and improvement of the coding system's plausibility and face validity. It also lays the groundwork for the subsequent detailed review of individual coding decisions. This is the second stage, where one or more coders (with appropriate qualifications and information), independently of the principal coder (usually the researcher/s), will review the standardization decisions. The degree of their convergence can be measured by quantitative indicators of inter-coder reliability/agreement (Krippendorff 2004). As a result of the review, the initial coding can be amended by changing the individual decisions and/or by creating new STV categories and recoding the respective items.

The second approach follows the logic of *construct validation* and *triangulation* (Maxwell 2012). The precondition is an underpinning theory or model which enables predicting how the measured variable or phenomenon representing the focal construct should behave in relation to measured variables which represent other constructs to which it should be logically related. Mohammed et al. (2000, p. 144) discuss this as an issue of cognitive methods' general ability to capture mental models. Projected to the level of a concrete CCM study, the issue is the representativeness of the emerging, usually aggregated, causal maps. Depending on the case, the question to assess differs. Perhaps in the majority of cases the issue is how accurately do the causal maps represent the respondent's belief patterns? In some cases the question is, are they theoretically or pragmatically plausible and useful models of the target real system? In the latter case, when mapping socio-technical systems (for example, Roberts 1976, Nelson et al. 2000), researchers usually start with a tentative preconception about the target system. This and the emerging causal maps enable a mind's eye simulation of the target system's behavior and counterfactuals under different conditions. These predictions can be tested with existing information and research findings or they point to suitable tests.

The idea of triangulation, essentially using relevant parallel evidence, can be applied to assessing aggregate causal maps, too. Because CCM deals with cross-subject knowledge and mental models, a potential but not absolute validity criterion is the extent to which the emerging standard concepts and causal notions are *shared*. *Ceteris paribus*, high commonality indicates the convergence and similarity of the underlying belief patterns and is thus *indirect* evidence of the method's and the findings' credibility. This is because it is simply not plausible that several respondents, who usually do not know each other and are located far from each other, could or would actively collude and agree *a priori* what they all will say or choose. There are, however, qualifiers to this idea. For one thing, it must be ensured that the emerging commonality is not an *artifact*, created by sloppy or too aggressive coding which puts too many original notions into illogical and/or very heterogeneous standard categories. This calls for appropriate evaluation and reviewing of the coding. In addition, the emerging sharedness is an *asymmetric* indicator of validity. Low commonality can be a valid result, meaning that there are indeed few shared belief patterns. However, it can also suggest that the method itself or, more usually, the way it was realized, in particular data elicitation and its coding, is in some respect flawed. This is one more reason to emphasize careful research planning and execution. In many CCM studies which use primary data, a useful manifestation of sharedness (or its absence) is the degree to which core concepts and patterns of causal beliefs begin to *saturate* with successive additions of new data, for example, by each new interview (Eisenhardt and Graebner 2007, Nelson et al. 2000). In some studies it makes sense to track the saturation (see Section 7.2, Figure 7.7) and use it to determine whether more data sources are necessary.

Finally, in CCM studies using primary or documentary data, it may be possible to use parallel previous evidence in the way of triangulation. Such data could be other, independent statements of the same respondents about the same domain or issue. They should consistently reflect the same belief patterns. Another strategy could be to use a different CCM method, for example, a structured approach, to corroborate a semi-structured interview-based CCM study. In the case of secondary documents, it is often possible to expand the document base to examine whether the emerging belief patterns begin to saturate, that is, the same causal statements occur repeatedly—a sign of consistency in belief system.

3.5 CCM Metrics: Counting the Countable

A key feature of CCM methods is that they convert covert cognitive phenomena (propositional knowledge/beliefs, mental models) into an overt form using an appropriate formalism (datatable, matrix) which supports cause-map-based mathematical operations. These can range from simple counting to matrix operations and calculation of combined relations and indicators, and eventual statistical analysis. Assuming valid data and causal maps, this enables a rigorous, *quantitative* description, analysis and comparison of the target phenomena. This is salient in psychometrically oriented, structured CCM studies. However, "counting the countable" (Cassell and Symon 1994) is important and arguably often even more relevant in *qualitative* CCM studies (Bluhm et al. 2011, Cassell and Symon 1994, Maxwell 2010). There the numbers can, first, *heuristically* pinpoint differences, unexpected anomalies, interpretation errors and tendencies such as accumulation or dispersion in the data and respondents. Second, numbers are often very useful for summarizing and descriptive purposes. This section first lists some of the usual metrics and numerical measures in CCM studies (Axelrod 1976, pp. 343ff, Clarkson and Hodgkinson 2005, Eden and Ackermann 1998, Mohammed et al. 2000, Nadkarni and Narayanan 2005). Second, it examines the descriptive and analytic purposes for which metrics have been used. Third, we discuss some of the preconditions of different metrics and how far quantification of causal maps is generally meaningful.

Typical numerical indicators or metrics used in CCM studies include the following:

1.   *Numbers of concepts and/or causal links* in a respondent's single or a collectivity's or subgroup's aggregated causal map. They can be calculated as absolute numbers or as average or median values, possibly with additional descriptive statistics showing the concentration or variance in the data.

2.   The *density of a cause map* can be defined as the ratio of the number of links between concepts to the total number of concepts, or as the ratio of the number of links in a specific cause map to all possible links. It is usually assumed that the nodes do not directly influence themselves, that is, there are no relationships of type A→A and the valency matrix diagonal always has zero values. Obviously, such causal influences can exist but they are assumed to be realized through feedback paths and effects in the underlying causal system. Notably, when calculating a density measure, the comparison base of all possible links can be defined to include or exclude *reciprocal* relationships (that is, only A→B, but not B←A). For example, the density measure in CMAP3 *excludes* such relationships.

3.   A *distance ratio* or *distance index* is an indicator of the (relative) *similarity/dissimilarity* of the studied individuals', their subgroups' or some collectivities' *elicited* causal maps, and thus, implicitly, of the underlying mental models or knowledge systems.

It is sometimes calculated using a complex formula which is based on the collected causal links and their specification data assuming identical numbers of map nodes (Langan-Fox et al. 2000, Markóczy and Goldberg 1995). In CMAP3, the *C/D-index* is a correspondence/distance measure, which is calculated automatically using a simple formula (Section 6.4). It is not sensitive to the number of concepts/nodes and it can be calculated using either the standard causal links (SCU) base or the standard node terms (SNT) base.

4.   So-called *in-, out-* and *total degrees* (Id, Od, Td) are typical causal map specific indicators. Their idea and calculation is best understood assuming that the underlying causal map is in the form of a *square matrix* (adjacency or valency matrix) (Axelrod 1976, pp. 349ff). Corresponding to the column sum, the *indegree* (Id) shows the number of causal links flowing into a causal map node/concept. Respectively, the row sum is the *outdegree* (Od) of that particular concept/node. Summing up the two for a concept/node gives its *total degree* (Td) in the specific causal map/matrix.

Quantifying, in practice knowing the metrics and how to calculate them, is as such not difficult in CCM. The problem is which indicators make research sense and for which purposes? This depends, first, on the target phenomena the causal maps are assumed to represent: are they models of some real socio-technical systems or representations of actors' or a collectivity's phenomenological and causal belief patterns? A metric can make sense only in either of these contexts but not both. A further condition is relevant and valid data. Weak data does not prevent calculating metrics, but makes their meaningfulness and the conclusions based on them problematic.

3.5.1 MODELING REAL SYSTEMS

In this case causal map data can be elicited as usual from documents or from persons who are assumed to know the target system and issues well. The latter route is usually necessary in explorative studies of previously uncharted domains and issues. However, irrespective of the source, the data consists of communicated causal statements and mirrors the data sources' *subjective* beliefs and ways of conceptualizing the domain. By using normal CCM methods of coding and processing, standardized aggregated causal maps will be created. In this case, they are defined explicitly as *models* of the respective *real socio-technical systems*, and thus assumed to depict at least tentatively the real phenomena and mechanisms in the domain, often to be corroborated in later studies.

In this type of CCM analysis, the initial, perhaps the main, approach is a *what-if* analysis based on a mind's eye *visual simulation* of the situation mechanisms as depicted in the aggregated causal map (Axelrod 1976, pp. 55ff, Roberts 1976). However, it is often heuristically useful to examine, first, the overall character of the causal map/system and, second, the *relative positions* and *types* of the individual map nodes (concepts, that is, variables and referents). For such purposes the focal cause map's nodes' *Id-*, *Od-* and *Td-values* can be calculated. Third, the decision-making or real implications of the mapped system can be analyzed.

The calculated link numbers can be used as indicators of *concept-level centrality* or *map-level centrality* (Nadkarni and Narayanan 2005). A concept with the highest Td-value would be the most central one in the mapped system. Map-level centrality on the other hand concerns how far the whole examined causal map/system is centered around a single concept, with most other concepts directly or indirectly connected to the central one as a cause or as an effect.

The cause map/system as a *socio-technical mechanism* can also be analyzed from a *means-ends* perspective. This mirrors the generic problem-solving strategy (Simon 2001), where the solver differentiates three main components in the task situation: one, the goals or *end* state to be achieved; two, the available *means* or different tools and levers; and three, the conditions or *givens* under which one operates and which cannot be changed, only factored in and perhaps utilized. Projected into a cause map/system, a node that has relatively many outgoing relationships, that is, a high out-degree (Od) value, suggests a *givens* type factor in the context which needs to be observed and adapted to. A node which has several ingoing relationships and thus a high in-degree (Id) value usually indicates an end or a goal and criterion type of variable. Finally, cause map nodes with a high total degree (Td), that is, sum of Id- and Od-values, can suggest *central* phenomena which the respondents consider important influencable lever factors, *means*. A high Od or Td could also refer to *trigger* or *threshold variables* in the overall causal mechanism.

The CCM study about local economic and entrepreneurship development (Figure 1.1) provides an example of the above type of analysis. In this case, salient ends-type variables are *new firm births*, *job supply* and a higher *attractivity* of the community, whilst central means or levers are the municipalities' *development strategies* and measures. These had high Id- and Od-values and a high centrality in the elicited and mapped system. Examples of givens type variable with low Id-values were things such as *economic policies, natural environment* or *market/ customer demands.*

A third approach is to analyze the *influence paths* in the mapped system (for example, Axelrod 1976, pp. 55ff, 349ff, Nelson et al. 2000). This can be done visually or by calculating one or more *reachability matrices* by multiplying the initial adjacency/valency matrix (Section 1.2). In this way it is possible to pinpoint the cumulative direct and indirect influences which a given node/variable has on other nodes/variables in the causal map/system. One can also locate eventual *feedback paths* and *loops* in the represented system from one variable back to itself. When undertaking quantitative exercises like these, it is obviously important to avoid reifying and over-interpreting the distilled causal maps. They are not the territory (or system) they depict, but artifacts which are derived and composed of causal statements from primary or secondary sources. Therefore, they are dependent on the elicited data and the processes of interpretation and compressive generation. One might ask oneself how far calculating this or that is tenable, can it say something worthwhile about the real world and its behavior, or is this just academic playing with numbers?

3.5.2 REPRESENTING MENTAL MODELS AND BELIEF SYSTEMS

Causal maps are, however, primarily used as representations not of real systems but of the phenomenological and causal *belief patterns, mental models,* of an actor or a collectivity. In this case, there are at least *four perspectives* and types of analysis where quantitative metrics have been used and where they may make sense, either in terms of comparative measurement or heuristically.

The first *structural perspective* parallels the above structural analysis of mapped real systems. In this case especially two viewpoints can be noted. One analyzes the cause maps' overall *structure* and the extent to which the represented mental models seem to be *centered* around some specific map nodes/variables. This is a centrality/dominance versus multipolar issue, which can be assumed to be linked to the elicited mental model's general richness or complexity. Another structural viewpoint is to examine the mapped models' apparent *means-ends structure.* Here, the question is what are the specific goals, levers and contingency factors which the actors individually or as a collective perceive? This is an important perspective because it concerns directly the causal *mechanisms*, not single relationships, which the respondents assume function in the context. An analysis of the Od/Id/Td-values can tentatively pinpoint the different node types, discussed above. However, to understand the actors' thinking, a visual causal map analysis and informed mind's eye simulation is usually necessary, too. It is of course also technically possible to calculate and analyze causal influence paths and feedback loops in causal maps which represent a person's or a collectivity's mental models or belief systems (see Axelrod 1976, pp. 55ff). In this case, the purpose might be, for example, to support optimal decisions or to explain or forecast them. It is, however, a moot issue how far that makes sense. In general, this seems problematic considering that the underlying mental models and causal beliefs are not "hardwired" and cannot be assumed to function as predictably as real causal mechanisms and tendencies. In addition, there are usually different social and contextual intervening factors. However, path analysis can sometimes be heuristically useful by suggesting hypotheses and questions for further analysis.

The second perspective is to examine the causal maps' or rather the represented mental models' or belief systems' *complexity* or richness, usually measured in terms of two dimensions. One is *comprehensiveness*, which can be expressed as the (relative) *number of concepts/nodes* in the causal map (Carley and Palmquist 1992). As maintained by Nadkarni and Narayanan (2005), this metric refers to the *differentiation* facet of complexity. In present terms, it represents the *phenomenological beliefs*, that is, which and how many different variables, factors, and so on the person or group discerns in the domain or about the issue. The other dimension is *density*, which captures the *integration* aspect in complexity. It is manifested in the *number of perceived causal relationships* in the mapped mental model and can be calculated as an absolute number or in relative terms. One option is to divide the number of causal links with the number of concepts in the causal map; the other is to calculate the relationship of the causal links to the maximum number of links in the map.

A third perspective is to examine the *similarity* (dissimilarity) of the elicited causal maps representing the individual mental models or belief systems. This can serve descriptive and comparison purposes. It also enables detecting and differentiating cognitively homogeneous *groups* of respondents. One way is to calculate the above noted *distance ratio* of Markóczy and Goldberg (1995). The measure has been used in some structured CCM studies (Langan-Fox et al. 2004, Langfield-Smith 1992, Markóczy and Goldberg 1995). It uses the numbers of identical causal links in the elicited causal maps and takes into account the individual specification (typically direction +/- and subjective weight) of the links assuming that all respondents select an identical number of concepts. Another distance/similarity measure is the *C/D-index* of CMAP3 (Section 6.4). It is based on calculating the number of nodes/concepts or causal relationships that a pair of respondents or predefined clusters *share* and comparing that with the total number of concepts or causal links they have in the data. This indicator is less precise but often adequate and perhaps also more realistic considering the volatility of the target phenomena and the inherent difficulties of cognitive measurement.

In principle, the above indicators of cause map structure, complexity and mutual distance can be used to *describe* and to *compare* the respondents or their clusters in cognitive terms individually or collectively. This enables "quasi-statistical" statements such as, for example, that respondent A's belief system is more "complex" or "richer" than that of B, or that A is closer or cognitively more similar to C than B in terms of their *elicited* mental models. A useful approach in many CCM studies is also to *categorize* the respondents into groups whose causal maps are mutually similar but differ from those of the other groups. If there are only a few respondents, the grouping may be technically feasible by a visual analysis of the distance measures. However, with a larger N, it is more practical to use, for example, statistical cluster analysis. Figure 3.4 contains a *dendrogram*, which was produced by SPSS *hierarchical cluster analysis* (for an un-mathematical explanation, see Mooi and Sarstedt 2011: Chapter 9). The underlying data is from the simulated CMAP3 default demo project (CCM_Case1), which has 9 respondents (S01-S09). The C/D index matrix was calculated on the causal link (SCU) basis and exported to SPSS. In this case, two clear clusters emerge, with two respondents (S08, S01) somewhat more loosely attached, corresponding to the two *a priori* defined respondent types in the data.

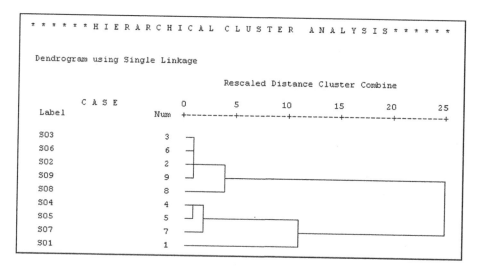

Figure 3.4   **CCM_Case1: S01-S09 hierarchical clusters (C/D index SCU)**

In real cases with larger Ns and NCU/NLU databases, the clusters would probably seldom be this clear-cut. However, a cluster analysis can be useful even so. Depending on the study, the statistical clustering can *confirm* but also suggest how to *modify* the *a priori* clustering, which was defined at the outset as perhaps expected on theoretical or pragmatic grounds. Second, statistical cluster analysis is useful *exploratively* to develop and test hypotheses about the background and reasons why there are just those groups which the data and the empirical cluster analysis seem to suggest. Third, it can be an indicator of the level of coding.

There is also a fourth perspective, where the respondents' mental models are compared against a *standard pattern* of concepts and causal relationships. This differs from analyzing cognitive complexity or distance-based clustering which take place *within* the sample and are based on the elicited cause map data. In contrast, assuming that we want to know which mental models or whose belief systems are "better" or more "optimal" from some perspective, additional data is required which is independent of and goes beyond the elicited belief system data. In general, this is the case in CCM studies which examine mental models' practical relevance or impact on decision-making or performance, that is, focus in one form or another on the complexity versus relevance issue discussed in Section 2.4.

Methodologically, for this case there are at least two alternative approaches. First, the comparison standard or causal map can be a *synthetic* one, constructed by the researcher. Depending on the case, it could be based on interviews and observations in the domain and represent, for example, current best practices, from which the causal map of a theoretical *"ideal actor"* could be inferred (Laukkanen 2001b). It could also be a causal map which summarizes the prevailing scientific or expert knowledge about the issue. The other alternative is to define the mental model/causal map of one or a group of respondents as the standard or "optimum". This assumes other evidence that just that particular belief system is preferable. An example is a CCM study which is based on other data showing that one respondent or a subset of respondents has been consistently more successful than the other respondents as small business managers (Laukkanen 1997). A case representing the second approach is when respondents' mental models are compared with an established expert or scientific view about the focal issue, such as health risks associated with radon or organization theory (Bostrom et al. 1992, Priem and Rosenstein 2000).

This type of analysis would describe and analyze the respondents' domain-related subjective thought patterns holistically as a causal system.

The apparently prevailing ideas and beliefs would be examined from different viewpoints, for example, how accurate they are in the standard terms or what practical or harmful implications could occur as a result of clearly inaccurate or lacking beliefs. In a computerized environment, this analysis can be realized by treating the standard cause map data as a *dummy respondent*. In the case of CMAP3, one would create two or three parallel projects: one containing all respondents plus the dummy, the other only the "real" ones, where the aggregate-level indicators would not be influenced by the template data, and the third only the dummy.

3.5.3 TO QUANTIFY OR NOT?

Whilst causal map metrics and numerical operations are technically not difficult, especially in computerized CCM, their meaningfulness and research utility is not obvious. This depends partly on the study's objectives and assumptions about what the causal maps should represent in each case. In addition, the study's data and methods influence which metrics are plausible in the traditional sense of "measuring what one claims to measure". In general, "we should not rely on measurements that cannot be made with validity and reliability" (Axelrod 1976, p. 70). At a deeper level, there are theoretical and methodological issues about the nature of the target phenomena and how far communication-based qualitative methods such as CCM can carry.

In CCM practice, the meaningfulness problem concerns mainly methods which emphasize *quantitative* causal map analysis, that is, the "psychometric" or structured measurement oriented variants of CCM. It is interesting that typical papers (Clarkson and Hodgkinson 2005, Hodgkinson and Clarkson 2005, Langan-Fox et al. 2000, Langfield-Smith 1992, Markóczy and Goldberg 1995, Mohammed et al. 2000) of this genre convey an impression that there are no serious ontological and epistemological problems involved in quantifying. They assume, first, that whatever the methods tap are "mental models" or "cognitive maps", which exist in the respondents' minds as distinct map-like entities, and can be reliably and validly tapped, known, measured and quantified. Second, related to this, it is implied that the methods themselves contain no significant constraining or biasing elements. As discussed in Sections 3.2 and 7.2, both assumptions can be problematic if a structured method is applied inappropriately. However, other CCM methods can also involve issues which must be observed when quantifying and drawing metrics-based conclusions.

As we have emphasized, a dilemma in all CCM concerns the objects of measurement. It is difficult to know unequivocally which cognitive sources and processes the respondents use when the data is produced. The *in situ* elicited or causal statements distilled from texts can reflect (measure, tap) recalled propositional knowledge and mental models, but also ad hoc reasoning and imagination. The latter can in the worst case produce unwarranted and highly volatile amounts of concepts and causal links as raw data. This is possible in structured and less structured elicitation methods, especially if the instructions are ambiguous and/or the administrators or interviewers are not careful and consistent. The obvious consequence is that indicators of comprehensiveness (number of concepts) or complexity (density), which must be based on *elicited* data, can measure or indicate different things without the researcher knowing what was actually measured. In addition, all subsequent data-based operations such as comparison or clustering of respondents will be influenced, too.

There are further issues. As discussed in Section 3.2, structured CCM methods must, on technical grounds, limit the number of concepts (for example, to 7–12) which the respondents select and process, sometimes also the number of causal links they are allowed to select (for example, to 3). Whilst administratively defensible, it also prevents the respondents' true comprehensiveness and complexity of knowledge and reasoning from surfacing. Moreover, if one uses a predefined number of concepts and density as a complexity measure, the only source of variance is the number of causal links, which is not necessarily the most relevant dimension. Finally, different techniques and heterogeneous concept list/pool contents in structured CCM can elicit systematically different and also volatile numbers of causal links.

What are the practical lessons? First, CCM is not about "measuring" people's *generic* cognitive capabilities or characteristics, nor about their *full* knowledge base. CCM can plausibly operationalize people's (pragmatic) knowledge or mental models about some *specific*, limited domains or issues. Whilst cause map metrics can reflect different aspects of the *elicited* belief systems, they are not convincing indicators of people's *general* cognitive characteristics such as aptitude or the extent of their knowledge or expertise, unless there is other independent evidence. Second, on the positive side, assuming a uniform, reliable and above all non-biased data acquisition, CCM indicators can be meaningfully applied for descriptive and comparative purposes within the *specific* study and its respondents. However, the metrics cannot be usually generalized beyond the specific study's context, unless there is additional evidence or the findings can be compared with studies using identical methods and comparable samples.

Third, a pragmatic tenet of qualitative studies, although not universally embraced, is to "count the countable" (Cassell and Symon 1994, Sandelowski 2001). Usually, this means simply that instead of statements like many, more or less, or typically—which are essentially quantitative—it is better to use, when possible, *descriptive numbers* which point to, support, summarize or sometimes contradict a given conclusion or observation. In addition, it is usually unwise to throw away the *heuristic* potential of numerical indicators like CCM distance metrics or density measures. They are not only tools for substantive topic-related description and comparative analysis. They can also support *generating* new ideas, pinpointing of anomalies and suggesting of fruitful questions and thus in general enable a more comprehensive and deeper analysis also in CCM studies (Gioia et al. 2013, Maxwell 2010, Seale and Silverman 1997). They also foster the quality of the study. For example, in coding-based CCM the ratios of raw to standardized data indicate the level of coding and data compression (Section 6.4). Observing them across data sources enables assessing and improving the uniformity of coding.

Finally, when using CCM metrics, the inferences drawn of them should perhaps generally be on the cautious side and observe the underlying conditions and eventual qualifiers. In general, one should also use common sense and avoid too detailed analysis and claims which would be based on essentially microscopic differences considering the typical measurement bases and objects. In CCM practice, this means, first, that the required values and differences of indicators, emerging patterns, clusters, and so on, should be significant and plausible in terms of common-sense face validity. Second, the observed patterns and notions should repeat themselves and have logical connections within the data and, if possible, be supported by parallel triangulating evidence.

3.6   Selecting a CCM Method

In principle, when planning a CCM study, one could first decide the approach and then adapt everything else, including the research questions, context and data type, to this premise. However, the more usual and prudent approach is not to think first about techniques but one's field, its research foci and practices and objectives and ask what research is theoretically and methodologically interesting and relevant and also technically feasible considering the research objectives, data and resources. In some cases the selection of a CCM method will be obvious; sometimes there are alternatives to choose from.

An obvious category of studies with few selection problems are those based on secondary *documentary* data. This is the case, for instance, in political science CCM studies, which have to use inductive coding-based methods (Section 3.1.1 and 7.1). The selection can appear more open in studies which must use primary data. This is fostered by the practice that CCM research papers seldom discuss the general applicability of different methods or their selection criteria. Fortunately, the selection problem is asymmetric and concerns mainly the applicability of *structured* CCM methods. *In situ* administered *low-* and *semi-structured interview-based* CCM methods can be usually used, assuming no resource restrictions and a normal access to respondents. Furthermore, if the focal topic is relatively narrow, *text-based* primary data acquisition could be an alternative, too.

In general, one usually begins with the research objectives and asks what research strategies are necessary in different cases. From this viewpoint, low- or semi-structured CCM methods represent an *inductive* strategy, which is needed when exploring new cognitive domains or socio-technical systems. Such CCM research asks what phenomena and notions do the actors define or see, what do they think, believe and know about the relevant causal mechanisms, are there widely shared belief patterns or core ideas, are there subgroups with characteristic ideas, and so on? In some studies it is important to find out what the actors do *not* think or are unaware of, although it would be advantageous for them for practical reasons. A third study type would be about tracking changes that happen in the thinking and beliefs of one or more actors.

In terms of research objectives, typical CCM studies (so far) are explorative and/or evocative, focused on tentative description, target conceptualization and on model/theory generation and local causal processes (Maxwell 2004a), but not on generating nomothetic findings generalizable into some population (see Eisenhardt and Graebner 2007, Maxwell 2012). By definition, in such studies the researcher usually knows little about the target phenomena at the outset, but has a strong interest to find out. Therefore, a stagewise, inductive approach based on low- or semi-structured CCM methods is necessary. They do not predefine what the cause map constructs are or how many nodes or links will emerge from each respondent or other data source. Consequently, the outcome—individual and aggregate causal maps—is not constrained *a priori*. They emerge from the *natural* data and reflect the target phenomena to be tapped, that is, the contents and complexity of the respondents' causal thinking and/or the key phenomena and mechanisms of the real target systems. However, there are practical constraints such as resources, access to respondents, their motivation, vigilance, and so on. For such reasons, the numbers of respondents will also be limited, effectively precluding the notion of sample-based quantitative generalization. Furthermore, these methods usually need interpretive/inductive coding. As a consequence, inductive CCM studies will often follow a *saturation* logic, where data is collected successively up to the point where new observations, that is, new original concepts and causal links, clearly seem to taper off. They must also use different strategies of validation, as discussed above and below.

As to structured CCM methods, the applicability criteria can be inferred of their technical characteristics. As noted in Section 3.1.4, structured CCM is based on a *predefined* short concept list (n = 7–15) or a larger concept pool (n = 30–50). The former variant elicits only the causal beliefs for the listed concepts. In the pool method, respondents first choose a short list of concepts from the pool and the causal links are elicited and usually also specified for this set. Structured methods can be administered *in situ* or using, for example, electronic techniques. Their advantages include no need of *ex post* coding and a relative ease of administration, which in principle enables larger samples of respondents. A downside is the preliminary work and tests which may be needed to prepare the concept list/pool and elicitation techniques.

However, structured CCM methods' main characteristics have important implications. First, even assuming that the pool or list concepts have been "localized", these methods do not, in a strict sense, elicit *original* expressions of the respondents. Instead, the data reflects their responses to and within the predefined list/pool. This can be a *validity issue* with important analytic consequences (Section 3.4). Second, the number of concepts accessed by the respondents must be small, usually around 7–15. This means that the *elicited* causal maps per respondent, as well as the aggregated causal maps, will be *small*. This restricts using them as representations of complex belief systems or as models of typical real domains. The question is when do such constraints favor structured CCM methods or at least make them feasible alternatives, and, conversely, when should a different, that is, less structured, CCM approach be used? There are perhaps at least three aspects to observe.

The first is related to the validity issue and concerns *representativeness*. Here one should ask how essential it is in the particular study that the elicited CCM data is known to reflect the respondents' *active* natural vocabulary and knowledge. If this is critical, a template-based CCM method seems defensible only if it can be *independently* ensured that concepts in the list/pool are indeed actively used and relevant to the study's *respondents* themselves, not their colleagues or appear otherwise common in the context, and so on. Such evidence could be obtained by observing the same respondents in action, by examining their other communications or by using previous findings about these persons. However, that can be difficult. Therefore, pilot studies of other persons in assumedly similar positions or examining relevant media or similar sources could be used as substitutes. Although this is strictly only indicative evidence, it may be sufficient, especially in explorative studies.

The second obvious criterion is that the studied issue or system must have a *reasonable scope*. This means that it must be possible and normal in the context to capture at least its essential substance with a limited number of concepts. Thus, there is an inverse relationship between structured CCM methods' applicability and the "terminological" richness or real complexity and width of target phenomena or systems. Consequently, structured CCM methods are less appropriate for capturing *general*, inherently variable and fuzzy idea systems such as *dominant wide* belief patterns in an organization or an industry or for defining cognitively homogeneous actor clusters in such contexts. It is a different matter that such studies are of course *technically* doable, but they will be dubious theoretically and in terms of findings. The self-evident reason, discussed already in Section 2.5, is that an adult person's, let alone a professional's, causal and phenomenological beliefs and reasoning patterns, not even their work-related parts, are too extensive to be plausibly represented with a mere 7–15 concepts. Whan structured CCM methods can operationalize, aggregate and compare are causal belief patterns about specific, relatively *narrow* domains, systems or issues, that is, phenomena which a normal person can cognitively represent and comprehend by creating and accessing a corresponding mental model.

However, having said this, it is also important to notice that a "reasonable scope" does not mean that the target system or issue must be insignificant, too. This can be seen, for example, in the recent debates about financial austerity policies in the EU or the mechanisms and methods of fighting global warming. Whilst the underlying mechanisms there are extremely complicated, the related public debates manage to do with very small numbers of concepts. Different positions are defended (or attacked) mainly by positing or rejecting some specific causal relationships, less by problematizing the existence of some particular phenomena. A different issue is how useful such highly general models are in theoretical or pragmatic terms. Here the point is simply that they can often be captured with the small causal maps which structured CCM methods allow, of course also less structured CCM.

Third, closely related to the above point, the studied issue or belief system should be inherently logical and coherent—in a word, *"modellable"* cognitively. This means that a normal respondent can be assumed to have/recall and/or create a relevant mental model to make sense about or to describe the focal issue or domain under inquiry. Methodologically, it follows that the concepts in the list or pool must both *make contextual sense* and be *coherent* in the meaning that there are plausible causal relationships and mechanisms which could connect them or at least many of them. It seems that this particular point has not been adequately observed in the literature, rather the contrary. For example, it has been maintained that putting irrelevant, even mindless notions in the concept pool is harmless, as long as all participants can freely and uniformly select their own concept sets (Markóczy and Goldberg 1995, p. 310). In a recent case (Clarkson and Hodgkinson 2006), the pool was reportedly picked from MOC theoretical and research papers and literature concerning the focal organizations (call centers) (Clarkson and Hodgkinson 2005, p. 324).

It is useful to once more point out the implicit assumptions of the structured methods (Section 3.4). The first is that whatever a respondent selects is, by definition, an active, authentic part of their subjective belief/concept system. This must not obviously be so. It is entirely possible for a respondent to select concepts and causal links which they do not know well or at all or to select using irrelevant and random criteria. For instance, vaguely familiar or currently salient, modish concepts in the pool will often draw more attention and trigger a selection response. The second implicit assumption is that the majority of the pool concepts and at least the selected concepts do necessarily belong to a coherent mental model (cognitive map, belief system) which exists in the person's memory and can be retrieved from there and "mapped" one-to-one. Again, because the concept pool setup, selection and their causal linking are *separated* tasks and processes it is quite possible that the list/pool concepts actually belong to several *different* mental models. Third, it seems also implied that selecting concepts and indicating causal relationships is only an exercise in memory recall. As argued earlier, the two tasks, which moreover are performed separately and after a shorter or longer time interval, can be expected to trigger not only memory recall but *different* parallel and/or sequential cognitive operations such as active reasoning and imagination. This can be expected to happen in particular when inquiring about the perceived causal relationships. These issues will be discussed again in Section 7.3.

What would happen if a structured CCM method is used without observing the above criteria? One result is a biased instrument and thus data which provides a dubious base for aggregation and comparative analysis. In particular, the more the list/pool concepts stem from *different* sources, the likelier they will represent different, mutually more or less distant conceptual systems, mental models or naïve theories. Such concepts can have few meaningful mutual causal relationships. Consequently, the participants' responses can be expected to be random and varying depending, for example, on how the person interprets the idea of causality or how familiar they are with the list/pool concepts. Furthermore, the more general the list/pool concepts are, the likelier they will trigger *more* causal relationship candidates in the minds of the respondents. This occurs when the pool concepts are acquired, for example, from general scientific literature, textsbooks or have a momentarily high salience in public media. In general, broad and inherently fuzzy and ambiguous notions such as "motivation", "corporate strategy", "equal rights" or "organizational culture" or global ones such as "economic policies", "recession" or "energy prices" are often perceived to influence almost everything else, especially in the minds of laypersons. It does not appear to matter that the underlying causal mechanisms are unclear to them. It suffices that one has an intuitive idea of salience and *some* connections to indicate a causal relation for "just in case", unless the instructions limit this.

The visible manifestation of violating the above criteria is that the emerging individual causal maps will have *low commonality* because many of the elicited causal relationships will be random and idiosyncratic. It will also be difficult to *aggregate* causal maps which could plausibly represent the respondents' typical thought patterns. The method itself precludes that. The non-emergence of shared patterns may explain why structured CCM studies often shun *substantive* and *aggregative analysis*, emphasizing instead *quantitative* analysis using structural indicators such as cause map density or distance (see, for example, Clarkson and Hodgkinson 2006). It seems that, for example, Markóczy and Goldberg were well aware of this issue. They recommend *limiting* the number of selectable concepts, because otherwise there may not be enough "overlap" of selected items to meaningfully compare the maps (Markóczy and Goldberg 1995, p. 310). However, the idea that the researcher "creates" or ensures commonality by limiting something can be problematic in the same way as if one would use aggressive coding to collapse together original items which have little in common. However, the more likely culprit of the low commonality/sharedness is probably usually an incoherent concept list/pool, and, more generally, the initial decision to use a structured CCM method for a task to which it is less suited.

To summarize, structured CCM methods seem appropriate when the studied belief system or socio-technical domain is relatively *narrow* and coherently *"modellable"*. As emphasized, this does not imply unimportant target systems or issues. Interesting objects could be, for example, distinct paradigms of thought or belief systems which often underlie different policy regimes, professional factions or groups in conflict. In such cases, the differences are often more about the causal mechanisms and less about whether some specific phenomena or factors exist. In such a context, even small cause maps and few nodes/concepts can cover the relevant phenomena and the critical causal relationships and/or thus enable differentiating and categorizing the respondents in the cognitive terms. However, it is may be a good idea also to ascertain whether the same information could be more economically gathered by more conventional methods such as questionnaires.

In addition to the theoretical and methodological criteria, a further selection viewpoint seems to be a mundane one: the assumed labor required in CCM research, either in general or in different method approaches. For example, Mohammed et al. (2000, p. 148, see also Clarkson and Hodgkinson 2005, p. 334), echoing Huff and Fletcher (1990), maintain that (all) cause mapping in general is labor intensive and time consuming. As evidence they refer to interview-based CCM studies, noting that typical durations varied from 45 minutes to two hours. In contrast, Bougon et al. (1977, p. 607) noted that the pairwise comparison of their 17 variables and the specification of the noted causal links took up to four hours per respondent. In the case of Markóczy and Goldberg (1995), collecting (specified) causal relationships between a set of 10 constructs took around one hour per respondent. The SBA study discussed in Section 7.2 elicited small business advisors' mental models using semi-structured interviews. These lasted, including the collection of background data, between 1.2 and 1.5 hours per participant.

Although perhaps understandable, selecting research methods predominantly in terms of labor or interview time obviously oversimplifies and sidetracks the issue. First, interviewing or any other form of collecting primary data is only one component and, although a salient one, usually not the most critical in terms of time and effort compared with tasks such as preparing the research, reading, logistics, analysis of data, review and validation. It is more useful to ask, "labor intensive" compared with what? Is an interview of one or two hours little, normal or too much? Where is the limit? Moreover, *all* serious research, social or otherwise, is laborious and demands resources in many areas. If a researcher is intrigued about a problem and committed to their research field, one must and will gladly do what is required. This, however, is obvious, and not really the point.

A more constructive reading of the contention that causal mapping in general or a specific CCM approach is "labor intensive" and "time consuming" is that there is a "better way" of doing the *same* thing. This can first be framed as an issue of causal mapping methods' applicability compared with, say, survey or narrative methods (see, for example, Eriksson and Kovalainen 2008, Maxwell 2012, Merriam 2009). This is an important, complex topic, whose wider examination is beyond the present scope. However, here the real issue is which CCM approach is necessary for the research task at hand, not which is "better" in terms of labor and some other derivative characteristics. This does not mean, however, that the labor and time requirements are unimportant. As can be seen when comparing different CCM approaches, they vary and usually entail trade-offs. For example, a careful construction and validation of the predetermined concept list/pool in structured CCM research is laborious. In low- or semi-structured CCM research this stage is not needed at all because they elicit original data, and call for more data processing and coding. The work in coding varies, too, depending on the type and amount of data, the level and purposes of coding, the number and complexity of issues addressed, the number of data sources, and so on. In practice, the most important single factor is usually the type of raw data. Handling open interview transcripts, original books or other documents which contain rich text is much more demanding than the data elicited by semi-structured interviewing because the latter consists mainly of causal statements.

An important yet often overlooked labor factor is the *technical method* and platform. Handling, analyzing and coding large volumes of rich text such as interview transcripts with manual methods is arduous indeed (Levins and Silver 2007, Maxwell 2012). Whilst small-scale idiographic causal mapping or concept/idea mapping for heuristic purposes is manageable using manual drawing, typical CCM studies require *computerizing* (Laukkanen 2012). In low- and semi-structured CCM, appropriate software enables an efficient and transparent entry of data, iterative coding of the original expressions and a fast processing of causal map output data. In structured CCM, using larger samples, computerizing makes both data entry and its processing more efficient. In both approaches, software supports selective analysis of output cause maps, the use of quantitative indicators and the visual representation of causal maps.

Depending on the computer skills of the researcher, some CCM tasks can be handled by standard office software. For example, database applications can store the original concepts and sort them by coding categories, thus supporting coding. Spreadsheet software can do some database operations, too, but are better adapted to numerical tasks such as processing matrices or calculating indicators including basic statistics. Graphic and drawing software is necessary for constructing visual causal maps based on text form output.

Another option in CCM may be to use so-called CAQDAS (computer-assisted qualitative data analysis software) applications such as *Atlas.ti* or *Nvivo*. These have become widespread among qualitative researchers and are typically used for handling and analyzing rich text data (see Evers et al. 2011, Levins and Silver 2007, Maxwell 2012). In CCM, however, at least the present CAQDAS tools do not seem to support well the key CCM tasks such as comparison, aggregation, calculation of numerical measures, and construction of visual causal maps as efficiently as CCM-specific software. Currently, there are two widely available software of this category: *Cognizer*™, which is a commercial application developed exclusively for the structured concept pool approach (see Clarkson and Hodgkinson 2005), and *CMAP3*, a non-commercial free application which can be adapted to different types of data and methods. This book is about using CMAP3.

Chapter 4

Computerizing CCM
with CMAP3

The CMAP3 software application consists of several integrated modules. They facilitate the basic CCM tasks of entering raw causal statement data, coding of original expressions, analysis of raw data, generation of standardized (coded) output and calculation of quantitative indicators, and, finally, the analysis and production of cause maps. In principle, CMAP3 supports all CCM method approaches discussed earlier. In other words, it is adaptable to document-based and semi- or low-structured as well as structured CCM projects as long as the number of respondents or other distinct data sources in the project is N =< 50. The techniques of data entry, coding and data processing vary by the CCM approach.

4.1 CMAP3: An Overview

To grasp CMAP3's operating logic and practices, the following points and features should be noted:

1. CMAP3 is based on the notion that causal maps can be *decomposed* into sets of pairs of nodes (A, B) which (more accurately: the entities to which they refer) are assumed to be typically causally or temporally linked to each other (A→B→C, and so on). The interlinked node dyads can be handled and analyzed individually and aggregated, and, when useful, put together again and represented, for example as a visual causal map.

2. CMAP3 uses *databases* which are automatically created when the project is first set up (see below). The first database stores the original cause map *nodes* (original concepts), termed *natural language units* (NLU); the second is for the original node-dyad information, called *natural causal units* (NCU); and the third is for the *standard term*

vocabulary (STV), which is used in coding the NLUs. In addition, CMAP3 creates two output databases: one for the *standard node terms* (SNT) (as coded), the other for *standard causal units* (SCU), that is, the coded node-dyad information. Using the corresponding module the researcher can access any database and, if necessary, *export* them as spreadsheet files (xls, xlsx), which can be, in turn, processed and *printed* by MS Excel. In addition, there is a *Project Log* file (a text file) and a database for the project's definitions and parameters (editable by the Project Manager module; see below). When processing and analyzing data—for example, calculating numerical indicators of the SNT and SCU databases or creating Focal Maps—CMAP3 generates *interim* databases, which are temporary and thus *not* stored permanently. However, as long as the respective module displays them, they too can be exported and, if necessary, edited, saved or printed as spreadsheet files.

3.   CMAP3 provides a platform and tools for *standardizing (coding)* of NLUs. In practice, standardizing assigns each NLU a relevant standard term signifier (STAG). By "stagging" the NLUs, the coder categorizes the NLUs into groups which are interpreted as homogeneous or at least associated in terms of their meanings or referents. The STAG and the corresponding standard vocabulary term will "replace" and represent the group's NLUs in the subsequent processing when the SNT and SCU databases are generated. This enables CMAP3 to *convert* (map) the raw data (NLUs) into a common notation system, represented by the project's standard term vocabulary (STV). The output—the SCU and SNT databases—will contain those SNTs which (the respective NLUs) occur in the raw data (as coded). The standardized databases will also contain information about which respondent/s or data source/s contained the respectively coded NLUs and, thus, the related NCUs.

4.   CMAP3 enables a reliable and transparent processing of data. Provided appropriate techniques are used in raw data acquisition, transcription and keyboard entry of data, CMAP3 creates an *audit trail* from standardized output back to the original raw data. This is one precondition of reliability and validity (trustworthiness) in qualitative studies as it enables the researchers and external reviewers to track the origins of coding and findings back to their raw data sources and examine and assess the coding decisions' background.

5.   CMAP3 was originally designed for exploratory (qualitative, ideographic, case,) small sample studies. In such cases, researchers typically interview several respondents or use other data sources such as secondary documents, sometimes in parallel with the primary data. Thus, the number (N) of respondents or other distinct data sources (S) cannot usually be large and the data may be unstructured, rich and voluminous. Reflecting this background, the number of data sources in a single CMAP3 project is limited, currently to $N/S =< 50$. This, however, seems to be (more than) adequate considering so far typical CCM studies. If necessary, the N limitation can sometimes be circumvented by using two or more parallel projects which typically would share a common standard vocabulary.

6.   The present version of CMAP3 can also support *structured* CCM research (the fixed list or concept pool CCM methods). This was made possible by adding the function of *importing* list and matrix raw data in spreadsheet file format. If parallel projects are used, this mode of data entry enables larger-scale causal mapping studies with traditional nomothetic objectives.

7.   CMAP3 also supports combinatory tasks in CCM research which enables generating *composite causal maps* of documentary sources. In this case, keyboard entry or spreadsheet file importing can be used. As above, CMAP3 preserves information about the distinct data sources such as documents, which enables one to analyze them for descriptive or explanatory purposes.

8.   Instead of producing visual causal maps, CMAP3 uses an indirect method of *exporting* causal map components (SCU sets) to an external drawing application such as *CmapTools* or presentation software such as MS PowerPoint. The same principle applies for *printing* CMAP3 datatables. They are first exported to MS Excel and formatted there and then printed as the user sees fit. The indirect approach provides much more functionality and options for creating visual causal maps and printing datatables than would be possible by a necessarily somehow constrained integrated graphic and printing capability.

9.   CMAP3 (current version) is designed for and operates exclusively in Windows computers (PCs) with Windows XP, Vista, 7 and 8 or 8.1

(not 8 RT or 8.1 RT) operating system. Functions such as exporting and importing data or printing the contents of a database file require that MS Excel has been installed and is available on the same computer. The same applies to drawing causal maps with *CmapTools* or MS PowerPoint.

4.2   Installing and Starting CMAP3

Installing CMAP3 is automatic using the CMAP3 setup file. It is very important that the file (and later the installed CMAP3) are opened and run as a System Administrator (command line under Open in the right-click submenu). Setup installs the application and support files (e.g., Uninstall) and creates the CMAP3 application folder and a Documents subfolder called CMAP3 Data, where the project files will be stored by default. In addition, the setup installs two CCM projects (CCM_Case1, CCM_Case2) for demonstration purposes. Details of them can be found in their Project Logs. Should the user wish to preserve the default projects intact, but test and change them, the demo projects can be first duplicated, that is, saved under a different file name, and the new projects used for testing.

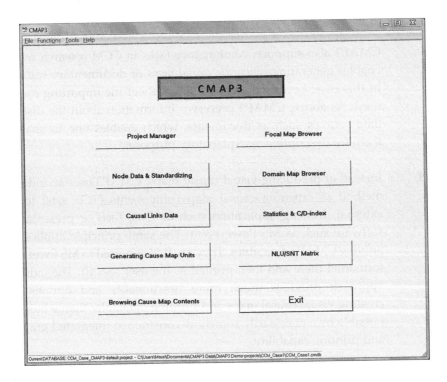

Figure 4.1   CMAP3 opening interface — main menu (v.3.1.2)

When CMAP3 is started for the first time, an information window appears with contact addresses and CMAP3 displays the *Main menu* (Figure 4.1) consisting of command buttons for the different modules. They are used to launch the corresponding function in a CCM/CMAP process. The modules are also accessible in the Functions menu or by pressing the appropriate function key, for example, F2 for the Project Manager. The information window can be turned off in the Tools/Settings menu and accessed again in Help/About.

In *Tools/Settings*, the user can set CMAP3 to start so that the opening screen is the Start screen (Main menu), the Project Manager or the last opened module. When working with a given project, it may be convenient to use the last option. Furthermore, two font sizes can be chosen.

When starting, CMAP3 always opens the last accessed project. The bottom row displays the active project and its file path and name. At the beginning, the default is one of the automatically installed demo projects (CCM_Case1.cmdb). When new projects are available, a project can be activated by the *File/Open* command. This opens the CMAP Data folder and displays the available project files. If a different folder was used, which is of course also possible, the last accessed project will be located and opened there.

4.3   Defining CMAP3 Projects

In CMAP3, a project corresponds to and represents a CCM study case, which has a given number of respondents or other data sources such as separate documents. In computer terms, a CMAP3 project is a set of database files which will contain the raw data, the generated output data and researcher-defined information and parameters about the study. The databases (datatables) are stored as a single *project* file[1] (file extension *cmdb*). In addition, there is a simple project *log file* (a txt file, also accessible directly).

A new CMAP3 project is set up using the *Project Manager* module, as displayed in Figure 4.2, in this case the default project (CCM_Case1.cmdb). The module can be accessed through the Main Menu, or it opens automatically when a new project starts (command *File/New*). In the new project, all fields are empty except for the date (set to the current date). The user can give the project any name.

---

1   When accessed a number of times a database file size tends to grow even if the contents are not changed. If the user wishes to simply compact the file to save disk space, there is a special command (<File/Compact project database>). Compacting the file does not change the database's contents.

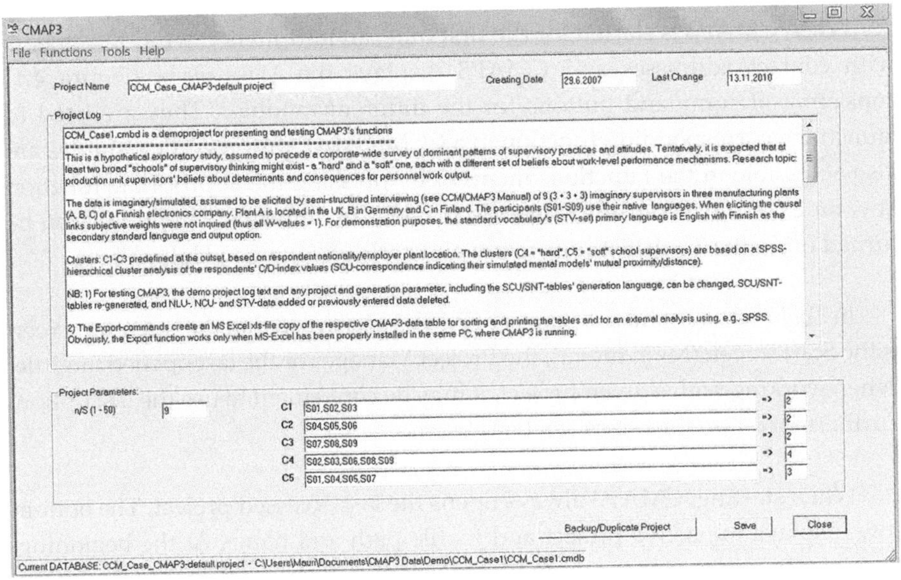

Figure 4.2   CMAP3 Project Manager

There is no upper limit to the number of projects. Although CMAP3 projects are operatively independent of each other, two or more projects can share data. This is possible for example by copying/duplicating (see below) an existing project and saving it under a different project name. That can be important, for example, when using the same raw data or standard vocabulary in two or more projects which have different parameters or a different level of coding.

The *Project Log* window is used to describe the project and its tasks, assumptions, data, various operations and stages, testing, keeping notes about next tasks, and so on. The log's text can be copy/pasted to other documents (and vice versa). It can also be accessed/edited directly by opening the project's *log file* in the CMAP3 data folder. Please note that when setting up a project, there must be *some* text entered in the *Project Log* window; it cannot be left empty.

The only other compulsory information when setting up the project is the *number of respondents* (S) or data sources. As mentioned, the current version of CMAP3 allows for an N of maximally 50 (S01–S50). In a typical research case, defining the S number is not a problem as the research plan usually determines the identity and number of respondents (data sources). However, in sequentially progressing studies such as those based on observed saturation of data, the number of S cannot be known at the outset. For such cases, CMAP3 enables an *upwards* adjustment of the S number. As to composite causal mapping, differentiating separate Ss/data sources is of course unnecessary if only one S (S01) is defined. However, if it is important to keep track of multiple data sources, each source (for example, a document) can be assigned its own S number.

Although the S number can be altered **(up or down)** later, if necessary, it is a good idea to try to define it correctly and at least avoid setting the number too low. When the S number is changed later, CMAP3 issues an alert. One reason is that the number of Ss defines the respective datatable structures. If the new value is set *lower* than the original one, the original datatable structure will be downsized to reflect the smaller S number. This means that if there was NLU and NCU data for the Ss with the higher numbers, that part of the entered raw data will be erased permanently and so will the eventually generated SCU and SNT tables. Conversely, if the new S number is set *higher*, there is no NLU and NCU data to delete. Only the contents of the SCU and SNT tables will be erased, but they can be quickly regenerated with no loss.

Finally, the Project Manager offers the option of defining *a priori Clusters*. This too is not obligatory, but often useful. The researcher can predefine up to five groups or clusters of respondents and an appropriate inclusion criterion. Technically, the clusters are defined simply by entering the respective list of Ss into a corresponding field (NB: S01, S02, and so on, *separated by comma*), followed by a threshold inclusion value. In Figure 5.1, for example, C1 was defined as consisting of three Ss with a threshold value of => 2. CMAP3 observes this when generating the SCU/SNT output. For example, for an SCU to be considered "owned" by C1, two of those Ss must possess an NCU which corresponds to an SCU (as coded). Together, those SCUs would constitute the C1's causal map.

From a research point of view, the study objectives and/or theoretical criteria and hypotheses decide which clusters, if any, will be defined and on which grounds. A typical case might be to define the S clusters so that they correspond to an *a priori* known difference or an assumed explanatory factor, for example, the Ss representing groups which are in a conflict or are assumed or known to have divergent "world views" or experiential backgrounds. This was the case in the first default project, whose clustering logic is explained in its log text. A further possibility is to define the clusters later based on the C/D (correspondence/distance) *index* (see below) or on a statistical (cluster) analysis of the C/D index (Section 3.5). Notably, it is technically possible that the *same* S is included in more than one cluster. Importantly, the researcher can also change the cluster definitions and test (by regenerating the output SNT and SCU tables) what different cluster compositions and/or inclusion criteria values would imply for the SCU/SNT output.

The Project Screen has three command buttons. *Close* shuts the Project Manager and opens the Main Menu. *Save* saves the project log and parameter data, including any changes made to them. The *Backup/Duplicate Project* button is basically a Windows *Save As* command. Naming the button thus reminds, first, that it is a good idea to keep regular backups of the project (= the cmdb- and log. txt- files). Especially in large projects, it is the raw data entry and coding—that is, NLU input, STV creation, NLU standardizing and entry of NCUs—which demand the main work and time. In contrast, the output for analysis and cause maps, that is, the SCU and SNT tables and the interim numerical tables, can be generated and regenerated in seconds once the standardized raw data is available. Therefore, regular backups of the project file during data entry make sense not only to protect one's work in environments with computer or electricity problems but also to prevent consequences of unintended moves and errors by the researcher. There are inexpensive devices such as USB sticks for that purpose. If necessary, the project files (NB: *both* the cmdb and txt file) can be later copied back to the CMAP3 Data folder to be accessible again.

In addition to backup purposes, duplicating a project can serve also research objectives by creating one or more *parallel projects* with a different title. From a research point of view, the uses and needs of duplicate parallel projects vary. A typical reason is the need to use *different STV-/standardization vocabularies*. That would enable, for example, using both a low-level and a high-level concept/coding system, the former for context/praxis-near description, the latter for more theoretic purposes. Another need might arise if the user wants to test different standardizing/coding strategies so as to find a "right" solution. A third context would be when the researcher uses a *dummy respondent* as a comparison template (Section 3.5).

To completely *remove* a CMAP3 project from the computer, the procedure is the standard Windows one: the project's cmdb and log txt files are located and deleted. Before doing so it is, however, a good idea to see that this project is not the active one. This can be seen and changed in the Project Manager window. If an active project is deleted, however, nothing fatal happens. When CMAP3 starts and cannot find the default project it last accessed, it alerts the user, who must open an existing different project, which becomes the new default, or create a new one. Needless to add, as in any radical file operations, it makes sense to ensure that potentially important data will not be irreversibly deleted or that there are backup copies.

Chapter 5

From Raw Data to
Analyzable Output

Raw data in CCM studies consists essentially of causal assertions that something influences or is dependent on or follows from or after something else. In Section 3.1 we examined the different ways of acquiring such data. This chapter describes what happens next and the procedures when using CMAP3.

The process begins by getting the raw data first into a form which enables its entering into the project's database controlled by CMAP3. After that, the original concepts will usually be coded (standardized) to enable generating the standardized output, SNT and SCU tables, and the subsequent cause map analysis. Let us first assume that the raw data was elicited by semi-structured interviewing (Section 3.1.5). However, the procedures will be more or less similar if the acquisition is based on open interviews and their transcripts or if the causal assertions are extracted from primary texts or secondary documents. Notably, CMAP3 also offers the possibility of *importing* raw data in a spreadsheet file (xls, xlsx). This means alternative methods for raw data entry, especially in structured CCM. This will be discussed in Section 5.3 later.

5.1   Preparing Raw Data

At the outset, the raw data must be converted (transcribed) into a practical interim form which enables an efficient and reliable *keyboard entry* into CMAP3. As an important byproduct, this creates an intermediate data stage as well as an *audit trail*, which enables the tracking of the origins of the standardized output (SNT, SCU) and findings based on them back to the original data.

In the case of CMAP3, an interim form which has proved practical is the *Raw Data Sheet* (RDS) in Figure 5.1. The specimen corresponds to the *Interview Note Sheet* (INS) in Figure 3.2 (Section 3.1.5). The displayed INS and RDS examples belong to the default project (CCM_Case1), installed when setting up CMAP3.

PROJECT: CCM_Test		S: 01 DATE: /18.07 P: /11	
ROW-#	NLU	→ E-ROW-#	STAG / REM
1	output /person	2, 8	P01
2	unit's output	3	001
3	firm's performance		002
4	personal effort	1, 5	P02
5	work quality	1	P03
6	supervision intensity	4, 5, 9	003
7	in/out selection	4, 10, 11	004
8	control tools /info	6, 9	005
9	rewards /level	4, 5, 11	006
10	skills /person	4, 5,	P04
11	personal attitude	4, 5, 6-	P05
12			

Figure 5.1   Raw data sheet (RDS) for keyboard entry

An RDS has an upper information row and four main columns with titles. There are *exactly* 50 numbered rows (explained below) and below them (not shown in Figure 5.1) rows for researchers' notes. Like the INSs, it is easy to make and print the necessary number of RDSs using a word processing or spreadsheet application. In the SBA study (7.2), for example, there were usually three to four RDSs per respondent. This depends of course on the number of anchor themes, too.

The point of using RDSs, as shown in Figure 5.1, is to note down, by writing, the original concepts (that is, the As, Bs, and so on) and their causal links (A→B), as elicited from a respondent or a source document. As noted, the original concepts (cause map nodes) are called NLUs (natural language units), for example, *output/person* in the above example. They are handwritten into the NLU column, as shown above. The original data's causal link assertions, called NCUs (natural causal units), will be noted simply by writing the row number of the *effect NLU* on the *cause NLU's* row. For instance, the NLU on row 01 (*output/person*) influences (according to the respondent named S01) the phenomena/NLUs on row 02 (= *unit's output*) and 08 (= *control tools/info*). Furthermore, the three NCU entries on row 11 indicate S01's belief that a team member's personal attitude leads to three effects. Two of them are *direct*, implying that "good/improved" attitude enhances a person's level of effort and quality of work. One of S01's causal links is *inverse*, implying that the "better" a person's attitude, the less intensive supervision is necessary. The inverse link is indicated by the *minus* sign and will be later entered with that NCU (NB: in CMAP3 the plus (+) sign is *default* and does not need to be entered).

In newer versions of CMAP3, it is possible to use, in addition to the information about causal direction, a second link characteristic or dimension with a value magnitude from 1 to 5 (value 1 is default and does not need to be entered). A typical use of this option is to ask the respondents to indicate the subjective *weight* or *importance* they attach to a particular causal link.

A couple of further conventions should be noted. First, to enable and ensure a systematic and consistent data entry, audit trail and processing, CMAP3 assumes that a single RDS page contains data for only *one* respondent or data source (S) and has maximally *50* NLUs/rows. This does not mean that exactly 50 NLUs must be entered; there can be fewer *but not more* than 50 NLUs per one RDS. If an S has much more NLUs, as usually happens, one simply uses *more RDSs*. The maximum number of RDS per S is =< 99. This has proved amply sufficient because it enables a total of 4,950 NLUs per S. The number of *NCUs* is *not limited*.

Why such conventions? They are necessary for processing the data and to create an audit trail. By systematic numbering of respondents (data sources) by RDSs and the RDS rows and allowing/entering only one NLU per row enables defining for each NLU a *unique identifier*, called an *NTAG*, which consists of six digits (for example, 010112). The first two digits indicate the respondent or distinct data source (S01 in the example), the middle two digits the respective RDS sheet (page 1), and the last two the RDS row number (row 12). The NTAGs will be stored, along with the NLU, and eventual researcher remarks will be entered about it in the project's cmdb file/datatables and will be used in the later operations such as sorting/browsing raw data and standard output generation. The conventions do not constrain the raw data entry. For example, if the researcher must later add new data for a particular S, one simply creates a new RDS page and enters the new NLU and NCU data there. Similarly, if all 50 RDS rows are full, more NLUs and NCUs can be entered on a new RDS created for that S. Notably, in CMAP3 it is not at all harmful if the *same NLU* is entered on several RDSs and is input several times into CMAP3, as long as they all are *coded consistently* with the same STAG. The SCU/SNT generation process will observe all NLUs and NCUs but the repeated NLUs or NCUs will not influence the number of *generated* SNTs and SCUs. However, all NLUs entered into the NLU database will stay there and will be included, for example, in the NLU matrix.

A further point to note is that preparing interim data such as the RDSs often overlaps with coding (standardizing). In practice, the interviewees' transcriptions and interview note sheets or secondary documents often contain much wordier expressions than those in the above example. In the simulated example, the researcher is assumed to have interpreted and decided that these NLUs capture the essence of what, say, S01 said and thought, namely, for example, that a team member's output influences the whole production unit's output and that this will be captured by the production information systems. In general, it is possible and practical to perform this kind of early interpretation or preliminary coding. It is, however, important that the *exact* wordings of the participants stay available in the respective INS and, ideally, in voice recordings, as they necessarily will be in the documentary or primary text sources.

The RDS has another connection to standardizing/coding. As shown in Figure 5.1, the fourth RDS column is reserved for *STAGs*. A STAG consists of *a capital letter* and *two digits* (for example, P01). It is a shorthand identifier of the respective *Standard Term* (ST), which will be or was entered into the project's standard term vocabulary (STV) database and will be located there by CMAP3 when generating standardized output. The idea of coding/standardizing has been discussed above and will be examined below from a practice viewpoint. In the example case, the STV was assumed to be created in parallel with the NLUs' RDS transcription. As will be discussed below, in real CCM cases, the STV (coding scheme) is typically created *iteratively*, beginning with *broad preliminary categories* into which NLUs having a similar or logically associated meaning or referent will be tentatively coded. The main advantage of the initial rough coding is that the STAGs can be *entered simultaneously* with the NLUs into CMAP3.

It should be mentioned that the handwriting based RDS method was developed for keyboard entry of manually transcribed raw data and before the worksheet data import of CMAP3 was available. It is easy to see that the RDS technique can also be computerized and realized digitally by using raw data *worksheets* (RDWS). Thereby, first, it is still very important to observe the RDS conventions, discussed above and below in Section 5.3, concerning the STV and NLU/CSL *data import* techniques. When using an RDWS it would have (at least) the same columns as the RDS (Figure 5.1), but perhaps in a different order and the REM column separated, if it is necessary. Furthermore, the *row numbering* in the RDWSs should follow the above RDS convention of maximally 50 entries per RDS in cases where there are more than 50 NLUs in an RDWS of a respondent or other data source (NB: the maximum N/NLUs = 1,000 NLUs per RDWS). As noted above, CMAP3 creates for each NLU an NTAG assuming that RDSs have a maximum of 50 NLU rows. This is also so when CMAP3 imports NLUs from a CSL. Assuming that the NCU entry will be based on an RDWS which is kept open together with CMAP3's NCU module in their separate workstation windows, it is practical that there are corresponding NTAGs in the RDWS and in the imported NLU database when it is accessed by the NCU module. Therefore, in the RDWSs row numbering the first 50 NLUs in the RDWS would have row numbers (NB: as text) from 0101 to 0150, the next

50 NLUs 0201 to 0250, and so on. The RDWS file name and worksheet titles tell to which respondent/data source (S) the RDWS belongs. As to NCU entry in this case, it must still be done using the normal keyboard/mouse method described below, but now "paperless" when the RDWSs containing the causal link data (NCUs, compare with, E-Row-# in Figure 5.1) and NCU entry module are accessible simultaneously in their separate PC screen windows.

The advantages of using RDWSs are obvious. First, the coding and the standard term vocabulary (STV) can be iteratively developed out of the NLU base using MS Excel. Second, the NLUs and the STV can be sorted and copy/pasted using the data in the RDWS columns. Third, by copy/pasting the appropriate RDWS columns, the researcher can create the new *STV* and *CSL worksheets/books*, which enable *importing* first the STV and then the NLUs into CMAP3, as discussed below in Section 5.3. This can save time and prevents errors. Furthermore, in studies based on documentary data (see Section 7.1), the NLUs can often be copy/pasted to the RDWS NLU column from data sources which are in (or were converted into) *digital* form and are simultaneously accessible in the same workstation.

5.2   Keyboard Entry

In CMAP3, as noted, there are two ways to enter raw data. One is to enter data using the PC's keyboard and mouse and the appropriate CMAP3 module (NLU, NCU). There is also a new method of *importing* data from a spreadsheet file (xls, xlsx), where the researcher, sometimes the respondents (see Section 7.3), have entered the data first. Which is appropriate depends on the research case. This section discusses keyboard entry.

CMAP3 has two modules for raw data entry. The first, *Node Data & Standardizing* module, hereafter called the NLU module, is used for entering the original concepts, NLUs. It is also used for entering the project's standard term vocabulary (STV) and for the actual coding of the NLUs, as discussed in Section 5.5. Figure 5.2 displays the NLU module's input screen, with data based on the above-mentioned example.

The module's upper window displays the contents of the *NLU datatable*, empty at the outset. The user enters the first NLU by giving the S number, the RDS and row numbers and types in the respective NLU. There is an REM field for eventual comments about the NLU. Furthermore, assuming the standard term vocabulary (STV) is available (in a preliminary or final form), the user locates the relevant standard term in the lower STV Input/Edit window and mouse clicks it. This brings

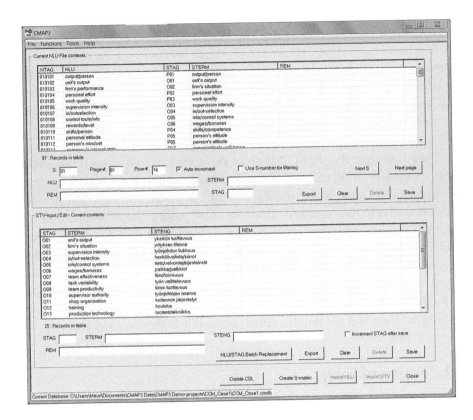

Figure 5.2   Node Data & Standardizing (NLU) Module

the selected standard term (STAG and STERM) into the NLU's respective field. By clicking the <*Save*> button, CMAP3 creates a signifier called *NTAG* for the NLU and enters the NTAG, the NLU, the eventual REM text, and STAG and its corresponding STERM into the NLU datatable. It will then appear in the upper NLU window.

There are some practical points. First, as noted, it is possible to enter the NLUs *without standardizing*, in which case the standardizing/coding will be done later (see below). Second, if an *entry error* occurs and was saved, clicking the respective NLU row in the upper window brings the previously entered contents into the respective editing cells. This enables adding remarks, changing the wording of the NLU or selecting a different ST/STAG. Third, to speed up keyboard entry, it is practical to check (activate) the *Auto increment* function. This keeps the entered S and RDS numbers intact but increments automatically to the next RDS row number so that it does not need to be entered manually. It is also convenient to select/check the *USE S-number for filtering* option. This makes the NLU window display only the NLUs which belong to a specific

S. Fourth, as long as the NLU fields' entries have not been saved, entered data can be removed from the editing windows by the <Clear> command. A new S or RDS page can be entered by commands <Next S> and <Next page>. The <Delete> command removes the selected NLU from the database.

Needless to point out, manual NLU entry does not always mean literally *typing* the NLUs into the module's entry window. Sometimes they can be *copy/pasted*, when the original data (NLUs) is available in the same PC in a digital form such as a PDF document, a transcript or a scanned OCR document. In this case, however, the researcher must see to it that the systematic NLU numbering, NTAGs, will be created which observes the above RDS conventions. Thus, a consistent and correct NCU input will be enabled, too. These technical details are discussed briefly in Section 7.1.

- *Browsing and sorting.* Assuming all or most NLUs are entered and at least tentatively coded with STAGs, the researcher can view the database and sort the NLUs by any of the window column titles by mouse clicking. In particular, by clicking the STAG column title, the NLU contents will be ordered alphabetically according to the STAGs, thus displaying all entered NLUs in a given ST category. This is obviously useful for examining the standardizing's consistency, accuracy, appropriateness, and so on.

- *Exporting the NLU database.* As most raw data and output tables in CMAP3, the NLU data file can be exported by clicking the <Export> button. Thereby, the file/table contents will not be altered. Obviously, this facility requires that the MS Excel spreadsheet application is available on the same PC. The <Export> command creates a worksheet and opens MS Excel, displaying the datatable's contents in the order just displayed in CMAP3. For example, it is possible to filter and export only the NLUs of a given S or C and in STAG order.

- *Converting* CMAP3 datatables into a spreadsheet file format has important uses. First, the browsing and analysis of a large datatable is often more convenient in MS Excel than in CMAP3 because one can see more of the contents. Second, the datatable's contents can be sorted and manipulated, including counting and logical operations. Third, the CMAP3 datatables can be formatted and *printed* using the PC's printer facility. This offers more formatting options and explains why CMAP3 does not have an integrated printing function.

- After NLU entry, the next step is the *manual entry* of the project's *natural causal units* (NCUs). Here it is assumed again that the raw NCUs are available in the transcribed RDSs as discussed in Section 5.1 (Figure 5.1) or in an RDWS. This contains the information about the causal links, and, depending on the study, there may also be data about causal link specification (+/-, W).

- The *Causal Links Data* module, called hereafter the NCU module, accesses the NCU datatable and is opened using the Main Menu or F4 command. The interface screen is shown in Figure 5.3. The upper window opens the NLU datatable, giving access to the entered NLUs, which are needed to define the NCUs. The lower window displays the NCU datatable.

- *Entering NCUs* is simple and fast in CMAP3. In the upper NLU window, the user first chooses the *Preceding NLU*. This brings the selected "cause" NTAG and NLU to the editing cells. Then, observing the link information on the respective RDS row, the *following NLU* or "effect" (that is it's NTAG, showing the row number) is chosen. It will then appear in the lower cell. If the study uses specification

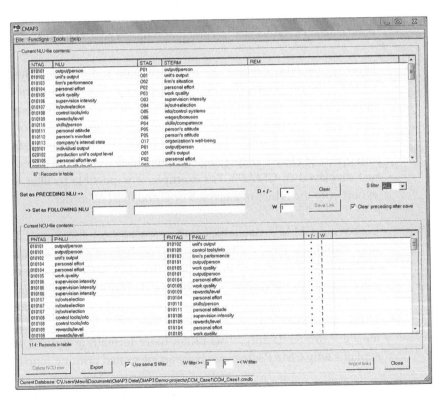

Figure 5.3   Causal Links Data (NCU) Module

information, and the causal link is an *inverse* one, the user must change the default value/direction (= direct = +) by clicking the < *D +/-* >. This *toggles* the plus sign into a minus sign. If the W (Weight) indicator is used, too, the appropriate W value must be keyboard entered into its cell if it differs from default value W = 1. When done, the user clicks <*Save*> and CMAP3 adds this NLU-NLU pair and its specification data to the NCU datatable. It will then appear in the lower NCU window.

- As in NLU entry, the command <*Clear*> erases erroneous entries before saving. If the user wishes to remove an NCU from the NCU database, this is done by selecting that NCU in the lower NCU window and the < *Delete NCU row*> command. Furthermore, there is an <*S filter*>, which enables displaying all Ss' or only a specific S's NLUs and NCUs. The filter affects both NLU and NCU windows. Using it makes it easier to pick the right NLUs and to check that the NCU entry is what was intended and that it was correctly saved into the NCU datatable.

- A further useful NCU entry command is <*Clear preceding after save*>. This is used when entering NCUs of those NLUs which have several effects, that is, "E-rows" (see Figure 5.1). In such cases it is convenient not to clear all NLU entries after saving, but to keep the <*Preceding NLU*> contents unchanged by choosing the appropriate option in the tick box, that is, keeping it unticked if there are predominantly several E-rows/NLU.

- *Specifying causal links (+/-, W).* The practice of detailed characterization of original causal links has been customary in structured CCM studies, as discussed in Sections 3.1 and 3.4. In general, it was maintained there that, instead of just following a tradition, the practice should be well grounded, weighing its overall meaningfulness against its costs in respondent time and less opportunity to cover more cognitive ground. From a purely technical viewpoint, CMAP3 has no problems with causal links' specification.

- *Batch deleting of NLU and NCU data.* In keyboard entry of data, occasional errors are unavoidable. They are usually detected quickly and corrected by changing the NLU input or by deleting and re-entering the individual NLU and/or NCU. There may also be cases where the user needs to delete NLU and NCU data either *completely* or for *a given S* but to keep the project's data otherwise intact. A reason for this could be, for example, that there has been a design error or that the data of a given source has unforeseen problems.

In such cases starting again with a clean slate or removing the dubious S data can be practical.

- CMAP3 has also a facility for erasing *all* raw datatables' (NLU, NCU, STV) contents in the < *Tools* > menu. Using it, the project and its datatables remain structurally and as files intact, but their contents will be erased either completely or only for a given S in case of NLU and NCU datatables. The benefit is that erroneous S data can be easily replaced. It is important to note that when erasing all NLU datatable contents or individual NLU data, the respective NCU data must also be deleted (but not the other way around) to prevent processing conflicts. CMAP3 does this automatically. Furthermore, when STV datatable contents are erased, NLU and thus also NCU datatables must/will be erased. This is necessary because of the NLU, NCU and STV datatables' interdependence. Thus, one should think before acting and often ensure that there are up-to-date backup copies of the project's file. Needless to add, there is no need to erase the output datatables (SCU, SNT). They will be simply regenerated based on the new data, which will overwrite these datatables' previous contents.

5.3   Importing Data

Initially, the *data import* facility was added to CMAP3 to enable *structured CCM* studies using the concept pool or the fixed list methods (Section 3.1.4). However, importing techniques also have other uses, as discussed above and in Section 7.1. To illustrate how importing works, we first assume that a variant of the concept pool method is used in an email-based elicitation (see Section 7.3). This also corresponds to the second demo project (*CCM_Case2*). Using CMAP3, such a study and data entry would require the following stages:

1. As in other CCM cases, a *CMAP3 project* is first set up. This includes determining the respondent number (max S01–S50) and their eventual clusters. The normal databases will be created automatically.

2. The researcher constructs the *concept pool* (or *fixed concept list*) as the project's *standard term vocabulary* (STV) (see Section 5.5 below). The STV can be entered manually using the NLU module or created using Excel and imported then from the respective worksheet file (for file conventions, see below) by using the <*Import STV*> command in the NLU module.

3. A *concept selection list (CSL)* is created for each respondent in the study using the *<Create CSL>* command in the NLU module. This command creates the CSLs as *spreadsheet* files, which are therefore identical with the concept pool, which in this case also equals the project's STV. In the *fixed list method*, CSLs are not necessary because only causal links will be elicited using the square matrices (see below).

4. The CSLs can be presented to the Ss in printed form or electronically (see Section 7.3) or filled in by an interviewer *in situ*. The concepts the Ss select correspond to the NLUs and will be *imported* from the CSL spreadsheet files directly to the project's NLU database using the NLU module's command *<Import NLU>*. In the fixed list method, although all Ss have the same number and identical concepts, for technical reasons, all Ss must have the NLUs in the NLU database under their name so that the NTAGs are correct and contain their S number. In this case, the NLUs can be imported into CMAP3 using the same CSL file but by giving it successively a different file name, which corresponds to the respective S.

5. To elicit the causal links (NCUs), the researcher first uses the NLU module's command *<Create S-matrix>*. This produces, in worksheet format, a *square matrix* of each S's personal concept sets (NLUs) which they selected of the CSL. In the fixed list case, the NLUs will be the same for all Ss but the NTAGs will have their S number. The created file is called a *pairwise comparison matrix* (PCM). The entry of the Ss' NCUs in the matrices/files is similar in the concept pool and the fixed list methods and can be done by Ss themselves on a printed matrix or on computer screen (see Section 7.3), by the interviewer (for example, using a notebook or tablet PC) or by using forms to be completed by the Ss or by the interviewer, and so on. An option is to combine freehand drawing and PCMs, whereby the Ss do the drawing and the researcher enters their NCU data to the PCMs and imports the data into the project's NCU database. However, in all cases, for each S there must eventually exist a PCM which can/will be imported to CMAP3 in creating the project's NCU database. The importing is done by using the command *<Import links>* in the NCU module.

6.   When all data has been imported, the next steps will be the same as in other CCM cases using CMAP3. In other words, the standard SCU and SNT tables will be generated and analyzed, focal or domain maps created, structural statistics and proximity data calculated, and so on. Finally, selected SCU sets can be imported to CmapTools for generating visual cause maps.

As noted, when importing data into CMAP3, the STV, NLU and NCU data must be available as Excel worksheet files. They must follow some conventions so that CMAP3 will recognize the files and import their data correctly. The Excel files can be in the *xls* format (Excel 97–2003) or the newer *xlsx* format. The conventions are as follows:

1.   *Entry of the concept pool = standard term vocabulary* (STV). This is the first task and precedes importing NLUs (below). Formally, there must be *at least one* (1) STAG/STERM in the STV and, moreover, a STAG which will be entered with all NLUs. However, in a normal case, the full concept pool will be entered as the STV by keyboard or Excel importing. If the user imports the STV, the workbook must use the following *conventions* (Figure 5.4):

   a)   The workbook's *file name* must contain the STV and the project name. A valid file name is, for example, STV CCM_Case2 (see the files installed for the demo case).

   b)   The workbook must contain one (1) *worksheet* with the name *DATA* (in *CAPITAL* letters). The first row of the worksheet *must* include three (3) columns with *titles STAG, STERM* and *STENG*. The STAGs *must* consist of one *capital* letter A–Z (no special characters like Ä, Ö, Å, and so on) and *two digits 01–99* (for example, A01, P12). Which letters are used and what they signify is open and will be discussed below in standardizing. The STERM column *must contain text* (that is, text, not numbers in Excel terms), that is, the pool/list concepts. The third (STENG) column, also text, is for the eventual second STV language. If that is not needed in the study, the third column can be left empty, but the title STENG must be there.

   c)   The STV/pool/list DATA worksheet must not contain data, formulas, and so on, *after* the last active row: that is, all rows after the last STAG/STERM must be left empty. If necessary, the

A	B	C
1 STAG	STERM	STENG
2 O01	unit perfomance	yksikön tuottavuus
3 O02	firm's profitability	yrityksen kannattavuus
4 O03	supervision intensity	työnjohdon tiukkuus
5 O04	hiring/dismissal	henkilövalinta/siirrot
6 O05	info/control systems	tieto/valvontajärjestelmät
7 O06	wages/incentives	palkka/palkkiot
8 O07	team effectiveness	tiimi/toimivuus
9 O08	task satisfaction	työn antoisuus
10 O09	team productivity	tiimin tuottavuus
11 O10	supervisor authority	työnjohtajan asema
12 O11	shop organisation	tuotannon järjestelyt
13 O12	training	koulutus
14 O13	production technology	tuotantotekniikka
15 O14	management support	yritysjohdon tuki
16 O15	team composition	tiimin rakenne
17 O16	product characteristics	tuotteen ominaisuudet
18 O17	organization's well-being	organisaation hyvinvointi
19 P01	output/person	tuotanto/henkilö
20 P02	personal effort/input	työpanos/henkilö
21 P03	work quality	työn laatu
22 P04	skills/competence	osaaminen/työtaidot
23 P05	personal attitude	asenteet/henkilö
24 P06	self-management	itseohjautuminen
25 P07	motivation/commitment	motivaatio/sitoutuminen
26 P08	work experience	työkokemus
27		

DATA

Figure 5.4   Concept pool/standard term vocabulary (STV) worksheet

user can have one or more worksheets in the same workbook, but they *must be differently* named (for example, Notes).

d)   When ready, the STV/concept pool is *imported* into the CMAP3 by mouse clicking the <*Import STV*> button in the NLU module. This will open a normal file selection window that enables locating the correct folder and opening the respective file (for example, STV CCM_Case2.xls). When opened, CMAP3 reads its contents (STAGs and STERMs, eventual STENGs) into the project's STV datatable. After this step, they will be displayed in the NLU module's lower STV window.

e)   If the researcher wants to *edit* or *delete* some of the STV/pool's concepts, this is perhaps best done using CMAP3 NLU module's STV editor. The STERM is selected by mouse clicking on the

STERM row and deleted or after editing saved again. If major changes are necessary, it is possible to delete the current STV (< *Tools/STV delete*>), redo the STV/concept pool using Excel, and reimport.

2.   *Concept selection lists* (CSL). These too are worksheet lists, from which the participants select their personal set of concepts from the pool. A CSL contains the entered concept *pool/STV* concepts and their STAGs and are the same for all Ss. A CSL is constructed using the command button < *Create CSL* > of the NLU module. This creates automatically an Excel workbook file with the obligatory three (3) columns with titles *STAG, NLU* and *0/1* on the first row (Figure 5.5). It is important for the subsequent importing that the column order stays as created and that the entries in the 0/1 column remain *text* as created (that is, are *not* changed into numbers). The created workbook has two worksheets: the one named DATA contains the CSL/concept pool, the other named GUIDE is reserved for eventual (not obligatory) instructions from the researcher to the respondent.

When created, the CSL file has at first no name. It must be named so that CMAP3 can recognize it as belonging to the project at hand and assigns the NLUs to the right respondent in the NLU datatable. For example, the CSL file for S01 would be named: *S01 NLU CCM_Case2*.

The *concept selection* itself when using CSLs is done by typing a 1 (NB: in this case, the 1 must be *text*, not number in Excel) instead of the default 0 in the third column. It is a different issue how the data elicitation (= Ss' choosing their own concept set) is done. As noted above, the CSLs could be, for example, presented to the Ss by an interviewer or emailed as attached Excel worksheets to the Ss (see Section 7.3), who select and mark their concepts on the list and email it back to the researcher. In the latter cases, if the study requires that the selectable concepts' number is fixed and must be uniform for all Ss, it may be useful to add a counter formula and *display the number* of concepts the respondent has selected. A simple way is to put text such as "*Already selected*" in cell D1 and an appropriate formula into cell E1 [for example, =(COUNT.IF(c2:c26;1)]. This reminds the Ss of the need to observe the required number of concepts (typically 10–15 concepts). Should an S mark more concepts than defined, this would cause extra work and unnecessary problems. The reminder text and counter data/formula that is located to the right of column C will be ignored by CMAP3. Thus, they must not but are best *removed* before importing.

◢	A	B	C	I
1	**STAG**	**NLU**	**0/1**	
2	O02	firm's profitability	0	
3	O04	hiring/dismissal	0	
4	O05	info/control systems	0	
5	O14	management support	0	
6	P07	motivation/commitment	0	
7	O17	organization's well-being	0	
8	P01	output/person	0	
9	P05	personal attitude	0	
10	P02	personal effort/input	0	
11	O16	product characteristics	0	
12	O13	production technology	0	
13	P06	self-management	0	
14	O11	shop organisation	0	
15	P04	skills/competence	0	
16	O03	supervision intensity	0	
17	O10	supervisor authority	0	
18	O08	task satisfaction	0	
19	O15	team composition	0	
20	O07	team effectiveness	0	
21	O09	team productivity	0	
22	O12	training	0	
23	O01	unit perfomance	0	
24	O06	wages/incentives	0	
25	P08	work experience	0	
26	P03	work quality	0	
27				

| ◄ ◄ ► ► | GUIDE | **DATA** |

Figure 5.5　　Concept selection list (CSL) in project CCM_Case2

To import CSL data, one clicks the < *Import NLU* > command button of the NLU module. This opens a normal Windows folder view to locate the respective CSL file in the PC and to open it by clicking. CMAP3 imports the NLUs/selected concepts for that particular respondent (above S01) to the NLU datatable and creates the appropriate NLU codes (NTAGs) and STAGs and STERMs. Finally, the number of imported concepts is displayed. This procedure is then repeated for all Ss. The *order* in which the different Ss' CSL/NLUs are important is free.

3.　　*Causal links data (NCUs).* In concept pool and fixed list based CCM, the number of concepts is relatively small. This allows importing causal links data in the form of a square matrix called a *pairwise comparison matrix* (PCM). A PCM contains the NLUs selected by the respective respondent arranged as *rows* and *columns*. As noted above, the PCMs are created by using the < *Create S-matrix* > command in the NLU module for each respondent, as defined in the upper window's S cell. CMAP3 creates an Excel workbook, which contains two worksheets (Figure 5.6): a DATA sheet (in *CAPITAL* letters) that has the S's concepts (NTAGs and NLUs) as a square matrix; and a GUIDE worksheet for eventual (non-obligatory) instructions and/or interviewer notes. Using the previous example (S01 NCU CCM_Case2.xls), the PCM shown in Figure 5.6 specifies 10 concepts and their causal links with +/- signs and W values (1–3). A zero (0) entry means no causal link. The matrix diagonal must remain *empty*, because it is assumed that the concepts do not influence themselves directly.

As in the case of CSLs, the researcher may want to define a maximum number of links per row and/or column. To display this and to give the respondents immediate feedback, the researcher can add *row and column sum counters* manually before sending the PCM to the respondents. This will show the Od/Out- and Id/In-degrees and the total number of links for each concept. If counting formulas are used, it must be observed that the matrix cell entries, although digits, are *text* (that is, not numbers for Excel). Furthermore, to prevent import problems, the eventual counter rows and columns *must be removed* before importing. If it is important to preserve them, one can copy the original contents (with the counter results) to a third worksheet with a different name and use a cleaned-up version for importing.

	A	B	C	D	E	F	G	H	I	J	K	L	M	N
1	NTAG	NLU	*firm's profitability*	*hiring/dismissal*	*management support*	*output/person*	*personal attitude*	*personal effort/input*	*supervision intensity*	*supervisor authority*	*unit performance*	*wages/incentives*		
2	010101	firm's profitability		-2	0	0	0	0	0	0	0	3		
3	010102	hiring/dismissal	0		0	0	1	0	0	0	0	0		
4	010103	management support	0	0		0	0	0	0	3	0	2		
5	010104	output/person	0	0	0		2	0	0	3	3	3		
6	010105	personal attitude	0	-2	0	0		3	0	0	0	0		
7	010106	personal effort/input	0	-3	0	3	0		0	0	0	0		
8	010107	supervision intensity	0	0	0	3	0	3		0	3	0		
9	010108	supervisor authority	0	2	0	0	2	0	0		0	0		
10	010109	unit performance	3	0	3	0	0	0	-3	3		3		
11	010110	wages/incentives	0	0	0	0	3	3	0	0	0			
12														

GUIDE **DATA**

Figure 5.6   The PCM of S01 in project CCM_Case2

CMAP3 cannot automatically name the PCM files. The researcher must assign the file name manually. For CMAP3 to correctly import the contents of the PCM file, the file name *must* contain the *S number*, the acronym *NCU*, and the project's name (to differentiate the file later from those of other projects). For example, *S01 NCU CCM_Case2*.xls is a valid PCM file name.

As in the case of CSLs, there are different ways of *entering NCU data* to the PCMs. The Ss could do that themselves using emailed PCM files (see Section 7.3), or an interviewer does it using printed forms or direct entry into a PC notebook. If the freehand drawing method is used to elicit NCUs, the researcher (assistant) can enter the drawn links data later to the respective S's PCM. To *import* PCM links data, one uses the NCU module's < *Import links* > command button. Before or during the importing process, CMAP3 will alert the user to invalid entries in DATA worksheet (see above for the formats).

Two final points about importing data should be added. First, the number of selected concepts in the imported CSLs can differ in CMAP3. The researcher can use the CSLs for entering concepts and allow or instruct the respondents to pick *different* numbers of pool concepts for their personal sets, although this has been unusual in structured hybrid CCM methods. In the latter case, the corresponding PCMs will (and can) also be of different size. This too is contrary to concept pool method practices, which require *identical* matrix sizes. However, it is *technically* possible in CMAP3 and could be useful in some CCM studies.

Second, during the importing process, incompatibility problems may occur if the processed Excel files differ in file formats—for example, when a respondent uses an application other than Excel to enter CSL and PCM data. To solve/avoid compatibility problems, it is recommended that before importing such CSL or PCM files, the researcher first opens them with their own Excel application, which was used in the preceding stages.

Third, as noted earlier, the technique of CSL importing is not confined to structured CCM in CMAP3. It can be used instead of the manual RDS/keyboard entry method for input of any original concepts/NLUs which have first been entered into worksheet format and saved as a workbook file using MS Excel. This was discussed in Section 5.1 as an alternative to the manual method using raw data sheets (RDS, Figure 5.1). This can be particularly useful when data is extracted from digital documentary sources for composite causal mapping (see Section 7.1). Apart from observing the above CSL file conventions, in particular that the concepts/ NLUs have *valid STAGs*, the only limitation is that a single CSL spreadsheet file (per a single respondent or other distinct data source) can have *maximally 1,000 NLUs*.

Moreover, as discussed in Section 5.1, when CMAP3 imports NLU data from a CSL file, it follows the original RDS convention that there are maximally 50 entries per RDS and will define the NTAGs of the imported NLUs accordingly. This should be observed when using the RDWS technique and its NLU row numbering. As to standardizing/coding, obviously, CMAP3 does not mind if the STV/STAG system is a tentative one or even includes only one STAG/STERM which is used for all imported NLUs. In general, the import function can be practical in studies where the actors' and/or documents' original concepts are the main focus. Depending on the computer, using Excel, more concepts can be visible and their sorting or editing is more convenient than in CMAP3. As to the causal links data input, the NCUs would in these cases be entered manually, as described in Section 5.2. A practical method for this is to simultaneously access the CSL-imported NLUs in CMAP3 NCU module and to access in an Excel window the respective RDWS (assuming of course it contains the NCU information as in the RDS method).

5.4   Standard Term Vocabulary

The idea and objectives of CCM coding (standardizing) were discussed in Section 3.2. This section focuses on the related technical issues, in particular the inductive building of the coding scheme, called the *standard term vocabulary* (STV) in CMAP3. A conceptual bridge binding these two sections and discussions together is the idea of a *level* of standardizing. STOP

In practice, coding is basically about detecting and defining *distinct* concepts and notions (NLUs) or their logical higher-level groups in the original data. The NLUs represent the phenomena, entities, variables and notions in the actors' thought/belief patterns. The process eventually creates the project's standard term vocabulary, which is entered into the project's STV database using the NLU module. This enables the actual coding of the individual NLUs, that is, defining them as same denoting with the respective standard term and thus as belonging to the same homogeneous or internally associated group. Technically, this is done by linking the NLU with the relevant standard term by entering its STAG into the NLU's row in the NLU database when the NLUs are input or later as a separate stage.

Importantly, the STAGs/STERMs/STENGs in the STV and the STAG codings of any or all NLUs can be *changed* if and as often as necessary. For example, more appropriate STs can be created and entered into the project's STV and selected to recode the respective NLUs. In CMAP3, the STV database is independent. It contains the active STERMs, which have been linked to the NLU database with the respective STAG, but it can contain also passive

STERMs, which are/were used provisionally or not at all. This would be the case when all provisional STAGs/STERMs are replaced with the final ones. Thus, there is no need to remove passive standard terms from the STV database. As long as they are not used in active coding the NLUs, they will not influence the standardized outcome.

In some CCM studies the STV may be fully available or it can be defined to a large extent at the outset of the study. This would be the case when the CCM study is about comparing some respondents' beliefs with an ideal pattern or template. In more typical cases, however, the STV can at first be known only indicatively, in rough outline. For example, in CCM studies using low- or semi-structured interviewing, there may be, based on preliminary interviews or research, a rather good idea of the respondents' probable terminology in addition to the anchor topics.

Usually, coding/standardizing must therefore proceed iteratively. This means creating first a rough initial grouping and ordering of the original concepts. This provides the necessary transparency and a broad idea of the substantive issues, notions and meanings in the data. In the next stages, the coding progresses stepwise towards the final solution. A typical standardizing process can be thought of as consisting of three overlapping stages.

5.4.1 STAGE 1: TENTATIVE STANDARDIZING: PROVISIONAL STANDARD TERM VOCABULARY

The iterative top–down process begins by creating a preliminary system of broad categories which will be represented by the first tentative standard term vocabulary (STV). Typically, the researcher examines the raw data to observe the kinds of natural language terms (NLUs) contained therein and their meanings and referents. In practice, this often happens in parallel with data acquisition. This enables starting to build a tentative standard term vocabulary (STV) as a first approximation of the project's coding/standardizing scheme.

The standard terms in the preliminary STV can be considered *tentative labels* of *broad concept/meaning "baskets"*. The main purpose is to group together closely related phenomena and notions which have more or less similar connotations or referents. The objective of the tentative standard terms/baskets is to enable organizing the NLUs into broad and relatively homogeneous groups. They will be more transparent and thus easier to analyze and break down for further development. Instead of trying to make sense of tens or hundreds of NLUs, the researcher can focus on considerably smaller sets of NLUs.

The above process continues as long as the interviewing goes on and the interview notes (see above) are being *transcribed*. This usually continuously points to new concepts, phenomena and aspects to be differentiated and added to the provisional standard terms. Using the NLU module, the tentative STVs are typed in to create the projects' STV database (Figure 5.2) *before* entering the NLUs. The other option is to use the STV import method.

There is no general rule for the number of tentative STs. It is flexible and changeable, and depends on the study case, its level of abstraction, the number and coverage of the addressed domains/issues and the raw data. It is better to think about the first stage as an *iterative* process, where the first organizing categories can, if necessary, be very broad and thus consist of only a few STs. The preliminary categories will then be examined and gradually cleaved into more homogeneous categories standard baskets/concepts. Thus, these processes overlap with the second stage.

As noted, the project's standard term vocabulary must follow some conventions. Each *standard term* must have a *code*, called an *STAG*, which consists of a capital letter and two digits (for example, A01, A02, and so on), and a descriptive term or label called an STERM, which can consist of a single word or a couple of words. In many cases the STERMs are literally synthetic terms such as *F-growth/well-being* or *ED-activities* (see Figure 1.1). As will be shown below, the *generated* output datatables (SNT, SCU) and the export-based *visual maps* will use the STV's standard terminology, that is, the STERMs and/or, if available and selected, the second language's STENGs. For practical reasons, it is therefore useful to avoid long STERMs/STENGs. When choosing and naming the standard terms, including the tentative STs, the STAGs and the STERMs/STENGs should provide a good idea of the respective standard category's contents (NLUs), that is, their referents and phenomena. It is often practical to use terms that refer to broad domains or issues and their relevant sub-phenomena and subcategories. For instance, the tentative STs could sometimes group together NLUs that refer to a firm's management, financial situation, its organization, human resources, and so on. It is also often practical to select the STAGs' first letters so that STERMs, which are logically close to each other, will have the same initial letter. This practice too can often be adopted already when creating the tentative STV (for example, M01 / manager and management, F01 / financial situation, and so on), although in some cases it may be better to signal the STV's tentativeness (for example T01 / management issues, T02 / financial notions, and so on).

When the tentative STV has been created and entered into CMAP3, the actual NLU entry and the NLUs' simultaneous tentative coding of the NLUs can begin. As mentioned earlier, however, the NLUs can, if necessary, be entered without the STAGs, in which case the standardizing will be done later.

5.4.2 STAGE 2: INDUCTIVE CONSTRUCTION OF THE STV'S FIRST APPROXIMATION

When all NLUs have been entered and *tentatively* coded using provisional STs/STAGs, the coding and the STV can be developed further. What this means in each case depends on the *research objectives* and its corresponding *level of standardizing* (Section 3.2). This influences how far from or close to the original vernacular level the standard terms will be, and thus, how much of the original richness of expressions will be preserved or alternatively compressed together into the constructed standard categories/terms. This influence, for example, whether the standard terms differentiate polar states of variables (for example, low/high unemployment, high/weak motivation) or refer only to the variables as such, assuming that any variation is self-evident and more or less continuous.

Usually, the researcher has a good preliminary idea of the meaningful level of abstraction in the study. To advance towards that direction requires a detailed examination of the provisional broad NLU baskets to determine the *distinct* phenomena, entities or variables, to which the NLUs in the examined STAG/STERM category refer. To enable that, the NLU database contents can be ordered and examined in *STAG order* using the NLU module (Figure 5.2). This displays the NLU contents of each provisional STAG/STERM category. If the database is large, it may be more practical to *export* the NLUs into Excel in STAG order. Depending on the PC, this can provide a larger window than CMAP3 for NLU browsing. In addition, exporting enables using Excel's *sorting* tools and *printing* the NLUs, too. Printing the NLU database is often practical when developing the STV and NLU coding.

The examination of the provisionally coded NLU database will lead to different things. Occasionally, some NLUs are detected which were erroneously coded and should be in a different STAG/STERM category. These will be noted and recoded. The main task, however, in the second stage is to detect the distinct notions and referents to which the NLUs refer. As emphasized, what is distinct and should be differentiated into an independent standard term category depends also on the study's objectives and standardizing needs. As a general rule, it is usually better at this stage to err into the direction of *more differentiation*, that is, towards using more specific and thus more numerous standard terms rather than the other way round. This can always be corrected in the third stage if necessary.

When distinct referents, phenomena, notions or variables are detected and differentiated, the relevant new STAG and its standard term (STERM, possibly the STENG, too) will be created and entered into the project's STV database. After that the respective NLUs can be re-standardized, that is, the tentative STAG replaced with the new one. In practice, an option is to use the RDSs or an Excel printout of the NLU database for written notes of the new STAGs/STERMSs and to link them with the respective NLUs when recoding them using the NLU module. When creating new STERMs/STAGs, one can use the tentative STERM/STAGs as a starting point, assuming they were created systematically. This would mean, for example, expanding a management-related basket by using STAGs like M02, M03 or M10, M11, and so on. This will be very useful when the NLUs are re-examined again after re-standardizing.

After a recoding of the NLUs, the NLU datatable must be listed, possibly printed, in STAG order to display and examine the STAG/STERM categories' new contents. This will reveal eventual coding errors and omissions. Usually, special attention should be given both to the *larger* NLU/STAG groups and the *smaller* NLU/STAG groups which consist of only a few, perhaps just one or two, NLUs. As to the larger groups, the main issue is their homogeneity, that is, do its NLUs have essentially similar meanings and referents? As to the small STV groups, the researcher can assess the need and relevance of such obviously rare, more or less idiosyncratic, notions. In general, this stage is about defining possibly too narrow or too broad standard terms/concept categories from the research perspective. If there are too large and too heterogeneous categories, they will be taken apart, and new STAG/STERMs are created for the detected distinct phenomena/variables. On the other hand, the NLUs in the smaller categories are perhaps better assigned to a different existing STAG/STERM or one creates a new STAG/STERM by joining one or more previous standard categories which are close to each other in terms of meaning (see below *STAG batch replacement*). In practice, the second stage iteration can require several rounds, especially in large CCM studies with several respondents and focal issues.

5.4.3 STAGE 3: TOWARDS THE FINAL STV AND STANDARDIZATION SOLUTION

When the second stage STV building and NLU recoding have been done, the next (third) stage begins with *generating* the SCU and SNT tables (Section 5.5). Generating requires that the original causal links data (natural causal units, NCUs) has been entered, too, as discussed above.

The third stage's objective is to enable a first examination of the *standardized* output and thus of the operative consequences of the standard term vocabulary and of the individual NLU coding solutions. This is not possible without the project's standardized output of nodes and causal links. Essentially, the iterative analysis and development of coding continues but with the difference that the causal links data will now be observed. This enables the researcher to see the *standard node terms* (SNT) and the *standard causal links* (SCU) and their *incidence* by data source and total numbers.

From a coding perspective, the first question in the third stage is the sharedness and meaningfulness of the generated SCUs and SNTs. It depends on the raw data, that is, how similar or different are the original notions and belief patterns in terms of their meaning and referents? However, as emphasized in Section 3.2 on coding, the sharedness or commonality also depends on the standard term vocabulary's STERMs' level of generality and on the coding which assigns the NLUs into the STERM categories. In practice, thus, the first point is the realized level of sharedness: is it too high or too low considering the research task? In the former case, the standardizing collapses too many NLUs and NCUs together, hiding important detail. In the latter case, the STV's STERMs are too close to the original language, which produces small NLU/STERM groups and thus little commonality and fewer "owners" of the generated SCUs and SNTs, many of them belonging to only one or a few respondents/data sources. In other words, in the latter case the coding leaves too much of the original idiosyncrasy visible, in the former standardizing occurs at a higher level and combines relatively NLUs into the same STERM baskets, producing more commonality of the SNTs and SCUs.

A useful tool for an overall view of the realized coding is the *NLU/SNT Matrix*. It is accessible from the main menu or by <F11> (Figure 5.7). The table lists the active *standard node terms (SNT/STAG)*, which belong to the *last generated* SCU set. The matrix file will always be generated anew. If the researcher wishes to preserve the contents, the matrix table must be exported and saved as a workbook file.

The NLU/SNT Matrix columns display the active standard terms (STAG, SNT), the number and distribution of the respondents or data sources (S) that used an NLU which was coded into a given STERM category, and how many corresponding NLUs there were for a given S and in the whole NLU database. In other words, the matrix shows which SNTs/STERMs are widely shared and which are more unique, owned only by one or a few respondents.

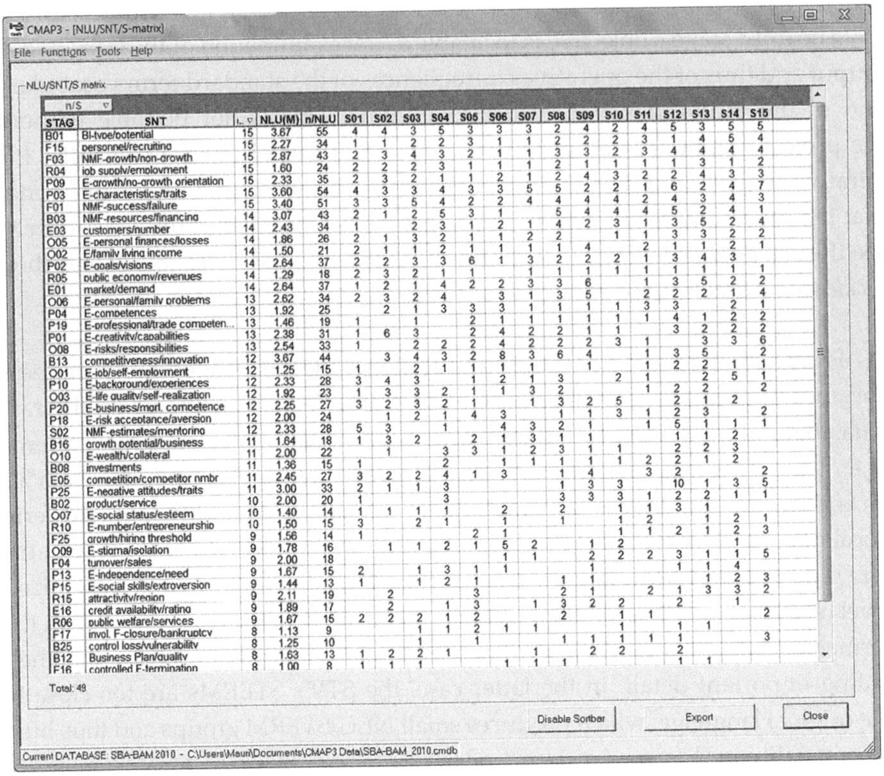

STAG	SNT	n	NLU(M)	n/NLU	S01	S02	S03	S04	S05	S06	S07	S08	S09	S10	S11	S12	S13	S14	S15
B01	Bi-type/potential	15	3.67	55	4	4	3	5	3	3	3	2	4	2	4	5	3	5	5
F15	personnel/recruiting	15	2.27	34	1	1	2	2	3	1	1	3	3	2	3	1	4	5	4
F03	NMF-growth/non-growth	15	2.87	43	2	3	4	3	2	1	1	3	3	2	3	4	4	4	4
R04	job supply/employment	15	1.60	24	2	2	2	3	1	1	1	2	1	1	1	3	1	2	3
P09	E-growth/no-growth orientation	15	2.33	35	2	3	2	1	1	2	1	2	4	3	2	2	4	3	3
P03	E-characteristics/traits	15	3.60	54	4	3	3	4	3	3	5	5	2	2	1	6	2	4	7
F01	NMF-success/failure	15	3.40	51	3	3	5	4	2	2	4	4	4	4	2	4	3	4	3
B03	NMF-resources/financing	14	3.07	43	2	1	2	5	3		5	4	4	4	4	5	2	4	1
E03	customers/number	14	2.43	34	1		2		2	1	1	4	2	3	1	3	5	2	2
O05	E-personal finances/losses	14	1.86	26	2	1	3	2	1	1	2	2		1	3	3	2	2	
O02	E/family living income	14	1.50	21	2	1	1	2	1	1	1			2	1	1	2	1	
P02	E-goals/visions	14	2.64	37	2	2	3	3	6	1	3	2	2	2	1	3	4	3	
R05	public economy/revenues	14	1.29	18	2	3	2	1		1	1	1		1	1	1			1
E01	market/demand	14	2.64	37	1	2	1	4	2	2	3	1	3	5		2	2	1	4
O06	E-personal/family problems	13	2.62	34	2	3	2	4		3		3	1	3	2	2	2	1	4
P04	E-competences	13	1.92	25			2	1	3		3	2	1	1	1	4	1	2	2
P19	E-professional/trade competen...	13	1.46	19	1			1			2	1	1	1	1	4	1	2	2
P01	E-creativity/capabilities	13	2.38	31	1		6	3			2	4	2	2	1	3	2	3	6
O08	E-risks/responsibilities	13	2.54	33	1			2	2	2	4	2	2	2	3	1	3	3	6
B13	competitiveness/innovation	12	3.67	44				2	1	1	1	2	8	3	6	4	1	1	
O01	E-job/self-employment	12	1.25	15			1	2	1	1	1	2	1			2	5	1	
P10	E-background/experiences	12	2.33	28	3	4	3			1	2	1	3		1	2	2		2
O03	E-life quality/self-realization	12	1.92	23	1	3	3	2	1		1	3	2		2	1	2		
P20	E-business/mgrl. competence	12	2.25	27	3	2	3	2	1		1	3	2	5		2	1	2	
P18	E-risk acceptance/aversion	12	2.00	24		1	2	1	4	3		1	1	3	1	2	3	1	1
S02	NMF-estimates/mentoring	12	2.33	28	5	3		1			4	3	2	1		1	5	1	1
B16	growth potential/business	11	1.64	18	1		3	2		2	2	1	3	1	1		1	2	
O10	E-wealth/collateral	11	2.00	22			1		3	3	1	1	1	1	2	2	1	2	
B08	investments	11	1.36	15	1				2		1	1	1	4		3	2		2
E05	competition/competitor nmbr	11	2.45	27	3	2	2	4	1	3		1	4		3	2			2
P25	E-negative attitudes/traits	11	3.00	33	2	1	1	3				1	3	3		10	1	3	5
B02	product/service	10	2.00	20			1	3				3	3	3	1	2	3	1	
O07	E-social status/esteem	10	1.40	14	1	1		1	1		2		2		1		1	2	1
R10	E-number/entrepreneurship	10	1.50	15	3		2	1			2	1			1	2	1	2	3
F25	growth/hiring threshold	9	1.56	14	1			1		1	2	1	5	2			2	3	1
O09	E-stigma/isolation	9	1.78	16			1	1	2	1	5	2		1	2	2	2	3	1	1
F04	turnover/sales	9	2.00	18							1	1		1		1	1	1	4
P13	E-independence/need	9	1.67	15	2		1	3	1	1		1		1		1	1	2	3
P15	E-social skills/extroversion	9	1.44	13	1		1	2	1			1		1	2	1	1	3	3	2
R15	attractivity/region	9	2.11	19		2				3		1	3	2	2		2		1
E16	credit availability/rating	9	1.89	17		2	2		1	3	1	1	2		1	1	2		2
R06	public welfare/services	9	1.67	15	2		2	1	1	2	1	1				1	1		
F17	invol. F-closure/bankruptcy	8	1.13	9				1	1	2	1	1		1	1	1	1		3
B25	control loss/vulnerability	8	1.25	10				1		1		1	1	1	1	1	2		
B12	Business Plan/quality	8	1.63	13	1	2	2	1				1		1	2	2	2		
F16	controlled F-termination	8	1.00	8	1	1	1			1	1	1				1	1		

Total: 48

Figure 5.7   NLU/SNT matrix in a CCM project

Both indicate standard term categories whose contents may deserve a detailed examination and eventual recoding of the respective NLUs. First, STAG/SNTs containing many NLUs may have issues of homogeneity. Second, the small categories/SNTs with fewer NLUs and/or S owners should be assessed to see if they really represent unique phenomena which deserve a distinct STAG/SNT or should they be recoded into a larger existing or new STAG/SNT group.

In practice, the goal in the third stage is to gravitate towards a solution which the researcher (and eventual external reviewers) considers satisfactory in terms of the research task. In most cases, this requires some rounds of iterative testing and successive changes in the standardizing vocabulary and the individual standardizing decisions. The advantage of using CMAP3 is that the necessary or possibly useful changes in the STV and/or NLU coding can be detected, tested and done and also undone quickly by regenerating the SCU and SNT tables to examine the changes' impact. In general, the objective is to achieve a meaningful level of sharedness of the output SNT/SCUs, but at the same time to

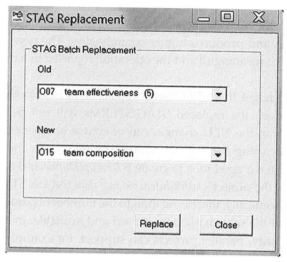

Figure 5.8   NLU/STAG batch replacement tool

preserve and display the valid differences and unique phenomena and notions in the raw data. Technically, if the emerging commonality seems too high, the solution is to create new STERMs/STAGs with less sharedness and generality. The respective NLUs' previous STAGs will be substituted with new ones. In the case of too low sharedness, the high idiosyncrasy can be reduced by joining the smaller STERM/STAG groups, either into new higher-level and thus more encompassing STAG/STERMs or into an existing STAG/STERM category (see *STAG Replacement* below). Both will increase the output SNT/SCUs' commonality.

As noted earlier, changes of *single* NLUs' coding are usually best made using the NLU module. However, CMAP3 has a special tool for changing simultaneously the coding of several NLUs. Mouse clicking the *NLU/STAG Batch Replacement* button in the NLU module or the *<F12>* function key opens this tool's window (Figure 5.8). In the upper (Old) row, the currently active STs/STAGs are listed with the number of NLUs coded using each STAG in parentheses. The lower row (New) accesses the project's standard term vocabulary and shows all STAG/STERMs in the active project's STV. This method is practical for merging *several* NLUs into a different STAG/STERM group or for correcting systematic coding errors.

Perhaps needless to point out, imported data's coding can also be changed, if necessary. A reason to do so could be a too low sharedness of the elicited causal beliefs, which could result if the pool's concepts (that is, the NLUs and STERMs) are too close to the natural jargon and not general enough. In this case, the respective STV/pool concepts can be combined and the corresponding NLUs recoded through the *Node Data and Standardizing* module. This collapses also the respective NCUs and produces higher commonality. The new standard terms must obviously be meaningful and the operation reported in a transparent way.

It should be noted that STAG batch replacement is *irreversible* in the NLU database. However, the replaced STAG/STERMs will not be removed from the STV. Moreover, the NLU changes can of course be *redone* by recoding the respective NLUs using the normal manual techniques in the NLU module. However, it is often a good idea to create (*<Backup/Duplicate>*) a parallel project which preserves the project's *work-intensive raw data* (NLUs, STV, NCUs) in the original form. Technically, there is no limit to the number of parallel projects. The advantage is that the same basic data is used and available. In addition to data backup and security, parallel projects can support, for example, using *different standardizing strategies/vocabularies* at higher or lower levels.

It should be emphasized that the validity, accuracy and semantic appropriateness of the coding and the level of the standard term vocabulary depend on the research questions and objectives, assuming no major errors of coding and data entry. As in qualitative research generally, a proper assessment of validity and coding requires theoretical expertise to understand what the study seeks to accomplish. Ideally, the study's coding and active standard term vocabulary will be commented on by peers and finally assessed by external and independent knowledgeable reviewers. The main issue to assess is usually the *semantic* and *face validity* and the *consistency* or *reliability* of the study's coding scheme (STV) and especially of the most critical standardizing decisions which affect the emerging level of sharedness (or its apparent lack). Different approaches to reviewing are discussed in qualitative and content analysis method sources (for example, Krippendorff 2004, Merriam 2009). Usually, one or more reviewers (with appropriate qualifications and information) assess the coding scheme (STV) and the standardization decisions. Thereby, it is possible to calculate quantitative indicators of reviewers' and/or multiple coders' mutual correspondence (inter-coder reliability/agreement). After such reviews, the previous coding can be supported or amended by changing the individual standardizing decisions or creating new STV categories.

5.5   Generating Output Data

Standardizing assigns the NLU database's original concepts into categories of standard terms, which have been defined homogeneous in terms of their meaning or referents. The generation process in CMAP3 builds upon this basis. It metaphorically converts the original concepts and the causal assertions (NCUs) into a parallel new and more compressed upper-level set of *standard causal units* (SCUs) and *standard node terms* (SNT). In addition, the process identifies and calculates which and how many respondents possess a given SCU and SNT, that is, had one or more correspondingly standardized NLU and NCU in the original data. This enables constructing sets of SCUs (standardized causal maps) which are shared by a specified number or predefined cluster of respondents. Moreover, the Id, Od and Td values of the active SNTs will be calculated and entered into the standardized output SCU and SNT datatables.

Generating can start when the raw data (= NLUs, NCUs) has been entered and *all* entered NLUs have been standardized at least tentatively for *all* Ss defined for/in the project. Generation is possible even if data for some data source (S) has not been entered. Technically, the generation process uses the STV, the NLU and the NCU databases. The NCUs in particular regulate whether an NLU (more accurately its SNT) will be included in the generated output SNT table. If an NLU is not linked with at least one other NLU as an NCU pair, that NLU will not be observed in the generation process.

To begin the standardized output's generation, click in the Main Menu or use key <F5> to open the *Generating Cause Map Units* module (Figure 5.9). The window first displays information about the project and the source datatables' current condition. To obtain this data, CMAP3 checks the integrity and status of the source datatables (NLU, NCU, STV). If the datatables are in order, an Ok note is issued. If data for one or more Ss is missing, this will appear after the respective database's name. Technically, it is required that all respondents/data sources (Ss) have at least one NLU and that all NLUs have been *standardized* with a valid STAG/STERM, validity defined as existing in the project's STV. As noted, the input STAGs' validity in this meaning will be automatically checked with the respective NLU entry, but NLUs can also be entered untagged. However, it is also possible that the STV has been changed or the previous SNT/STAG has been removed *after* NLU standardizing. In that case, the user must make corresponding changes to the NLU database. If CMAP3 meets NLUs with no STAG or a non-existing STAG, it issues an error message and the user must locate and correct those errors before proceeding. In addition, CMAP3 checks that every S has at least one NCU in the source NCU file. If NCUs for a given S are found missing, an alert will show, but the researcher can start the generation as usual but based only on the available data. This can be useful and intentional, for example, when using dummy Ss, so there is no point in blocking the generation in such a case.

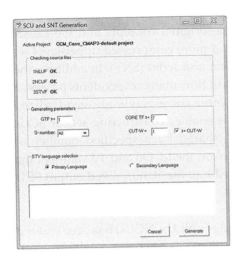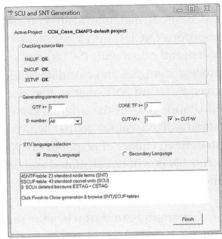

Figure 5.9   Generating Cause Map Units Module (before and after generation)

At the outset, the researcher must define some *parameters*. The first (compulsory) is the *<GTF >=* (Generating Total Frequency). Its value range is from 1 to the maximum number of respondents/data sources defined in the project. The GTF sets a threshold by which the researcher can regulate how fine-grained (idiosyncratic) versus highly shared the output of SCUs and SNTs will be. If GTF equals 1, the generated SCUs and the SNTs (which depend on the generated SCUs) will contain *all* available standardized data, including the SCUs, which are unique to only one respondent (S). However, in CCM studies which are interested mainly in shared causal patterns, setting a higher value of GTF may be useful so as to exclude "outliers," that is, highly idiosyncratic SCUs and SNTs. As most other parameters, the GTF can also be changed and the consequences of different GTF values observed by regenerating the SCU and SNT output files. In this way, the impact of different or parallel solutions can be tested.

The second definable, but optional, parameter is the *<S-number>*. Its default value is *<All>*, which means that data for all defined respondents or data sources (Ss) will be observed in the generation. However, the researcher also occasionally has the useful option of generating the SCU and SNT datatables and to thus produce an analysis basis and cause maps only for a single specific respondent.

The third and compulsory parameter is the *<CORE TF >=>*. The available value range is from 1 to the maximum number of Ss (1 =< CORE =< number of S). The result of the CORE calculation will appear in the CR column of the SCU and

SNT tables (Figure 6.1). The digit 1 will be displayed for those SCUs and SNTs which are shared at least by the respective number of respondents/data sources. From a research perspective, a given core value represents the researcher's idea or definition, presumably grounded, of how many Ss of the study must have the same SCU so it can be considered a typical, widely shared or "core" belief or notion among the sample. For example, in a CCM study of 10 respondents, a plausible CORE TF could be >= 8, representing roughly 80 percent. The CR value can be used as a filter, and the core SCUs would constitute a core causal map. As other parameters, the *CORE TF* and the output files can be changed quickly, so that the impact of a different core value is easily examined.

Fourth, if the researcher uses *W (weight)* values for the NCUs in the study, the <*CUT-W* => box and its tick box will control the processing of NCUs into the SCU database. The CUT-W defines a lower threshold W value, which will be observed in generation. If this option is not used, the CUT-W takes the default value 1, which is the same as the default value of W by NCU entry. If the tick box marked <>=*CUT-W*> box is *ticked* (= default), all NCUs with W values *equal to* or *higher than* the W value defined by the researcher in the box will be observed in generation. If there are different W values in the NCUs which will be standardized into the same SCU, the SCU will take an *averaged* W value calculated based on the respective W values. However, if the *tick* in the box is *removed*, CMAP3 will observe *only* those NCUs which have the *specified* W value (including 0) and use them when generating the SCU/SNT tables.

In research terms, using W values and their interpretation is a question of the CCM study's needs and the researcher's preferences. For instance, assuming that W = 2 indicates an "important" causal influence and W = 1 a "normal" one and the researcher sets the value of W at 2, only the "important" NCUs would be observed in generating SCU/SNT output. Instead, using W = 1 would include all NCUs in the NCU database and increase the number of output SCUs. Consequently, the SNT datatable, eventual DM and FM sets and the Statistics/CD-index tables, which are all based on the generated SCU set, would also be different. They would obviously also be different if the tick box is unmarked.

Depending on research needs, a final selectable option is the *output language*. In practice this means whether the SCU and SNTs datatables will use the STV's *primary* language (STERMs), which is the default, or the *secondary* language (STENGs), assuming it is available in the STV. Using two output languages can be useful, even imperative, in studies involving different languages. For example, a study submitted to a UK or US journal might have Finnish or Chinese data sources (Chapter 7). In such cases it would not be possible to use original language in the output. However, using parallel languages has its own problems, such as risks of *mistranslation*, which the second-degree mapping from one culture sphere and meaning system to a different one can imply. This introduces a further semantic dimension and may require special validation.

The Generation module has two command buttons: *<Cancel>* (= return to the Project Manager) and *<Generate>*. The duration of the generation varies and depends on the sizes of source files (NLU, NCU, STV) and the PC's processing speed. Using a modern PC, even in the case of relatively large databases like those in the SBA study (Section 7.2), the generation is usually a matter of seconds, not minutes.

When the generation is done, CMAP3 changes the window to show that the process was successful. It also summarizes the main statistics of generated SCU and SNT datatables (Figure 5.9, right). In addition, CMAP3 also reports the number of eventually *deleted SCUs*. This is usually because CMAP3 precludes SCUs which assert that a phenomenon (when coded) influences itself directly. This would be the case if an NCU's two NLUs have been coded in to the same standard term category, that is, their input STAGs are identical—not unusual when standardizing rich original data. As an example, let us assume that two respondents used the NLUs "motivation" and "commitment", which were coded using a synthetic STERM "Motivation/Commitment". One S said that "Motivation increases commitment" and the other S that "Commitment depends on motivation". Both statements will be entered as NCUs. In this case, however, the resulting initial SCU would be "Motivation/commitment → Motivation/commitment." CMAP3 checks for such links and removes them from the final SCU database.

To leave the generation process, the *<Finish>* button is clicked. This opens the SCU/SNT browsing window (Figure 6.1). The module *<Browsing Cause Map Contents>* is accessible also from the Main Menu and by <F6>. It is a central tool in CMAP3 CCM analysis and will be discussed next.

Chapter 6

Cause Map Analysis Tools in CMAP3

This chapter discusses the generated output of SCUs and SNTs and the different alternatives and tools for their further processing and analysis. To illustrate, the datatables in the figures are based on the output data of the automatically installed two *demo projects* and can therefore be generated when testing CMAP3.

6.1 Standard Causal Units

The *<Browsing Cause Map Contents>* module opens automatically after the generation process. For brevity, it will be called the *SCU/SNT module*. It can also be accessed from the Main Menu or by function key <F6>. As shown in Figure 6.1, the module has two windows. The upper window, *Map Node Links-SCU-file*, displays the contents of the recently generated SCU datatable; the lower window, titled *Map Nodes-SNT-file*, shows the standard node terms (SNTs). They are *active* standard concepts which exist in the SCU datatable as a preceding (cause) or as a following (effect) concept.

It will be remembered that the SCUs represent the data's *node-node pairs* (A→B, B→C, and so on) using the standard vocabulary's language (SNTs). Thus, they are a result on the one hand of the underlying original data and how it was *standardized* and of the generating process and researcher-defined parameters such as the GTF value or selected output language on the other hand. The generation subsumes and metaphorically converts and compresses the original NLUs into the more compact SNT categories. Furthermore, the numerous original causal assertions (NCUs) will also be converted and replaced by a more compact set of standardized causal units (SCUs) with additional information such as their S incidence. Needless to add, the original NLU and NCU datatables remain as they are. The standardized datatables can be thought of as a more or less higher-level mirror conceptual system, which will be the basis of the subsequent analysis.

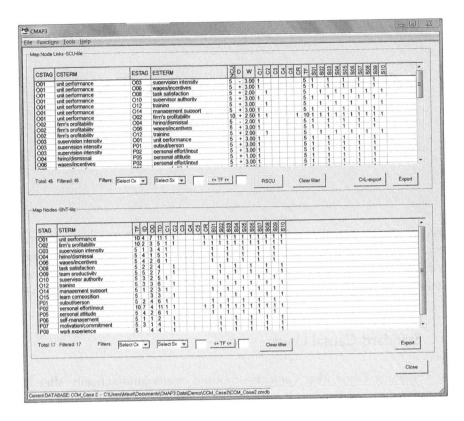

Figure 6.1   Standard Causal Unit (SCU) and Standard Node Term (SNT) browsing module

The upper window of the SCU/SNT module lists the generated SCUs ordered first alphabetically by the SCUs' CSTAGs and corresponding CSTERMs, that is, the "cause" or "antecedent" notions of the standard causal unit. Respectively, the ESTAG and ESTERM columns list the "effects" or "consequences" (E = effect) of the preceding cause standard node term. Clicking the column titles changes the order of display.

The first row under the SCU window shows the total number of SCUs in the datatable. A selective *display filter* can be used (below) to define which SCUs will be displayed. For example, the filter in Figure 6.1 was set at TF <= 6, which excludes (hides) 11 SCUs out of the total of 46. Using an SCU (or any other) filter does not alter the content of the generated datatables.

The column <NCU> shows the number of NCUs which underlie or were subsumed into each SCU. Usually, the NCU number equals the TF, but it can be higher if the corresponding original causal notions were repeated by one or more respondents in the NCU database, which is common in CCM studies based on rich interview data. The respondents typically repeat notions and causal ideas that are subjectively important or for some other reason salient in the context. Thereby, respondents may use the identical or some synonymous original concepts (NLUs), which will be coded under the same standard node term (SNT). The existence of same denoting NCUs in the NCU database does not affect the generated standard output. The generated SCU datatable will include all distinct standardized causal statements which exist in the raw NCU database *and* correspond to the STV and coding decisions. The SCU datatable shows all respondents who have at least one corresponding NCU and the number (TF) of respondents.

Depending on the CCM study, especially the richness of its data and the method of acquisition, NCU numbers can provide information about the background and characteristics of the SCUs. The NCU number indicates how frequently a given causal assertion occurs in the data and can therefore provide a (rough) measure of the *salience* and relative *weight* of the respective causal ideas in the respondents' mental models. This could in some cases be an empirical alternative to inquiring about the NCUs' weights (W values).

Column <*D*> (direction) displays the direction (+/-) sign of NCU and thus that of the SCU. In case there are similarly coded NCUs, some of which are direct (+) and some inverse (-) relationships, CMAP3 will generate two corresponding SCUs, one direct, one inverse.

The <*W*> column displays the corresponding attribute of the SCU such as, for example, the assigned weight of the original link in the NCU database. As explained in Section 5.5, depending on how the CUT-W is used, the displayed W value will be either an *average* of the NCUs' original W values or a *definite* W value, which was used as the generating filter.

The value in columns *C1 to C5* (C = cluster) is 1 when the SCU is possessed by the cluster/s as it was defined in the Project Manager. In the example above, the fifth SCU is owned by both C1 and C2. This means that the threshold number of respondents (Ss) assigned to that cluster possess a respective NCU. The same logic applies to the column *CR*, that is, the Core, except that the CORE-TF value is defined at generation as noted above. In the example, one core SCU is visible, obviously the one belonging to C1 and C2.

The <*TF*> (Total Frequency) column shows the number of respondents or data sources that share a given SCU as the NCUs were coded. The maximum value of TF equals the number of Ss in the project, TF = 1 obviously indicating an SCU owned by only one S. As noted, the GTF threshold can be set higher (>1) to exclude outlier SCUs. This can be useful for pruning large N datasets in those CCM studies, where unique (idiosyncratic) concepts and causal notions are not important. Generally, if the GTF is set higher, the SCU datatable will also often be much smaller if there are many idiosyncratic NCUs. The impact is also reflected in the SNT datatable and other datatables and numerical indicators, which are always calculated based on the *most recent* SCU database. The S *columns* are self-explanatory. They display a value of 1 if a particular respondent's or data source's NCU data contains an NCU which was coded as that particular SCU.

When browsing, setting a *filter* enables focusing on different aspects and specific contents of the SCU datatable. The first filter is based on the *clusters* (*C1 – C5*) and the *Core*. For example, if *Core* is set as the filter, only the SCUs possessed by the corresponding number of Ss (see Section 5.5) will be displayed. The second filter is the S *number* (default is all Ss) to show the SCUs of a specific respondent or data source only. The third filter (*<= TF <=*) uses the calculated total frequency (TF), that is, the number of Ss who possess a given SCU. The TF filter can be set to display SCUs with a minimum or maximum TF. Figure 6.1 shows what would happen in the demo project when the TF is set to show the SCUs of *at least* 6 Ss (6 =< TF). The window displays a message about the active filter and the number of SCUs passing that criterion. Notably, different filters can be *combined* by selecting another filter without clearing the previous one. This makes the selection narrower. If this is not intended, the previous filter/s must be *deactivated* by clicking the *<Clear filter>* button.

The button < *RSCU* > is a special filter which enables detecting and displaying eventual *reciprocal* SCUs in the database. As noted earlier, a reciprocal or two-way standardized causal unit (RSCU) refers to a SCU pair which occurs because the raw data contains at least *two* NCUs, one maintaining that A→B, the other B→A, that is, that there is a *mutual* influence relationship, where the standardized NLUs appear both as a cause and as a consequence of each other. Figure 6.2 shows the result of applying this filter in the demo project.

From a research viewpoint, RSCUs can be important. They may have different backgrounds and also different implications. Sometimes RSCUs represent valid original causal beliefs. For example, it is not unusual that interviewees perceive a positive (virtuous) circle such as "good results will increase a person's motivation, and vice versa". Sometimes RSCUs result of NLU coding. Whilst RSCUs seem generally rare in low- and semi-structured or TBCM CCM data, they occur frequently in structured CCM studies using *pairwise comparison* (PCM). The dilemma is that some of these RSCUs (that is, the underlying NCUs) may be dubious. They

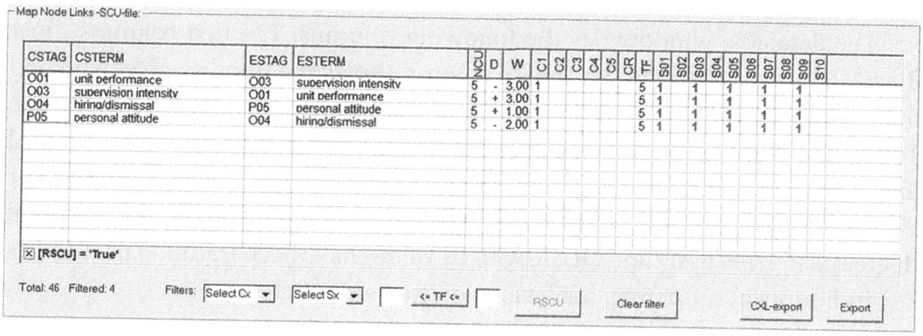

Map Node Links -SCU-file:

CSTAG	CSTERM	ESTAG	ESTERM	NCU	D	W	C1	C2	C3	C4	C5	CR	TF	S01	S02	S03	S04	S05	S06	S07	S08	S09	S10
O01	unit performance	O03	supervision intensity	5	-	3.00	1						5	1	1	1	1	1				
O03	supervision intensity	O01	unit performance	5	+	3.00	1						5	1	1	1	1	1				
O04	hiring/dismissal	P05	personal attitude	5	+	1.00	1						5	1	1	1	1	1				
P05	personal attitude	O04	hiring/dismissal	5	-	2.00	1						5	1	1	1	1	1				

[x] [RSCU] = 'True'

Total: 46   Filtered: 4   Filters: [Select Cx ▼] [Select Sx ▼] [ ] [<• TF <•] [ ]   [RSCU]   [Clear filter]   [CXL-export]   [Export]

Figure 6.2   Reciprocal standard causal units (RSCU) in the SCU window

inflate the SCU database and above all lead to erroneous conclusions and findings, for example, about the complexity of respondents' belief patterns. We will discuss these issues in Section 7.3.

There are two more options in the upper window. First, clicking the *<Export>* buttons creates a worksheet file of the SCU datatable and opens it in MS Excel. If the SCU datatable is displayed using a filter, only the filtered set will be exported. The SCUs will be exported in the displayed order. Exporting enables the user to print or copy the datatable or to embed it in worksheet format into other Windows applications. Furthermore, using Excel can be more practical for browsing and analysis purposes. It can display more of the datatable and enables sorting it by any column, and to manipulate the SCU data in many ways.

Second, the *<CXL-export>* button creates a cxl file of the displayed (filtered or unfiltered) SCU datatable. Using this file format the datatable (as filtered) can be imported to *CmapTools* and displayed and edited there in visual form. This provides a practical route for creating visual (graphic) causal maps, as discussed more below in Section 6.5.

6.2   Standard Node Terms

The lower window of the SCU/SNT module, titled *Map Nodes SNT-file*, displays the active *standard node terms* (SNT), which exist in the just created SCU datatable (Figure 6.1). The SNT datatable is automatically created immediately after the SCU datatable. Thus, the SNTs contained there, the S distribution and all numerical data in the database are based on the SCU datatable as generated and observing the defined parameters.

The datatable window has the following columns. The first columns show the SNTs' *STAG* and *STERM*. The *TF* column shows the number of Ss who had this particular SNT as a preceding or a consequence notion in the SCU datatable. The columns *ID* and *OD* (indegree, outdegree) display the number of causal links (cause map arrows) that, respectively, flow *into* a cause map node (SNT) or *from* an SNT node (based on the *full* unfiltered SCU table). The column *TD* (total degree) is the *sum* of ID and OD. Id/Od/Td values have been traditionally used as key indicators in cause map analysis as discussed in Section 3.5.

The SNT window too has columns for the predefined *clusters* (C1 – C5), and for the *Core* (CR), assuming they are used/defined in the study. Finally, there are *S columns* for respondents/data sources in the project. The column title enables sorting the SNTs according to the respective dimension.

The SNT datatable has three optional *filters*. The first is used to select and display the SNTs which belong to a specific cluster or the core. The second displays the SNTs owned by a specific respondent or data source. Third, the SNTs can be filtered using different TF values.

The displayed (filtered or unfiltered) SNTs, too, can be *exported* in spreadsheet format. This starts MS Excel and the respective new workbook/ sheet will open automatically after clicking the *<Export>* button. The SNT datatable can then be formatted or printed or copied to other applications or analyzed using Excel's sorting tools and calculating functions.

The SCU and SNT datatables and their filtering, display and export facilities provide a set of basic tools and options for CCM analysis. What is done in practice depends on the research questions and the researcher's needs and analytical preferences and skills. Some of the general aspects and approaches have been discussed above. Typically, the SCU and SNT datatables are analyzed at least for two broad types of questions. First, the respondents or documentary data sources or their clusters will be *compared* in terms of the emerging standardized belief patterns. A typical objective is, for example, to locate the widely *shared* core SCUs among the respondents by iteratively setting and testing different selection filters (TF or C). In many cases it is useful to export the full or filtered SCU subsets as cxl files into CmapTools and display and analyze them as a visual causal map. Visualizing provides a holistic view of the mapped belief systems and helps understand the respondents' subjective thinking or mentally simulate the target real system.

The second type of analysis focuses on the *substance*, that is, the cause map contents and the mapped system or the mechanisms and their different factors and phenomena, which the standard node terms (SNTs) and causal units (SCUs) represent. In this respect, first, the Id/Od data of the individual SNTs can serve as rough indicators of the relative roles of the different factors. Second, the S distribution of the SNTs can be illuminating. A deeper and more holistic view of the SNTs and causal mechanisms, however, requires a more detailed analysis of the causal relationships in the standardized data. The *Focal Map* and *Domain Map Browser* modules provide tools for such tasks.

6.3   Focal and Domain Maps

In addition to the SCU/SNT module, CMAP3 has two additional tools for causal map analysis: *Focal Map Browser* and *Domain Map Browser*. The Focal Map (FM) module (Figure 6.3) has two windows: *A: Preceding Nodes – "Causes"* and *B: Linked Nodes – "Effects"*. A standard node term (SNT) and selection window will appear in the middle after it has been selected by mouse clicking from the

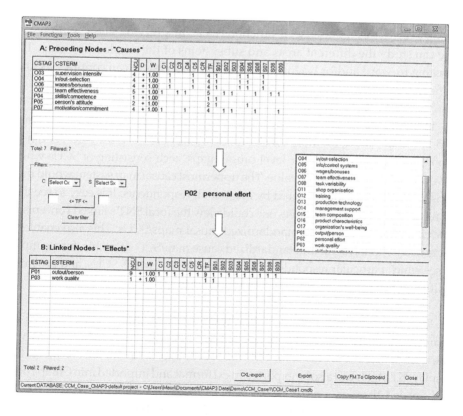

Figure 6.3   Focal Map (FM) browser

SNT list (middle/right). The usual filters (Core/Cluster, S/all, and lower and upper limits for TF) are available, too.

Technically, a Focal Map consists of those standard node terms which are *directly* causally linked to a specific focal SNT selected by the researcher and are available in the last-generated SCU database. For example, as shown in Figure 6.3, selecting the concept *"P02 personal effort"* will display its "cause" SNTs in the upper window and its "effect" standard concepts in the lower window.

Why use Focal Maps? Let us assume a large SCU datatable with well over 100 SNTs resulting of rich raw data from several respondents and a low generating GTF filter (GTF => 1). Many of the resulting SNTs and SCUs will be idiosyncratic or shared at most by a couple of data sources. Assuming the full SCU set converted into a visual causal map, it would have a large number of nodes and links, and be difficult, if not impossible, to comprehend and analyze as a whole. Instead, the analysis would have to focus on some specific areas of the causal map which correspond to interesting issues or mechanisms, probably doing this successively one area after another. The Focal Map Browser enables doing exactly this. In a sense, it functions as a "magnifying glass" with which one can study the different areas and subsystems of the whole cause map. The tracking forward and/or backward in the mapped system can continue as long as necessary by defining new SNTs as the next focal phenomenon to study.

However, the Focal Map Browser has other functions as well. If the causal map and FM in the above example consists of SCUs with TF => 1, the SCU set can be thought to also include higher-level causal maps, each consisting of SCUs which have a successively higher TF value. The uppermost causal map system would then consist of SCUs which are shared by most or all respondents. It is easy to see that by using the FM Browser's filters one could view the focal SNT's linked concepts in *differently shared* layers of the standardized causal maps/SCUs. This also enables a more detailed analysis of the standardized cause map/SCU datatable, for example, to see which particular respondents or clusters possess which SCUs, and provides a different viewpoint for analysis than browsing the SCU and SNT datatables.

The displayed and filtered or unfiltered Focal Map SCU sets, too, can be *exported* as a spreadsheet file and opened in MS Excel. This is also necessary if one wishes to *save* the particular FM contents or to *print* them. Furthermore, the displayed FM sets can also be exported in cxl format and imported into CmapTools and opened there as a *visual causal map*, as discussed below in Section 6.5. In addition, the FM contents can be *copy/pasted* into another Windows application for drawing. In this case the displayed SNTs will be converted and transferred as plain text, the two windows' contents staying separated from each other.

The *Domain Map Browser* (Figure 6.4) is functionally similar to the FM module, but it enables selecting a larger causally interlinked subset of SCUs from the SCU database. These SCU sets are called Domain Maps. There are three types of DMs. The first is the *full* DM (DM-F = default). If this option is selected, CMAP3 first generates, around the selected seed SNT, a subset of SCUs, which is the same as a Focal Map. It then locates those SCUs which add to the FM base the "causes of the FM's causes" and the "effects of the FM's effects". The other DM options produce narrower SCU sets. The user can select either the *cause* component (DM-C) or the *effect* component (DM-E) to be added to the FM base. The displayed SCU rows have different colors depending on which cause map component they represent.

To generate a Domain Map, one first decides the type (DM-F, DM-C, DM-E), the eventual filters and selects the appropriate seed *concept* (from SNT) around which the domain map will be constructed. What will be selected depends entirely on research purposes and analytic and presentation needs.

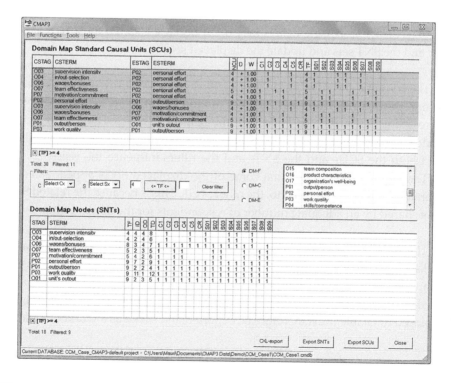

Figure 6.4   Domain Map (DM) browser

The DM's main function is to represent and help analyze sub-areas or mechanisms in a larger causal map system in CCM studies, in particular in cases when the full SCU/causal map would be too large and thus difficult or even meaningless to display and analyze as a whole. The seed SNTs refer usually to a central or critical phenomenon or factor in the analyzed domain or issue. Such SNTs/ variables can be assumed to have important causal relationships and linkages to other variables in the SCU database. In the example in Figure 6.4, the SNT *personal effort* was given as the seed SNT. In this case, this SNT represents clearly a critical issue considering the examined belief systems. The DM type depends on the analytic needs. For example, if one examines the issue from an impact and criteria viewpoint, a DM-E would perhaps be chosen. If the influence mechanisms and tool factors are more relevant, a DM-C would probably be selected and analyzed.

Using DMs and FMs pinpoints the factors and issues represented by the respective standard concepts and causal relationships that are most relevant in research terms. Sometimes, similar results as with using DMs can be reached by successive sets of Focal Maps which share SNTs on the cause or the effect side. Using the DM tool may be faster. In the case of large SCU databases (say more than 1,000 SCUs) and/or a highly central seed SNT with many links, the resulting DMs, especially DM-Fs, can be large, too. When the researcher uses several filters simultaneously, processing delays may occur because CMAP3 must recreate the SCU and the SNT sets and update the displayed sets.

The columns and filtering/display options in the DM browser are similar to those in the SCU/SNT and FM Browser modules. The upper window displays the resulting SCUs and the lower one the respective SNTs. The SNT selection window and the filter options are in the middle. Notably, the DM Browser filters affect both the SCUs and the SNTs and the filters influence the *generated* DM set. Therefore, it can happen that some of the displayed SNTs appear as being separated from, not connected to, the other SNTs. This is because the related SCU is not shared by an adequate number of respondents for the applied filter level.

The DMs' SCU and SNT sets (filtered or unfiltered) can be *exported* to create a worksheet file or exported as cxl files to be edited into visual causal maps using CmapTools. As the Focal Maps, the Domain Maps too are always generated anew based on the active project's SCU database. To preserve the contents of a DM, the displayed datatable must therefore be exported and saved as a workbook file.

6.4 Statistics Module

A key advantage of CCM and the CMAP3 database approach is to facilitate a cause-map-based quantitative analysis (see Section 3.5). For this purpose, CMAP3 has an integrated *Statistics & C/D Index* (Figure 6.5) module, which calculates a set of numerical indicators for the active CCM project. In addition, the numerical analysis can be considerably extended by exporting the relevant databases or generated quantitative data to external software such as MS Excel or SPSS and using their analytic and statistical functions.

The statistics module calculates two interim databases which are displayed in the module's two windows. The upper one shows *Project Statistics*, which summarize the contents of the NLU/NCU and SCU/SNT datatables and display a set of relationship indicators. The lower window shows the *C/D Index* in matrix form. It is a correspondence or distance indicator of the degree to which either the SCUs or the SNTs overlap across data sources (S). The numbers and

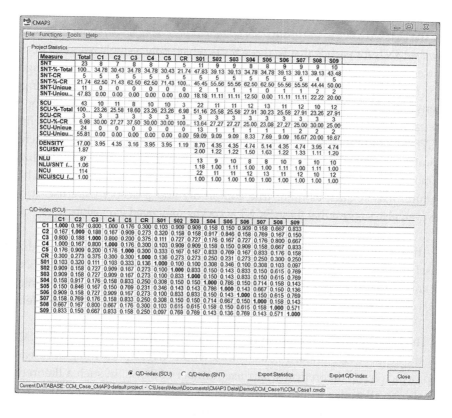

Figure 6.5   CMAP3 statistics & C/D index module

measures are calculated based on the *last generated* full SCU and SNT datatables and each time anew when the statistics module is accessed. Therefore, again, if the researcher wants to preserve the displayed numerical data, the contents of the respective window must be exported and saved as a workbook Excel file.

Figure 6.5 shows the statistics module content based on the default CCM_Case1 project. The upper *Project Statistics* window displays first information about the generated standard node terms (SNT): the *total* number of SNTs, their numbers for each active *cluster* (C1–C5), the *core* (Cr), and for each respondent/data source (Sn).

On the row titled *SNT-%-Total* the clusters', the core's and the respondents/ data sources' (S) SNT numbers are compared with the SNT Total (in percentages). For example, S01 possesses 47.83 percent of all SNTs, that is, almost half. The next row, *SNT-CR*, shows how many of the SNTs are *core* SNTs, that is, belong to the SCU set, which meets the Core criterion as defined for the SCU/SNT generation. The *SNT-%-CR* row gives (in percentages) the share of each cluster's or S's *core* SNTs as compared with the respective cluster's or S's all SNTs.

The last two rows in the group (*SNT-Unique, SNT-Unique-%*) show the number of *unique SNTs* for each S, that is, those SNTs which only a single respondent/data source has in the generated SNT datatable. The lower row shows the percentage of an S's *unique SNTs* as compared with the number of that S's all SNTs. "Uniqueness" means in this case that some SNTs belong to only one S. Thus, the clusters or the core cannot have unique SNTs. Obviously, if the generation threshold is defined at GTF >= 2 or higher, there will be no unique SNTs (or SCUs). The uniqueness indicator is useful especially when iterating towards an appropriate standardizing solution by pinpointing Ss who have relatively many unique SNTs. This can have a natural reason, such as more true complexity and a deeper expertise. It can, however, also suggest that these Ss' NLU coding may need a revision.

The second or *SCU* set displays parallel numerical data for the standardized causal units, SCUs. As can be seen, the indicators correspond to those of the SNTs, but are calculated for the SCU database. In this case, too, a higher share of unique SCUs can have an authentic explanation or suggest a possible coding problem.

The *Density* row indicates (in percentages) the degree of how far the SCUs and the respective standard causal map would overlap an imaginary cause map, which has a theoretically *maximal* number of SCUs. In such a theoretical causal map all nodes would be linked to all other nodes, although in CMAP3 in *one direction* only, that is, direct reciprocal links are not observed in the underlying formula. In the example, the theoretic maximum SCU number is

= 253 (= 23*(23-1)/2). Accordingly, the relative density of, say, S01, is = 8.70 (= 22/253*100). For the whole SCU set the density is respectively 17.0 (42/253*100).

The *SCU/SNT* row shows the average number of SCUs per SNT in the generated full SCU datatable. The SCU/SNT relationship is calculated for the total and for each respondent/data source (S). This too can be used as a density indicator. It could pinpoint different categories or types of belief system, for example, those with characteristically fewer but influential, multiply linked concepts, or a belief system which has many concepts and few links. In addition, the SCU/SNT measure can be used to compare different elicitation methods (see Section 7.3).

The last four rows in the Statistics window contain the numbers of the original concepts (NLUs) and causal links (NCU) in the raw database for each respondent/data source and their sum (Total). Assuming a reliable and uniform elicitation of data, these numbers can also be used as indicators of *cognitive characteristics* such as complexity or expertise. Arguably, depending on the case, they could be occasionally more relevant and plausible than the customary density measures discussed in Section 3.5.

Furthermore, CMAP3 calculates the relationship measures NLU/SNT and NCU/SCU, that is, the ratio of all NLUs and NCUs to the number of respective standard node terms and standard causal units. They are calculated for each respondent/data source. In this case, the Total column shows the *mean* of the respondents/data sources' values. In inductive coding-based CCM, the NLU/SNT and NCU/SCU ratios reflect the realized *level of standardizing*. In the example in Figure 6.5, the NLU/SNT values are close to 1, which indicates practically a similarity of the NLUs and the SNTs, that is, a low level of standardizing. In contrast, in the SBA study discussed in Section 7.3, the NLU/SNT (M) was 1.88. This is somewhat higher, but still relatively low and suggests that its STV too is close to the original vernacular. These indicators can also be useful for analyzing the relative uniformity and realized compression effects of coding across respondents/data sources. Possibly, they may be used to compare different CCM studies and when analyzing the impact of major changes to the project's STV and standardizing.

The *Statistics* window's contents can be *exported* and opened as a worksheet by MS Excel. This can be useful, because thus a wider set of *statistical measures/formulas* will be available to support the CCM analysis. This can begin with calculating basic indicators such as the means and standard deviations of NLUs in the database, which may be descriptively useful also in an otherwise predominantly qualitative analysis. It is also easy to see that the researcher

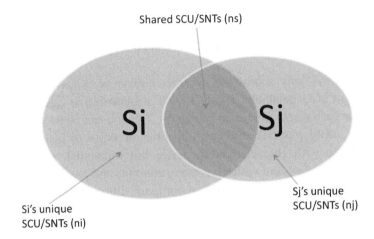

Figure 6.6   **Calculating the correspondence/distance (C/D) index in CMAP3**

can easily construct further indicators based on the NLU, NCU, SNT and SCU numbers and their distribution over respondents.

The lower window, titled *C/D-index*, displays, in matrix form, a measure of the active project's respondents' or clusters' mutual correspondence or distance. It indicates, in relative terms, the degree to which a given pair of Ss or Cs possesses the same SCUs or SNTs (Figure 6.6). The underlying formula is *C/D index = ns /(ns + ni + nj)*, where ns = number of *shared* causal links (SCUs) or concepts (SNT) and ni and nj the numbers of *unique* causal links (SCUs) or concepts (SNT) owned by two defined respondents, a given respondent and a predefined cluster, or two predefined clusters of respondents (Si, Sj). Notably, "unique" in the formula means uniqueness relative to the *compared* pair, that is, that the *other* cluster or respondent in the compared pair does not own those specific SCUs or SNTs. As noted earlier, uniqueness in the full SNT/SCU set in the SNT/SCU Statistics window means that only a given single S owns a set of SNTs or SCUs.

The C/D index can have values between one and zero. A value = 1.000 indicates that the causal maps (SCU sets) or SNT bases of the two compared respondents (or clusters) are *identical* and overlap perfectly. A C/D index value = 0 means that the compared respondents or clusters have no SCUs or SNTs in common and there is no overlapping of the respective causal maps or SNT bases. If necessary, the C/D index values can be converted into a more distance-oriented measure by subtracting the matrix values from 1 (using Excel).

It is important to note that CMAP3 can calculate the C/D matrix using either the standardized causal units (SCU) or the standard node terms (SNT) as the comparison base. The user selects this by clicking the respective option. In most cases, the SNT base produces clearly *higher proximity values*. The reason is that a major source of variance, that based on the *causal* relationships, is not in play. In most cases the number and differences of the SCUs are considerably higher than those of the SNTs.

From a CCM research point of view, the SCU and SNT bases and thus the C/D index values reflect and are thus dependent not only on the existing "real" variance in the original NLU and NCU data but also on the conversion and compression impact of the project's coding scheme (STV) and the individual standardizing decisions. In addition, the GTF threshold value set at SNT/SCU-generation will obviously also influence the SCU and SNT databases and thus the C/D index. Technically, using a higher GTF value precludes the less shared SCUs (for example, TF = 1 or 2) from the generated SCU database. As a consequence, the apparent commonality and C/D index values will rise because a part of the original NLU/NCU variance will not be observed. What is appropriate depends, once again, on the research needs. In addition, it may often be a good idea to test and examine different solutions by regenerating or using *parallel projects* to see the impact of different strategies/levels of standardizing and GTF limits. Importantly, the reasoning, decisions and their implications must be clarified transparently when reporting the study's methods and findings.

The interpretation of the C/D index values depends on the study and its premises, too. Assuming a *cognitively* oriented CCM study, where the SCU and SNT databases represent the Ss' causal thinking and belief systems, the C/D index values measure the *overall* similarity or dissimilarity of the respondents' cognitions (knowledge, beliefs). In the above case, for example, there is a relatively high correspondence among the respondents belonging to C4 or C5, but more distance is visible when non-members are compared with each other. In real life, observations like these could suggest interesting subgroups of the respondents. In contrast, in *composite* or *systemic cause mapping*, the role of the C/D index would probably be different, if it is relevant at all. The objective in such studies is often to create a system description for analysis and pragmatic development or to extract the typical beliefs of key actors from several documentary sources. In such cases the correspondence or similarity across the data sources would probably matter less. What might matter more is that the study acquires valid data from as many sources as is necessary, but with as *little overlapping* as possible. In that case, the C/D measure's interpretation would stress maximal uniqueness and minimal overlapping and redundancy.

The statistics module's tables/matrices can also be *exported* and opened in worksheet format using the *Export* buttons for printing and saving the contents for later analysis or comparison. An advanced use of exporting is to transfer the C/D index data via MS Excel to statistical software such as SPSS for further analysis. As discussed in Section 3.5, this can help pinpoint empirically based groups of respondents who have similar or divergent causal belief systems. Technically, the C/D matrix exported in worksheet format must be prepared for importing. In the case of SPSS, for example, the worksheet's title and date texts, which will be created by CMAP3, must be removed. Usually the cluster and core data must be removed too so that the worksheet includes only the Ss' C/D index values with appropriate row and column titles to define the matrix.

6.5   Visual Cause Maps

In typical CCM studies, a visual graphic display of causal maps can augment the text or datatable and numerical indicator based analysis. This enables a *holistic* view and understanding of the typical thought patterns or the target domain or system, and thus an analysis by running them "in the mind's eye". In CMAP3, there are three ways for presenting and analyzing the standardized output as a visual causal map.

The first and simplest tool is the *Focal Map* tool described above. Although it uses a non-graphical textual and database format, it allows viewing the generated causal map's SCUs by displaying the proximately causally linked cause and effect SNTs of the focal SNT. By using sequentially different SNT seeds, the generated causal map can be viewed in full, if necessary. Furthermore, the FM views can be filtered to display FMs of a specific cluster or S. In addition, FM contents can be copy/pasted to a Windows graphics application or imported into CmapTools and viewed as a visual causal map.

The FM method has obvious limitations. If larger and in particular more specified causal maps are required for presentation or publication purposes, it is better to use a specialized drawing application. CMAP3 supports this by enabling copy/pasting or exporting the relevant cause maps' SCU sets. For practical reasons, CMAP3 does not have an integrated graphic capability. First, specialized graphic and presentation applications provide much more versatile and practical drawing and editing capabilities than could be built into a necessarily constrained integrated facility. Second, from a CCM research and publishing perspective, whilst visual analysis can be dominant in some pragmatic and composite CM approaches (see Bryson et al. 2004, Cossette 2002), in typical comparative causal

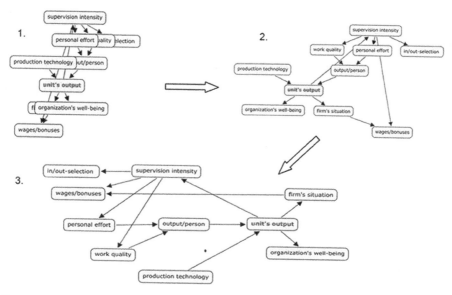

Figure 6.7   A DM-F causal map (CCM_Case 1, focal concept O01 unit's output) created using CmapTools and CMAP3 cxl-export facility

mapping studies visual causal maps have a secondary role. Instead, it is the theoretic issues and the comparative and quantitative analysis of belief patterns that dominate. Moreover, the visualization needs vary and the researchers and journals may have different analytic and subjective visualizing preferences.

When using CMAP3, the perhaps most convenient way of producing visual causal maps is to use *IHMC CmapTools,* a popular and freely downloadable software application for concept (idea) mapping.[1] Importantly, CmapTools can read exported cxl format files (created by the SCU, FM and DM modules) from CMAP3 and convert them to visual maps.

In CmapTools, importing is simple (*File/Import/Cmap from CXL file*). After importing, the viewer opens the file. At the outset the imported interlinked SCUs will be initially displayed as a more or less cluttered set (stage 1 in Figure 6.7). To create a readable causal map, it usually needs some editing. A first approximation can often be created using the *Format/Auto-layout* command (Ctrl-L) (stage 2). To further edit the cause map, the concepts (SNTs) can be moved with a mouse to more appropriate places, whereby the connecting arrows will automatically

---

1   http://cmap.ihmc.us/download/.

follow (stage 3). CmapTools has a number of further editing and formatting options for the texts and arrows/lines.

As an example, Figure 6.7 shows a DM based on the CCM_Case1-project data using *01 unit's output* as the focal seed concept. This is an unusually simple cause map and contains only the most basic information (SNTs, SCUs) in the base DM-F. Depending on the task and preferences, however, this can be adequate as such at least for tentative visual representation and analysis or as a first approximation. To create more complex causal maps, one can edit and format the concepts and arrows, for example, add specification information, use different fonts and types and styles of arrows, to add text annotations, and so on. The graphic maps created in CmapTools can be saved and exported as graphic files (for example, BMP or JPG), PDF files or as text propositions (SNT-SNT), which can be copy/pasted further if necessary. A practical method for publication is simply to copy or screen capture the cause map in CmapTools' viewer window and embed it into another document, as was done in Figure 6.7.

However, when drawing one or at most a couple of larger and more specified causal maps for publication, it may be better to use a dedicated drawing or presentation application such as, for example, MS PowerPoint. A work-saving method in this case is to *successively* copy FM sets or SCUs from a spreadsheet file and paste the contents into text boxes created in the application. The single SNTs in the box can then be copy/pasted into further text boxes and finally arranged into their appropriate locations and meaningful pattern for the causal map. The active "hot" points of the text boxes (with or without borders) can be connected with "sticky" arrow connectors to represent the causal links. When the SNTs/boxes are moved, the connected arrows move, too, making editing the map's layout easy. Moreover, different types of arrows and text styles, and so on, are available. The cause maps created in this way can be saved in different file formats and embedded into other documents.

Drawing causal maps is, to some extent, a matter of personal inventiveness and preferences, but perhaps not entirely. When creating causal maps for publication or a presentation, the objective is not to artistically impress the audience, but to report, in *visual* form, the study's findings and/or to convey the essence of a person's or a collectivity's causal beliefs and overall mindset about the focal issue or domain. A point to remember thereby is that graphic and abstract models such as causal maps may not be obvious to everybody. Some readers need explanations and examples to grasp even the very idea of *visually* representing somebody's causal thinking or the structure and mechanisms of a socio-technical system. Furthermore, readers must not be overburdened with overly complex and dense causal maps.

In addition, whilst there may be no absolute rules for drawing a causal map, there are some common-sense notions. First, the dictum "less is more" is often a very useful guideline. Visual causal maps should focus on clear and specific issues or domains. In CMAP3, this can be realized by generating a correspondingly focused Domain Map or even a Focal Map, which are exported to underpin the causal maps. Another, often parallel, tool is to use filtering. This enables displaying a truncated SCU set or a Domain or Focal Map as visual causal maps, which represent just the specific patterns which the researcher wants to capture and show.

Second, the layout of a causal map is not entirely a question of personal preferences. A specific layout and ordering of concepts can foster but also obstruct comprehension. For example, when drawing graphical models like causal maps, it is a tradition and a good practice that causality is displayed flowing *horizontally* and *from left to right*. This means that nodes/variables representing outcomes or goals will be placed on the right side of the causal map and the factors and mechanisms leading to them on the left side, their positions possibly roughly indicating their relative significance. This corresponds also to normal human problem-solving, which is built around means and ends and givens in the represented situation or system, as pointed out earlier.

Occasionally, there is a problem of how to represent differences and changes in the *same* causal map. For example, the researcher wants to show the longitudinal changes of the belief patterns or display the different located groups or "schools" of respondents, who have both common belief elements and some non-shared, even diametrically different, notions. One solution in this case may be to place the shared or unchanged elements in the middle and the older and new or divergent causal notions in the upper and lower parts of the causal map respectively (Laukkanen 2001). Another one is to display the differences or the different origins of causal notions by using different text type or different types or thicknesses of the arrow lines. However, packing too much information into the causal map should be avoided. Sometimes it may be better to draw two or three causal maps, which have otherwise identical layouts, but show the changes or differences.

Chapter 7
CCM Research in Practice

This final chapter presents three research cases which represent typical methods and strategies in comparative and composite causal mapping. The idea is to discuss concrete examples of applying different CCM methods and thereby of some of the often emerging methodological issues. The first case (Section 7.1) represents the traditional "Axelrodian" approach to CCM. The study by Mingde Wang derives composite causal maps from documentary data, in this case published foreign policy speeches of Deng Xiaoping, China's paramount leader after Mao. The objective was to model and reconstruct the official belief system about international politics in contemporary China. The second study (Section 7.2) is by Mauri Laukkanen. It is based on semi-structured CCM interviewing and attempts to elicit and describe the typical belief patterns of Finnish small businesses advisors (SBAs) concerning the performance and growth of nascent small firms (NMF). The third case (Section 7.3) is a study also by Mauri Laukkanen. It uses two variants of the structured (concept pool) CCM approach, again with Finnish SBAs as participants. This study enables a comparison of two structured CCM approaches and the semi-structured CCM method. From a method selection viewpoint, this study shows that CCM methods can produce different data and also divergent findings. Thus, they are not necessarily interchangeable and freely selectable as method alternatives.

7.1 Document-based CCM: Mapping Chinese Foreign Policy Beliefs

Since causal mapping emerged as a systematic research strategy for analyzing documents (Axelrod 1976), documentary analysis remains a dominant category of research in the CCM tradition. To augment the discussion in Section 3.1.1, this section provides a more technical guide to document-based causal mapping (DBCM) studies. We will illustrate the complete process from the question-specific selection of data to the final construction and analysis of causal maps. For this purpose, we use a study example drawn from international relations (IR) research: the analysis of China's foreign policy beliefs embedded in

Deng Xiaoping Wenxuan (*Selected Works of Deng Xiaoping*). CMAP3 serves as the main technical means by which data generation and map construction will be realized.

7.1.1   DBCM STUDIES IN IR

In international relations scholarship, DBCM has been largely employed in (but not limited to) three categories of research. The first seeks to explore belief contents pertinent to rational decision-making. The second is more occupied with the psychological implications of individual beliefs. The third category focuses on shared beliefs within different collectivities.

The first, rational category represents studies for which causal mapping was originally created. In *Structure of Decision*, Axelrod argues that causal mapping is useful for constructing a model of a belief system as it is embedded in texts. He maintains that a causal map that accurately represents a person's beliefs can reflect how that person should make rational decisions, and possibly also indicate "how a person actually does perform certain cognitive operations" (Axelrod 1976, p. 56). It follows that causal maps can help a policy-maker to more effectively grasp the interrelationships and causal consequences among "the full complexity of his many interrelated beliefs," so that he can improve the quality of rational deductions (Axelrod 1976, p. 56). By understanding such normative patterns of beliefs in a systemic way, therefore, scholars may achieve a more accurate prediction of the behaviors of rational decision-makers. To facilitate this rationalist commitment, Axelrod also develops operations to calculate the causal influence of a sequence of concepts, and thus differentiate the ranking of choice paths quantitatively (for example, the utility effect of "paths" and "circles," Axelrod 1976, pp. 61–4).

In political psychology, in contrast, it is not assumed that people can observe strict rational-choice norms. Individual beliefs are also viewed as products of various cognitive biases and problem-solving shortcuts. Therefore, in political psychology, DBCM is largely employed to capture the cognitive features and organization of beliefs rather than cognitive content *per se* (Young 1996, Young and Schafer 1998). In addition, the methods are usually more integrated with psychological theories that focus specifically on a variety of mental models, such as historical analogies, political metaphors and causal attributions. An example of such research is the analysis of Japan's 1941 decision for war by Ariel Levi and Philip Tetlock (Levi and Tetlock 1980). They constructed causal maps from the statements of Japanese policy-makers, and derived from the maps a number of structural indexes of cognitive complexity (see Section 2.4 for a discussion of complexity in MOC research). Using the indexes as dependent variables, they were able to test the hypothesis that crisis-produced stress (measured by situational settings of the statements) can lead to a decrease in cognitive complexity and thus diminished performance in decision-making. Here, the style of information-processing rather than specific beliefs about causality is the researchers' primary concern. Another application of causal mapping in political psychology, the Operational Code, is based on Alexander George's theory that links a decision-maker's political orientation to a number of cognitive features, such as patterns of causal attribution, in their philosophical beliefs about the political life (George 1969, Walker et al. 1998). Thus, the Operational Code captures in political documents the balance between different categories of causal assertions and its implications for behavioral orientation. By quantifying the structural features, researchers can compare the decision-making orientation of world leaders from George W. Bush to Hu Jintao on a standardized scale (Walker et al. 1998, Schafer and Crichlow 2000, Schafer and Walker 2006, Feng 2007, Renshon 2008).

Third, DBCM is also employed in IR to examine beliefs that are shared by a collectivity defined at varying levels of analysis (for example from an organization to a state). Alastair Iain Johnston, for example, was the first to apply causal mapping to studying collective beliefs in the constructivist school of IR. In *Cultural Realism* (Johnston 1998), Johnston first demonstrates the argumentation structure of strategic discourses in the seven Chinese military classics (including the well-known *The Art of War*) which, as he assumes, constitute the Ming dynasty's intersubjective strategic culture, that is, the decision-making code on which the military calculus of political leaders is based. By comparing the cognitive maps extracted from the military writings and the content of the writings, Johnston reaches the surprising conclusion that the military classics' argumentation structures regarding offensive doctrines do not differ much from the *realpolitik* paradigm in the Western strategic culture (Johnston 1998, pp. 94–8, 145). Certainly, as noted earlier, studies in management and organization have also employed DBCM on a collective level. A recent example is Nadkarni and Narayanan (2007), who used CEOs' letters to shareholders by sampled companies to extract the strategic schemas (that is, mental models) shared by top management in a firm.

In this section, we will discuss a study of the third category: contemporary Chinese elites' *grand strategic beliefs*, which in international relations usually refer to the beliefs about a state's consistent pattern of foreign policies for a relatively long period (Dueck 2004, Goldstein 2005, Layne 1997). This example illustrates DBCM and enables discussing some of the related methodological issues.

7.1.2   MAPPING CHINESE GRAND STRATEGIC BELIEFS

An analysis of China's grand strategic beliefs here is useful for three reasons. First, along with the rise of China, Chinese elites' beliefs about foreign policy-making have become increasingly important as indicators of the country's long-term intention (Friedberg 2005, Goldstein 2005, Swaine and Tellis 2000). This highlights the potential of DBCM in policy-making analysis. Second, China's grand strategic beliefs have been frequently studied and interpreted by IR scholars employing conventional methods. This provides an excellent background for demonstrating the added value of causal mapping. In addition, there is a technical point: using original data in Chinese brings the multilingual functions of CMAP3 to researchers' attention.

As an object of scholarly inquiry, China's grand strategic beliefs raise many theoretical and empirical questions. However, to restrict the present discussion to a manageable scale, we will focus on only one issue: to what kinds of behavioral orientation do China's grand strategic beliefs predispose decision-makers? Conflict or cooperation? For such a question to have some real-life significance, it is necessary to assume, first, that political beliefs can exert significant causal effect on political decisions. Moreover, it is also assumed that those who internalize such beliefs also share each other's interpretations to a considerable degree. Although both premises should be demonstrated by empirical evidence, for the current purpose of illustration it is sufficient to take them for granted. Thus, we can focus on how to empirically extract the belief systems about China's grand strategy and to assess the behavioral orientation embedded in the beliefs.

7.1.3   DEFINITION AND DATA SELECTION

Locating a representative sample of China's grand strategic beliefs is not an easy task, given the country's diversity of foreign policy thoughts. Our selected sample is *Selected Works of Deng Xiaoping*: three volumes of collected speeches by Deng Xiaoping, the paramount Chinese leader who exerted an unrivalled personal influence over Chinese politics after Mao. *Selected Works* is a valid sample of Chinese grand strategic beliefs for two reasons. First, the Chinese Communist Party (CCP) has institutionalized the sanctification of paramount leaders and the canonization of their words for purposes of public indoctrination. Deng's *Selected Works* in particular has been dominant in contemporary official discourses concerning China's paths to modernization and its national strategies in international politics. His published speeches, epitomized by the term "Deng Xiaoping theory," for example, have had a far-reaching impact upon foreign policy discourses. Examples of this include the official catchword of China's current grand strategy "taoguang yanghui" (Hide our capacities, buy our time) and the well-known rhetoric of "China's peaceful rise" (Zheng 2006). Moreover, the nationwide diffusion of "Deng Xiaoping theory" has been extensive, as shown, for example, by the widespread use of *Selected Works* in China's educational system, bureaucracy and news press (Yan 1995). Thus, one can safely assume that Deng's ideas have been widely shared by China's political elites.

The very fact that *Selected Works* is at the heart of the CCP's propaganda, however, leads to questions of validity. First, do the political elites who produce and distribute such discourses really believe what they propagate? In addition, how can one ensure the authenticity of Deng's published speeches given the fact that propaganda publications in China go through strict censorship? Indeed, some caution is warranted. It is not unusual that political scientists encounter discrepancies between the publicly stated and privately held positions of decision-makers (Khong 1992, Marfleet 2000, Walker and Schafer 2000). On the other hand, the relevance of such questions depends on what one seeks to measure. Let us assume that a researcher is mainly interested in how Deng's beliefs affected his decision-making style. In this sense, the researcher should acquire and examine declassified archives, and check for the consistency between *Selected Works* and Deng's thoughts as they were revealed in more private settings. Utilizing automated content analysis software (Section 3.1.7), it is even possible to run a preliminary, quantitative test of a leader's public and private statements (Renshon 2009). In the present case, however, neither sincerity nor authenticity poses a problem, because we are focusing on the socially constructed effects of *Selected Works* upon the intersubjective structure of China's grand strategic beliefs.

After defining the data sources, the range was narrowed to a smaller portion of the volumes. The selection criteria were straightforward. First, we looked for Deng's speeches between 1977 and 1992, the starting and terminating years of Deng's leadership. We then marked all systematic discussions about China's foreign policy and international strategy. That means excluding texts which cover the focal theme only in passing or in a limited manner. For example, if a speech contains only a fragmented sentence with a key word "Chinese foreign policy", it was considered irrelevant. The result was a pool of 27 speeches which we assumed would contain the key elements of the belief systems about China's grand strategy in *Selected Works*.

7.1.4   CODING THE SPEECHES

To derive the relevant belief systems, two essential steps were necessary: (1) coding Deng's speeches, and (2) standardizing the coded results. Yet, different from the usages in Section 3.2, the terms coding and standardization are used here differently. Coding only refers to locating relevant causal statements and breaking them down into cause and effect components, standardizing to the follow-up step of merging concepts and assigning an STV. The choice of coding strategy depends on the theoretical interests, which defines the elements that are presumably the most important ones in a document. This study was mainly interested in the argumentation structure and the complexity of Deng's grand strategic beliefs. For this purpose, extracting a composite map from all his 27 speeches was the operative goal. Accordingly, an open-ended strategy was adopted for capturing the causal concepts in their natural language form. The level of standardization is equivalent to Level 1 specified in Section 3.2, corresponding to low- and semi-structured or text-based CCM studies. In a composite causal mapping study, this entails a sentence-by-sentence style of coding. The coder first identifies causal statements and then breaks them down into the causal components (cause and effect concepts) and relational components (directional links between the causes and the effects).

In a project aiming to compare respondents' beliefs (Section 7.2), a researcher may prefer to standardize coded results with CMAP3. However, in a study involving lengthy documents, an alternative option is to conduct both coding and standardization in a separate database with a spreadsheet application like MS Excel. This allows for an effective management of all coding records, and especially keeping track of coded sentences in their original sources, usually a whole passage. This was the method in the present study. An Excel database was created to facilitate coding and standardization. The result of each coded sentence was then entered into the database in the form of natural language (NLU) (corresponding to column F: *cause concept* and column E: *effect concept*). The Excel spreadsheet was also arranged in a format (Figure 7.1) that can be easily adjusted to creating concept selection list (CSL) for importing NLUs in a later stage (see *Data Importing and Map Generation* below).

speech	year	data	sterm_c		stag_c	Cause Concept		linkage		CR	sterm_e		stag_e	Effect Concept		source sentence	source paragraph
With Stable Polici	1989	9.4	Imperialist invasion	A10		Other's (developed countries) plot against China		implied by the use of		-	Utility of China	I02		Utility of China			If the United States	So far as the internati
With Stable Polici	1989	9.4	Politics of hegemon	B13		Developed countries'policy of bullying backward		logical connection		+	International war	C04		Wars between underdeveloped countries		The current wars be	So far as the internati
With Stable Polici	1989	9.4	International war	C04		Wars between underdeveloped countries		are...what...need		+	Utility of developed	I06		Utility of developed countries		The current wars be	So far as the internati
With Stable Polici	1989	9.4	Stability of China	F12		Failure to hold China's ground		or & grammatical stru		+	Imperialist invasion	A10		Developed countries'plot against China		China should hold it	So far as the internati
With Stable Polici	1989	9.4	Persistence of peac	P01		Fight between the United States and Soviet Unio		if...don't...there will be		+	International war	C04		World War		China should hold it	So far as the internati

Figure 7.1   Sample database for coding and standardization

Table 7.1 shows an example from Deng's speech on September 4, 1989. In this passage, Deng specifies his views about the international environment of China after the Tiananmen massacre. The coder's task is to identify each causal statement in the passage, and to separate cause phrases from effect phrases. The first pair of causal relations, for example, is based on the sentence: "If the United States and the Soviet Union don't fight each other, there will be no world war." The coded statement is expressed in the following format: "fighting between the United States and the Soviet Union" (cause) + (positive relation) "World War" (effect). This indicates that the cause concept increases the likelihood (or value) of the effect concept. After successive operations like this, the initial coding resulted in 499 causal relations with over 600 NLUs.

Table 7.1   Example of coding

So far as the international situation is concerned, there is a question of war. If the United States and the Soviet Union don't fight each other, there will be no world war, but small wars will be unavoidable. The current wars between underdeveloped countries are actually what the developed countries need. Their policy of bullying backward countries has not changed. China should hold its ground, or other will plot against us.

Cause Concept	Causal Linkage	Effect Concept
Fight between the United States and Soviet Union	(If...don't...there will be no...)	(The happening of) World War
Developed countries' policy of bullying backward countries	+ (logical connection)	(The existence of) Wars between underdeveloped countries
Wars between underdeveloped countries	+ (are...what...need)	Utility of developed countries
Failure to hold China's ground	+ (or & grammatical structure)	Developed countries' plot against China
Others' (developed countries) plot against China	− (implied by the use of 'plot')	Utility of China

An indispensable part of coding is a set of standard rules which specifies how a coder should analyze grammatical structures and, thus, helps enhance the reliability of the causal mapping method. Without coding rules, DBCM would be close to any interpretive approach. The chapter by Wrightson in *Structure of Decision* provides a good example of an open-ended coding scheme (Axelrod 1976, pp. 291–332), which this study also draws heavily on. However, the flexible nature of language implies that no rules can exhaust all linguistic phenomena. Coders must frequently rely on their own judgment. Therefore, coding rules should always correspond to the features of the language that coders are handling. This is the case of coding Chinese, a language that does not express causality in a Subject/Verb/Object sentence structure as is typical in English (Axelrod 1976, p. 292). Therefore, some of the rules observed by Axelrod (1976) had to be relaxed. An example is that causal linkages in Chinese sentences are often signified by an adjective. The Chinese version of Deng's words "if we did not uphold socialism [...] it would be even more difficult for us to develop" (a speech on June 16, 1989), for instance, is expressed in a sequence of Complex Subject/Object/Adjective.

Table 7.2   Example of standardization

		Causal Concept		
No.	**NLU Category**	**Standard Term**	**Negation**	**STag**
1	Fighting between the United States and the Soviet Union	Break of peace	Persistence of peace	P01
2	(The happening of) world war	International war	—	C04
3	Developed countries' policy of bullying backward countries	Politics of hegemonism	—	B13
4	Wars between underdeveloped countries	International war	—	C04
5	Utility of developed countries	(same)	—	I08
6	Failure to hold China's ground	Instability of China	Stability of China	F12
7	Developed countries' plot against China	Imperialist invasion	—	A10
8	Other's (developed countries) plot against China	Imperialist invasion	—	A10
9	Utility of China	(same)	—	I02

Standardization begins when all causal statements are broken down into NLUs. In this step, the coder should assign standard terms (corresponding to *sterm_c* and *sterm_e* in Figure 7.1) to distinctive concepts that will be displayed on the composite map. A standard tag (STAG, corresponding to *stag_c* and *stag_e* in Figure 7.1) is accordingly attached to each standard term for realizing data importing in CMAP3. Technically, this serves two purposes in this case: (1) Standardization helps the coder to avoid unnecessary confusion by emerging synonymous concepts. (2) At the same time, it reduces the total number of concepts appearing on the extracted map so that the causal map can become more accessible (see Section 3.2). The technical side of standardization is mainly driven by the identification of synonyms or similar concepts. In the converted data of the previous example (see Table 7.2), NLU no.7 and NLU no.8 are assigned the same standard term ("imperialist invasion") because the two original phrases differ only slightly in wording. During the merging process, the coder may occasionally want to transform a concept to its antonym. This makes sense if the antonymous expression is shared by a greater number of causal statements. An example is the concept "instability of China" (no.6). The reason is that its antonym "stability of China" is more frequent in the database. Obviously, when this is done, the direction value of the causal linkage must also be reversed.

Importantly, standardization also serves interpretative purposes. In this sense, a crucial factor is the level of generalization a coder's research question informs. In Table 7.2, for instance, NLU no.4 ("wars between underdeveloped countries") and NLU no.2 ("world war") are far from identical. If one is interested in understanding the causal beliefs about different types of war in *Selected Works*, one probably would choose to keep both concepts in their original forms. Yet, since the present research question is concerned with beliefs about conflict in general, it is justified to merge both types of war into a general category of "international war." Another example is assigning the standard term "politics of hegemonism" to NLU no.3 ("developed countries' policy of bullying backward countries"). Underlying this choice is the author's contextual knowledge of what is understood as "hegemonism" in Chinese political culture. An American IR scholar, for example, might fail to see the linkage as it stands, because "developed countries" and "hegemonism" are interpreted differently in the academic lexicon of international relations.

It is the necessity of interpretation and judgment that can make standardization both difficult and sometimes problematic from an outsider's perspective. Therefore, ensuring the validity and reliability of coding and that the coder does not subject the interpretation to his *a priori* knowledge or assumptions is an important step. The ideal solution is to have at least two coders in the same project, so that the intercoder reliability can be assessed. However, this is often difficult and costly. An alternative is to randomly sample a portion of the dataset (5–10%) and to find knowledgeable outside reviewers who will replicate the coding with the standard rules. This is often the second-best test of intercoder reliability. Furthermore, keeping the conversion records (from raw data to coded results) transparent is also important, as it enables a coder to easily move back and forth between different stages of data processing in correcting errors.

In this case, the standardization reduces over 600 NLUs in the dataset to around 112 standard terms—the causal nodes that would make up the final composite map of China's grand strategic beliefs. An important step that followed was that all those standard terms were entered into a separate Excel spreadsheet as standard term vocabulary (STV), which could be entered into CMAP3. The format of the STV should observe the conventions of the concept pool/STV worksheet discussed in Section 5.3 (Figure 5.5).

7.1.5   DATA IMPORTING AND MAP GENERATION

In addition to CMAP3, this study employs *CmapTools* to generate the visual composite causal maps. For CMAP3 to automatically construct a first-approximation causal map out of the SCU/SNT database (Section 4.2), a coder's major task here is to enter either manually or import the STV and NLUs into CMAP3. If keyboard entry is preferred, a researcher can carry out the task directly with the *Node Data & Standardizing* module (Section 5.2). To facilitate an organized entry, the researcher can use different approaches when preparing the data. For example, one can use either the method discussed below or the techniques based on the manual raw data sheet (RDS) and the computer-based CSL method and raw data worksheets (RDWS), as discussed in Section 5.1 and 5.3. An RDWS enables direct copy/pasting to the concept selection lists (CSLs) for NLU import. After entering the data, causal links and their values can then be entered into CMAP3 in the *Causal Links Data* module (Figure 7.3).

In this study, we chose to import the STV and the NLUs respectively with STV worksheet and concept selection list (CSL, see Sections 5.1 and 5.3). STV could be immediately imported and displayed in the NLU browser, given the preparation. However, importing NLUs requires some careful arrangement because the manner by which one formats CSL will affect the efficiency of

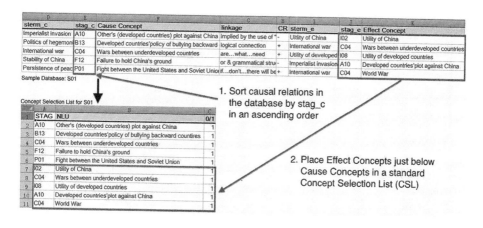

Figure 7.2   Example of data importing

entering causal links later on.[1] Thus, to begin with, we first defined a project containing 27 data sources (N/S = 27), whereby each data source (S) corresponds to one of the 27 coded speeches. The concepts (nodes) of each S/speech were then imported using the CSL technique. To illustrate, the previous example is again employed. Suppose that the coded results of Figure 7.1 constitute a data source S01, whose causal data is sorted by the STAGs of the cause concepts in an ascending order. The cause and effect concepts together with their STAGs can then be directly transferred from the database to a separate CSL named S01.xlsx (Figure 7.2). This CSL should, in turn, be organized into the following format where all the effect concepts are exactly placed below the cause concepts.

After using the NLU module's *Import* function, the NLU data can be viewed in both the NLU browser and the upper window of the *Causal Links Data* module in the order shown on the CSL in Figure 7.2. Then, one can start to manually fill in the causal links and their values. The particular format of CSL in Figure 7.2 speeds up data entry at this stage. First, the two rows of effect concepts (F-NLU) and their IDs (FNTAG) in the NCU browser should exactly correspond to the latter half of NLUs and their NTAGs in the NLU browser. Therefore, knowing the NTAG of the first effect concept, one can quickly identify the first causal link in *S01* (that is, the link between the first cause concept and the first effect concept). In this case, this is obtained by the formula: E1 = C1 + N/2 (E1 represents the first effect concept's NTAG, C1 the first cause concept's

---

1   As noted earlier (5.1, 5.3), using the RDS or RDWS techniques, the NCU information (row numbers) would be available in the RDSs or RDWSs for NCU keyboard entry with the NCU module (see 5.2). If the NLUs are imported, a CSL must first be created by copy/pasting the RDWS's appropriate columns. The method selection depends on type of data and user preferences.

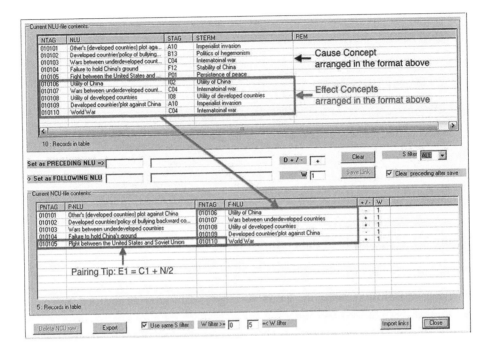

Figure 7.3   Example of NCU entry in CMAP3

NTAG, and N the sum of concepts in *S01*), that is, 010101 + 10/2 = 010106. The next causal link should be, in turn, 010102 + 10/2 = 010107, and so on. The advantage of this entry strategy is that one can, in the first round, quickly save all causal links without reading the concepts and even taking care of the links' values (there will be a default value "+" anyway). When all causal links have been entered one can, if necessary, fill in the negative values (–) of the causal links according to the original records in the database (column CR in Figure 7.2).

When all NCUs are created out of the NLUs, the final standardized map data can be obtained through the *Generating Cause Map Units* module. For the present research question, a composite causal map generated by setting *S-number* as "All" is necessary. A particularly useful function of CMAP3 in this case is that it allows one to construct the map in either English or Chinese. Thus, the author can code Chinese data first, and afterwards assign standard English terms (STENG) to standard terms in the *Node Data and Standardizing* module after the coding is finished. The record of STV-STENG translation is also kept as a separate Excel spreadsheet for checking accuracy and potentially revising.

7.1.6   MAP VISUALIZATION AND ANALYSIS

The major function of CMAP3 in the generating stage is to assign NLUs to SNTs, hence, NCUs to SCUs. As noted in Sections 3.2 and 5.4, a generated SNT will thus represent all NLUs it subsumes, as standardized. The number of NLUs compressed into an SNT can be viewed in both *NLU/SNT Matrix* and the NLU module in STAG order. In this case, the generation process ended up with a large composite map database of SCUs representing the belief system of China's grand strategy which was extracted from the 27 speeches of *Selected Works* (the SCU/SNT data can be viewed in *Browsing Cause Map Contents*). However, the large number of SNTs and SCUs in the map makes it almost inaccessible as a whole. Also, to examine the whole map may be redundant if its full complexity cannot reveal (would rather obscure) the cognitive features that are most pertinent to the research interest. Thus, to understand what is precisely wanted to make sense of in the belief system, it is necessary to focus on the various sub-systems in the composite system using domain maps (DM, Section 6.3).

In this study, the domain maps should largely represent the beliefs about the general and long-term relations between China and other states in the international system. This empirical interest follows directly from the research question: What kind of behavioral orientation is embedded in the belief system of *Selected Works*? It is also informed by the theories of international relations and social psychology which posit that the internalized beliefs about the self–other relationship predispose social actors, including nation states, to certain propensities of behavior: zero-sum perceptions eliciting tendencies of conflictual behavior and non-zero-sum ideas that of more cooperative behaviors (Brewer 2001, Wendt 1999). Accordingly, we use a DM around the concept "Utility of China" (I02) as an example of how the causal map can highlight our research question. The domain map was generated by selecting *I02* in *Domain Map Browser* as the seed concept (Figure 7.4) to capture all concepts which are relevant to China's national interest. Although there are other options, this seed concept was chosen because it can be reasonably assumed that the interests of "self" are closest to "self-identity" and thus the perceived relations to "others" can reveal the beliefs about the self–other relationship.

After importing the DM-SCU set to CmapTools (Section 6.5), 12 concepts were identified which both signify China's specific interests and contribute positively to *I02*: the more specific indicators of the self-identity in *Selected Works*, labelled as goal variables (*G01* to *G12*) on the visualized map. The DM is here displayed in a bottom–up manner (*self* concepts on the top, *other* concepts on the bottom), which deviates from the traditional order discussed in Section 6.5. This arrangement, however, serves arguably better the specific research

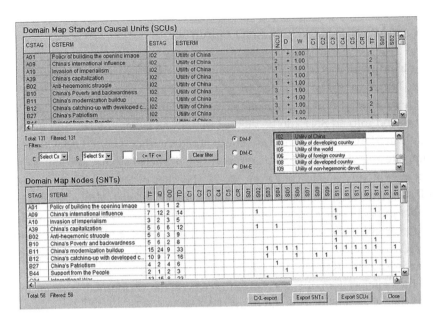

Figure 7.4 The domain map (DMF) around China's utility (I02)

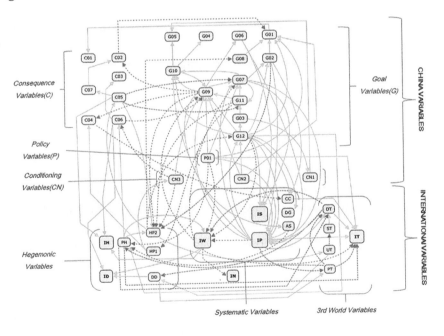

Figure 7.5 Domain map of China's strategic environment

Note: G cluster: China's national interests, C cluster: harmful consequences to G, IW: international war, IP: international peace, IH: utility of hegemonic states, ID: utility of developed countries, IT: utility of the third world.

interest here and the differentiation between *self* and *other* concepts to clarify the overall dynamics in between. The concepts are further organized around different clusters according to their shared attribute (for example, concepts related to developed countries and those related to third world countries). Figure 7.5 shows a simplified version of the DM (links to the abstract utility concept are removed for readability). The solid arrows represent positive causal relations and the dotted arrows represent the negative causal relations.

Overall, the DM displays the major factors that can be assumed to be observed when a reader of *Selected Works* reasons about China's national interest in international politics: war (IW) and peace (IP), the major players (hegemonic states and third world states), their interests and policies, and the consequences to China (C). One can notice the structural patterns of the map: (1) Overwhelming negative relations between G (China's interests) and hegemonic variables, and (2) overwhelming positive relations between hegemonic variables and C (harmful consequences to China). Both interactions are also channeled through C, IW, IP, and so on. In other words, dominating the causal map and the represented belief system is a zero-sum interaction between the major clusters representing China's interests (self) and the developed states (other). In comparison, non-zero-sum causal relations occupy a minor position on the DM (for example CN2: China's relations with foreign countries + G12: China's economic power).

The patterns in the domain map question some of the conventional interpretations of Deng's strategic thinking. For instance, Yongnian Zheng and Suisheng Zhao, two prominent scholars of Chinese nationalism, have argued that Deng's grand strategic beliefs indicate a defensive and status-quo nature of China's international behavior. They refer in particular to Deng's speeches on China's non-confrontational doctrine with the West and his emphasis on economic development as China's overarching international goal (Deng 1993, Zhao 2004, Zheng 1999). However, the argumentation structure in the cause map in Figure 7.5 does not support this view, but rather suggests that the two scholars may be selectively treating the discourses in *Selected Works* by emphasizing its cooperative components and downplaying the conflictual ones.

The above scholars have also suggested that, in Deng's belief system, economic interests override other interests. This issue can be examined by focusing on a sub-phenomenon in the domain map: the goal structure, which refers to the interlinks between the 12 goal variables on the domain map of the self–other relationship (Figure 7.6). The measures of the dynamics between those concepts, indegree (*Id*), outdegree (*Od*), and total degree (*Td*), have a useful role here (Section 3.5), as it is possible to infer their implications for means-ends differentiation by determining the hierarchy to which the goal concepts are clustering: a higher *Id* indicates a greater probability of a goal or key instrumental role, and a higher *Od* indicates a greater probability of instrumentality. The present finding is, strikingly, that the most explicit concept representing economic interest ("economic power," with an *Od* = 5) sits at the bottom of the goal hierarchy, while all concepts at the top concern mainly China's interests of security or international prestige (*Od* = 0). Some economy-related goals are high in the values of td (for example, "modernization build-up": *Td* = 5). While this reveals their saliency in the sub-system, the zero difference between *Id* and *Od* (*Id* – *Od* = 0) indicates a transitional role between higher- and lower-level goals. In other words, this pattern seems to support a contrary view. Economic development is in general an instrumental and rather low-ranking interest in the strategic beliefs of *Selected Works*. This does not obviously deny the objective significance of economic interest, but rather implies that it can be overridden by top interests, such as China's security or prestige.

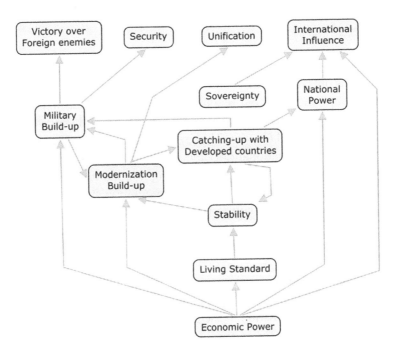

Figure 7.6   Domain map—goal structure

In general, causal maps can add to our understanding of actors' beliefs by providing an additional layer of evidence based on their structural features. As the analysis of *Selected Works'* belief systems shows, one can look into the structural dynamics between SNTs and the measurements of their respective saliency, namely, indegree, outdegree, total degree, and total frequency. Such indicators provide insights into the belief systems, which are not reachable by a linear, reading-based analysis. Moreover, those insights function as constraints on researchers' subjective and, often, wishful judgment of the discourses. However, one can be tempted to draw conclusions exclusively from the structural features of causal maps. To avoid this, one should be aware that the function of causal maps is to allow a researcher to examine beliefs in both their cognitive and textual context, but not to replace the latter. Therefore, a cautious analyst regularly returns to the original texts and checks the degree of convergence between the map findings and the context of the speeches. Such an interactive process may require several rounds of iteration, moving back and forth between the content and cognitive structure of beliefs in order to locate meaning at the crossroads.

7.1.7 WORKING WITH DBCMS

DBCMs can offer an effective instrument for scholars studying individual and collective belief systems—a commitment shared by many disciplines such as intellectual history, sociology, political science, and management and organization. Contrary to more conventional approaches such as discourse analysis, DBCM merits scholarly attention particularly for the following reasons: First, as a method it enables a considerable degree of replicability, hence, reliability. Second, it fosters a holistic, visual way of understanding which most linear interpretations cannot provide. Finally, it adds a cognitive dimension to our understanding of discourses and thus can help control for the subjective bias in traditional interpretation of textual data. Yet, applying DBCM is not free of risks. They result largely from the "composite" maps it produces of sources, which originally are separate. Thus, what will be "constructed" is to some extent guided by our theories, and may actually not exist or exert real causal effects. Unfortunately, it is impossible to completely eliminate such risks by examining the beliefs alone. One remedy is to integrate DBCM with relevant theories and behavioral evidence by using rigorous triangulating research such as examining the congruence of an agent's beliefs and actual behavior to corroborate or refute the findings based on composite causal maps.

7.2   Causal Mapping Professionals' Mental Models

This section discusses a CCM study of Finnish small business advisors' (SBA) belief patterns concerning the causes and consequences of two key phenomena: (1) nascent micro firms' (NMF) *success/failure* and (2) their *growth* or rather tendency to remain small. The focus is on the study's methodology, the emerging causal maps and map-based observations and inferences. Small business theory and the study's pragmatic implications are therefore discussed only in passing.

7.2.1   BACKGROUND OF THE SBA STUDY

In a modern economy, small business advisors (SBA) are usually unnoticed yet important actors. They influence aspiring entrepreneurs' start-up decisions and the new firms' performance, and thereby also economy-level phenomena such as rates and types of new firm formation, small business turbulence, supply of jobs, and the public's attitude towards entrepreneurship. The SBAs (N = 15) participating in this study are from the Finnish Entrepreneurship Agencies (FEA). It is the country's leading and only nationwide operating NMF advisory organization. More than one-third of all Finnish NMFs use its services.

A typical SBA/FEA NMF client plans to start a micro or solo firm to realize personal goals or often because of an imminent loss of job. They need and expect professional assessment of their business and personal prospects and practical advice. This defines an SBA's main tasks and also the private criteria of their effectiveness. A typical advisory process takes two to four sessions, each of which lasts one to two hours and results (in a positive case) in a jointly developed business plan and the SBAs' recommendation for governmental start-up funding. However, the entrepreneur decides for themselves whether or not to follow the recommendations, including ignoring a negative one. The FEA system has a network of local experts and mentors which the SBAs and the entrepreneurs can use.

As to the motives of the SBA study, first, there is very little research of small business advisors in spite of their potential impact. SBAs' belief patterns, which influence their analyses and recommendations, have not been studied at all. Second, SBA institutions such as the FEA are facing an imminent strategic threat which is a result of the ongoing debate about which policies of entrepreneurship development should be followed (Audretsch and Keilbach 2006, Bennett 2014, Hoffmann 2007, Lundström and Stevenson 2005, Shane 2009, Storey 1994, 2006). Traditionally, entrepreneurship theorists and lay practitioners have usually posited that founding maximal numbers of *any* new firms is beneficial. As a strategic position, this implies extensive and unselective fostering of NMF founding. However, there are increasingly louder arguments that such a "blanket" approach is wasteful and should be replaced by selective support of mainly or only growth firms. For SBA service providers such as the FEA, whose legitimacy and financing so far is supported by the wide acceptance of the traditional dogma, the paradigm change is clearly a problem. Therefore, it was also pragmatically important to find out about and understand the SBAs' dominant existing beliefs. The third objective of the study was a methodological one of comparing semi-structured CCM with more conventional structured approaches. Whilst there have been some CCM comparisons, these particular CCM method types have not been contrasted empirically. The comparison studies will be discussed in Section 7.3.

7.2.2 METHODOLOGY

The SBA study uses the semi-structured CCM method. As noted in Section 3.1.5, key issues in this case are the selection of the respondents and the anchor topics, the interviewing process and the coding/standardizing operations to distil of the interview data the aggregated causal maps representing the SBAs' views of the focal issues. In addition, ensuring the study's validity is an important task.

Participants

At the study's time, FEA had 90 SBAs in 32 local units. The empirical objective was to locate the SBAs' *dominant* beliefs about the focal topics. In view of their work roles, it could be assumed that both topics were very familiar to them. Moreover, the SBAs have similar educational and business backgrounds[2] and similar NMF clients. Therefore, all SBAs could be considered equally potential participants.

At the outset, the FEA central organization's permission and recommendation were acquired. Two senior FEA officials with recent and extensive SBA experience were the first interviewees. They suggested four further SBAs (local unit heads) who were known as well informed and

---

2   The SBAs' mean age was 45.3 years (SD 8.76). There were six female and nine male SBAs. Seven SBAs work exclusively as SBAs, eight double as an SBA and manager of the local FEA unit. The average SBA experience was 7.87 years (SD 6.24). Twelve SBAs had a Master's or higher business degree, three a Bachelor degree, and all had several years of business experience, typically as an SB owner-manager or a family business background.

experienced. Three SBAs were selected at random from their units' SBAs. The rest of the SBAs (six) were randomly selected representing three other local FEA units. Initially, the idea was to make the sample size dependent on the *saturation* of dominant concepts, based on the cumulative contribution of each new interviewee. This could not be strictly observed as some interviews had to be fixed and, in view of the forthcoming feedback and comparison study, we did not want to cancel them. The final number of respondents was N = 15. In hindsight, as discussed below, probably eight, but at least ten, interviews would have been sufficient to elicit the dominant thought patterns.

Interviews

First, the project and the interview format were explained to the respondent. It was emphasized that the data will be used collectively and anonymously, and should focus on what they find most relevant in terms of the focal theme. The interviews followed the format and practices explained in Section 3.1.5. The anchor topics were probed by focusing separately on *NMF-success* and *NMF-failure* and *NMF-growth* and *NMF-smallness*. When standardizing the NLUs, the two poles were combined again. The interview produced first an initial layer of natural concepts, which the interviewed participant perceived as causally most proximate to the anchor variable. The format was repeated using the first-layer concepts as new anchors, focusing, however, only on the "causes of the causes" and "effects of the effects". This elicited a second and considerably larger layer of new NLUs, that is, factors and outcomes causally more distant from the anchor. The mean duration of the interviews for the two anchors (without the introduction) was M = 80.0 minutes (SD = 16.9) (range 0:53 – 1:44 hours). The data was first in the form of INS notes and voice recordings, which were then transcribed using the RDS technique and keyboard entered into CMAP3 (see Sections 3.1.5 and 5.1).

Coding/standardizing

The study's summarizing and descriptive task requires compressing the NLUs into compact standard variables, which capture the factors and phenomena noted by the SBAs, but exclude now less relevant details such as attributes, synonyms or antonyms typical in everyday discourse. Thus, the coding approach was at Level 1. As shown in Table 7.3, the STV is relatively close to the NLUs, but compacts them into analytically more useful yet understandable "synthetic" concepts. The compression rate is shown by the NLU/SNT indicator (Table 7.4), which has a low value (1.88). To ensure the (semantic) validity of coding, two reviewers assessed the STV and the individual standardizing decisions of the NLUs.

Table 7.3   Standardizing (coding) in the SBA study: key standard node terms' NLU contents

STAG	STANDARD NODE TERM	Typical SBA NLUs in the main SNT categories (orig. in Finnish)	TF	Id	Od	TF/CS
F03	NMF-growth/non-growth	firm's growth, growing, growth entrepreneurship, expansion, smallness	15	61	56	1
F01	NMF-success/failure	new firm's success, failure	15	56	47	15
P09	E-growth/no-growth orientation	will to grow, intention to grow, no growth willingness	15	55	15	0
B01	BI-type/potential	business idea, firm concept, a good idea, business type, realistic BI	15	34	28	11
P03	E-characteristics/traits	entrepreneur personality, personal characteristics, commitment	15	29	26	14
F15	personnel/recruiting	personnel, recruiting, hiring extra hands	15	20	21	2
R04	job supply/employment	jobs, employment, unemployment	15	17	8	2
P02	E-goals/visions	entrepreneur's goals, visions, motives, lifestyle, expectations, intentions	14	26	24	13
B03	NMF-resources/financing	financing, capital needs, resources, working capital, loan availability	14	26	20	10
E01	market/demand	demand, market, low demand, market situation, open niche, non-mature	14	30	14	12
E03	customers/number	customers, population, lack of customers, buying power, whom	14	29	8	12
O05	E-personal finances/losses	private financial losses, financial calamity, loss of property, indebtedness	14	21	12	6
O02	E-family living income	family livelihood, income, private consumption level, standard of living	14	9	6	7

Table 7.3   Standardizing (coding) in the SBA study: key standard node terms' NLU contents (*continued*)

STAG	STANDARD NODE TERM	Typical SBA NLUs in the main SNT categories (orig. in Finnish)	TF	Id	Od	TF/CS
R05	public economy/revenues	tax income, public revenue, community finances, health	14	7	4	0
P01	E-creativity/capabilities	competence, creativity, innovativeness, business/entrepreneur fit	13	31	20	12
P04	E-competences	entrepreneurial competences, type, lack of e-competence	13	18	18	12
O08	E-risks/responsibilities	employer risks, responsibilities to people, recruitment problems	13	16	15	2
O06	E-personal/family problems	health/psychic problems, family crises, divorce, giving up	13	15	9	6
P19	E-professional/trade competence	business line/trade competence, industry/niche know-how	13	9	13	12
P20	E-business/mgrl. competence	marketing and managerial competences, strategic understanding, leadership	12	18	23	12
S02	NMF-estimates/mentoring	SB advisory service, budget review, marketing and network support	12	14	23	0
B13	competitiveness/innovation	competitive edge, innovativeness, newness, originality, too early	12	19	15	0
P18	E-risk acceptance/aversion	entrepreneurial courage, timidity, risk and uncertainty avoidance, false beliefs	12	22	11	6
P10	E-background/experiences	family background, work and career experiences, hobbies	12	3	29	7
O03	E-life quality/self-realization	self-realization, self-esteem, life quality, satisfaction, "own money"	12	10	7	0

Table 7.3   Standardizing (coding) in the SBA study: key standard node terms' NLU contents (*concluded*)

STAG	STANDARD NODE TERM	Typical SBA NLUs in the main SNT categories (orig. in Finnish)	TF	Id	Od	TF/CS
O01	E-job/self-employment	self-employment, avoidance of unemployment	12	4	9	2
B16	growth potential/business	growth potential, lack of potential, market limited/BI	11	25	8	0
E05	competition/competitor nmbr	tight competition, few competitors, new competitors, saturated industry	11	15	13	9
P25	E-negative attid./traits	unrealistic, laziness, short-sighted, proudness, employee attitudes	11	11	14	0

Note: TF = total frequency, Id = Indegree, Od = Outdegree, TF/CS = Total frequency in the comparison study (Section 7.3)

Table 7.4 displays the SBA project's statistics data. The 15 interviews elicited 1,832 original concepts (NLU) and 2,720 original causal statements (NCU). When standardized and generated using GTF => 1, that is, including all NLU/NCU data, the result was 123 active standard concepts (SNTs) and 1,272 standard concept pairs (SCUs). In passing, it may be noted that GTF => 2 would have produced 106 SNTs and only 384 SCUs. This is typical of low compression standardizing, which understandably produces relatively many unique causal notions, as can be seen in the high share of unique SCUs (69.81 per cent).

Table 7.4 Summary of SBA study's raw and standardized data

Measure	Total	CR >= 8	S01	S02	S03	S04	S05	S06	S07	S08	S09	S10	S11	S12	S13	S14	S15	Mean	SD
SNT	123	67	67	69	76	63	54	54	59	78	70	61	52	63	70	71	65	65	7.60
SNT-%-Total	100.00	54.47	54.47	56.10	61.79	51.22	43.90	43.90	47.97	63.41	56.91	49.59	42.28	51.22	56.91	57.72	52.85	53	6.18
SNT-CR	67	67	48	47	53	47	47	47	43	53	51	46	44	49	53	51	47	48	3.07
SNT-%-CR	54.47	100.00	71.64	68.12	69.74	74.60	87.04	87.04	72.88	67.95	72.86	75.41	84.62	77.78	75.71	71.83	72.31	75	6.07
SNT-Unique	6	0	0	0	1	0	1	0	0	1	2	0	0	0	0	1	0	0	0.61
SNT-Unique-%	4.88	0.00	0.00	0.00	1.32	0.00	1.85	0.00	0.00	1.28	2.86	0.00	0.00	0.00	0.00	1.41	0.00	1	0.89
SCU	1,272	21	146	169	196	163	118	114	128	196	140	147	85	158	141	169	133	147	28.94
SCU-%-Total	100.00	1.65	11.48	13.29	15.41	12.81	9.28	8.96	10.06	15.41	11.01	11.56	6.68	12.42	11.08	13.29	10.46	12	2.28
SCU-CR	21	21	13	14	15	17	15	13	15	12	16	13	14	14	16	13	13	14	1.38
SCU-%-CR	1.65	100.00	8.90	8.28	7.65	10.43	12.71	11.40	11.72	6.12	11.43	8.84	16.47	8.86	11.35	7.69	9.77	10	2.46
SCU-Unique	888	0	54	67	94	67	41	40	46	89	49	65	25	62	54	86	49	59	18.77
SCU-Unique-%	69.81	0.00	36.99	39.64	47.96	41.10	34.75	35.09	35.94	45.41	35.00	44.22	29.41	39.24	38.30	50.89	36.84	39	5.49
DENSITY	16.95	0.28	1.95	2.25	2.61	2.17	1.57	1.52	1.71	2.61	1.87	1.96	1.13	2.11	1.88	2.25	1.77	2	0.39
SCU/SNT	10.34		2.18	2.45	2.58	2.59	2.19	2.11	2.17	2.51	2.00	2.41	1.63	2.51	2.01	2.38	2.05	2	0.26
NLU	1,832		111	127	136	136	96	99	98	150	130	100	84	146	133	146	140	122	21.12
NLU/SNT (M)	1.88		1.66	1.84	1.79	2.16	1.78	1.83	1.66	1.92	1.86	1.64	1.62	2.32	1.90	2.06	2.15	2	0.20
NCU	2,720		172	210	243	210	148	146	164	225	172	166	104	196	177	206	181	181	33.91
NCU/SCU (M)	1.24		1.18	1.24	1.24	1.29	1.25	1.28	1.28	1.15	1.23	1.13	1.22	1.24	1.26	1.22	1.36	1	0.05

Validity

The prerequisite of trustworthiness or dependability, validity in more conventional terms, is authentic and sincere raw data. In this case, authenticity seems evident and is confirmable by the voice recordings. As discussed in Section 3.4, sincerity—in other words, did the SBAs say what they think and know and mean what they say—can be assessed only indirectly. First, the interview themes were non-sensitive, professionally familiar and relevant, and the overall setting a normal workday one. Thus, there were no apparent *systematic* reasons for the SBAs to hold back or fabricate. Second, the rapid emergence and saturation of especially core concepts and causal beliefs is (asymmetric) evidence of validity in CCM studies focused on *shared* beliefs. It is not plausible that the SBAs, who did not know about each other's interviews, had colluded and agreed what they *all* will say in the interviews. The saturation of the concepts referring to distinct phenomena is shown in Figure 7.7. The majority (90.2 per cent) of the SNT base (N = 123) emerged already with the first three participants. The next five SBAs each added some common concepts, but after them practically no new notions came up. It is obvious that the saturation is dependent on the probed issue: a more diffuse topic would probably trigger more heterogeneous responses and thus a slower saturation. Finally, the comparison study (Section 7.3) also collected feedback about the cause maps from the present SBAs, confirming that the emerging causal maps, such as the one in Figure 7.8, do represent their views.

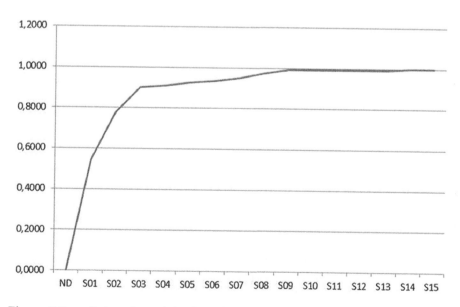

Figure 7.7   **Saturation of the SNT base (N = 123)**

7.2.3   VISUAL ANALYSIS: NMF-SUCCESS/FAILURE

In CCM studies of collectivities' belief systems, which the present SBA case represents, a typical first, often the only task is a valid and analytically useful *description* of the respondents' thought patterns using one or more aggregated causal maps (ACM). The initial, and often the main, analysis is based on the visual description. It enables grasping and understanding the respondents' thinking as a system of phenomena and causal relationships. However, it is often useful to augment the qualitative analysis by numbers, which highlight, for example, the distribution of different causal beliefs or the map concepts' type (Section 3.5).

What is "analytically relevant" now? This is a valid question. The SBA database supports different perspectives, not only that of locating dominant beliefs about the two anchor issues. For instance, one could focus on the mechanisms of success/failure or examine growth barriers in small business as perceived by the SBAs. In that case, one would probably use not only the most shared but also the more idiosyncratic SNTs/SCUs, accepting less representative results for, for example, hypothesis generation. In the SBA study, however, the analysis required using ACMs which capture the typical thought patterns. Therefore, larger causal maps were created and analyzed around the two focal issues.

The book's readers are probably less interested in the SBA study's substance and entrepreneurship or SBA-related issues. Therefore, we examine only one representative example of the different ACMs, which can be created from the SBA data. Figure 7.8 displays a domain map (DMF, see Section 6.3), generated around the focal topic *NMF-success/failure* of the full SBA database setting the filter at TF <= 7. This DMF has the additional advantage of also containing the most typical beliefs about *NMF-growth/non-growth*. The DMF was imported to CmapTools (see Section 6.5) to create the corresponding visual map.

Why use a threshold? Unfiltered, this particular DMF would contain 1,074 SCUs and 123 SNTs, that is, nearly the whole standardized database (Table 7.4) (84 per cent SCUs, 100 per cent SNTs). This is mainly because *NMF-success/failure* was an anchor topic and the DMF will thus closely correspond to what the semi-structured interview elicited. Whilst technically possible, it would be impractical to display such a large DMF as a single causal map. Thus, it must be filtered, but why just TF <= 7? This is a question of judgment, which observes practical criteria (beginning with simple readability) and the representation and analytic task. In this case, different TF values were tested and TF <= 7 emerged as a good compromise.

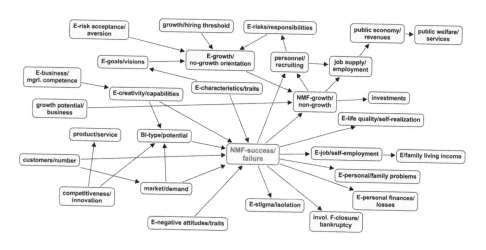

Figure 7.8   Causal map: SBAs' belief pattern of NMF-success/failure

The resulting DMF contains 35 SCUs and 29 SNTs, shared by nearly all SBAs (SNTs' TF median = 13). Thus, it can be argued to represent well the SBAs' belief patterns. A lower cut-off point would grow the DMF, a higher TF make it smaller. For instance, a DMF with TF => 6 would have 48 SCUs and 39 SNTs; a TF => 8 only 21 SCUs and 21 SNTs. The former would be too dense and detailed; the latter would exclude many highly shared notions. In general, a good solution depends on the representation task and will therefore vary case by case.

In passing it may be noted that this DMF could also be generated directly as SCU and SNT databases using GTF => 7. In this case all SCUs would be exported to CmapTools. If one needs to process more DMs, this approach and generally using a higher GTF generation cut-off point will be faster because of the smaller SCU database from which the DMFs are extracted. As emphasized in Section 5.5, these are no irrevocable decisions. The generation (and regeneration) of SCU/SNT databases is quick and easily repeatable. This enables also an easy testing of different cut-off points' impact.

To comment on the aggregated causal map in Figure 7.8 briefly, first, *NMF success* primarily means to the SBAs that the nascent entrepreneur creates a job and can employ themselves on a living income. Further positive outcomes include better quality of life, self-realization and the firm's growth. Symmetrically, *NMF failure* means that such positive things will not be realized. In addition, failure can lead to financial difficulties, bankruptcy, social stigma and isolation, and family problems. Typical SBAs clearly felt strongly about the negative consequences.

Second, the SBAs explain NMF success mainly by two groups of factors: the nascent entrepreneur's capabilities and traits and the overall economic soundness of the proposed business. However, the pattern of causal notions is more complex than on the outcome side. As to NMF failure, the SBAs attribute it first symmetrically to the lacking qualities of the entrepreneur and to problems in business factors such as an uncompetitive offering, intense competition, misjudged customer base, and so on. Second, as a specific failure factor, most SBAs (N = 11) note the dysfunctional attitudes and traits of the entrepreneur, summarized/coded as *E-negative attitudes/traits* (Table 7.3, STAG P25).

Although this DMF ACM focuses on NMF success/failure, it gives an overview as to how the SBAs think about *NMF growth/non-growth*. They believe that growth leads to more investments and jobs, which has a beneficial impact on public revenues and welfare and public services. From an entrepreneur's viewpoint, however, growth means recruiting personnel, more managerial tasks, responsibilities and risks. Combined with typical NMF clients' (usually) negative *E-growth/no-growth orientation*, the outcome is a low probability of growth aspirations and growth. Most SBAs (TF = 9) conceptualize the antigrowth syndrome in terms of a *growth/hiring threshold*. In addition, they discern additional factors such as personal goals and risk aversion which influence the initial growth attitudes, not only of their NMF clients but probably also their own.

7.2.4   THE SBA MINDSET

The DMF ACM can be further interpreted as indicating a typical SBA mindset. Its dominant feature is the idea of creating jobs through small, mainly solo, firm formation. As in traditional entrepreneurship theory (Bennett 2014, Bridge et al. 2003, Cressy 2006, Hebert and Link 2006, Storey 1994), the SBAs also think predominantly in *voluntarist* terms, emphasizing prospective entrepreneurs and their characteristics and traits. With the exception of stressing the role of customers and demand, they downplay deterministic elements such as environmental, situational and serendipity (luck) factors.

Furthermore, the SBAs mainly focus on *single* NMF projects and micro-level outcomes, whereas more general social and economic consequences receive less attention. In particular, potential negative consequences such as the risk of displacing existing firms and wasteful firm and job churning (Hoffmann 2007, Storey 2006) seem largely ignored or bypassed. Had there been a wide awareness of such issues this would have been visible in the aggregated causal maps.

Finally, the thought patterns indicate pronounced risk aversion. The SBAs are well aware of the potential hazards facing entrepreneurs. They stress their clients' assumed interests and security, considering themselves pilots in dangerous waters. Reflecting this and the overriding objective of job creation, the SBAs' emerging attitudes toward firm growth seem asymmetric, if not somewhat paranoid: growth is always risky, staying small is never so. *No* SBA noted the many negative aspects of staying a solo or micro firm, which is why such things do not appear in the aggregate causal map.

What are the pragmatic and strategic conclusions? In operative practice, the SBAs and the FEA can be assumed to serve their individual NMF clients well, at least those with no or limited growth aspirations. This is also supported by other evidence. The FEA's clients' cumulative satisfaction index (scale 4–10) is at 8.9, a high level considering the large number of clients. Furthermore, over 80 per cent of the FEA's clients have been found to be still in business after five years. For comparison, in Finland and internationally, the typical five year survival rate is around 50 per cent. As to the strategic implications, it must be first noted that SBA services are free to the NMF clients. The FEA's financing comes from public sources: the local communities, larger firms and the state budget, conceivably based on SBA services' (so far unquestioned) beneficial role as job creator. The public resourcing means logically that what the SBAs do and achieve is not a private, micro-level issue only. From a public perspective, the study suggests some grounds for concern. An issue is the SBAs' single client/job creation emphasis and bypassing of indirect social and economic effects such as displacement. Another problem is the SBAs' smallness and anti-growth bias, a result of emphasizing the creation of at least one job and the understandable wish to avoid risks and moves that could endanger that. This can, however, be counterproductive already at the micro level in the case of capable NMF clients. Strategically, it can become a serious legitimacy issue if/ when the new growth-oriented entrepreneurship policies eventually become a public norm. Fortunately, after this study, the FEA has become aware of such risks and launched countermeasures such as putting more emphasis on small firm growth and offering new services to existing small businesses.

7.3 Structured CCM: Comparing Methods

This section discusses a comparison study of three CCM approaches: (1) semi-structured interviewing (SIM) and two variants of structured CCM, (2) pairwise comparison (PCM) and (3) freehand drawing of causal links (FDM). The selection of these methods had two grounds. First, the SIM approach was used in the SBA study (Section 7.2). This provided a logical comparison base and a comparison study could also validate or refute the SBA study's findings. Second, only methods using *primary* data were considered, in particular polar types of CCM. SIM CCM acquires original data by *in situ* interviewing and uses *ex post* coding to compare and extract the respondents' shared causal thought patterns. PCM and FDM methods are based on respondents selecting concepts from a researcher-defined concept pool. There, causal relationship beliefs are elicited either by pairwise comparison or freehand drawing, which moreover must not take place locally. Therefore, the compared methods will differ mainly in terms of (1) the type of elicited data (original versus researcher defined), (2) settings and techniques of data acquisition, and as a corollary of these, (3) the extent and impact of researcher judgment (*ex post* coding versus building the concept pool).

Indirectly, the comparison study implicitly contrasts also divergent methodological and ontological positions. Semi- and low-structured CCM is predominantly qualitative, that is, interpretive and constructionist. Structured CCM is nomothetically and psychometrically oriented and uses routine, neutral techniques of data acquisition and (when computerized) mechanical processing and analysis of data. The technical rigor, lighter research needs, and no need of *ex post* coding, in principle enabling also large N studies, make structured methods appear more attractive, assuming that one believes that CCM approaches are substitutable and differ only in administrative and resource terms. However, the really critical issue in method selection is which CCM approach is more likely to provide more useful and valid results. This is not a technical question but requires comparative evidence about the *substantive outcomes* of different CCM approaches. The study's aim was to contribute to this goal.

7.3.1   RESEARCH PROCESS

Participants

The comparison study's respondents represent the same population as in the SIM study. The SBAs in both cohorts have similar positions and advisory and administrative tasks in the FEA organization. There was roughly one year between the SIM interviews and the PCM/FDM data elicitation. However, no salient events took place globally or nationally during that year. The strategic position and operative tasks of the FEA organization and the local SBA units remained the same, too.

The comparison study's respondents (N = 15) were selected at random. When compared with the SIM study, no such overt (demographic) differences[3] could be detected which could be assumed to significantly influence their response tendencies beyond the different data elicitation. The same focal topic as in the SBA study (nascent micro firms' success and failure, *F01 NMF success/ failure*) was used when probing and creating the cause maps. It could be argued that instead of selecting a new SBA cohort, the SIM study's SBAs should have participated also in the PCM/FDM comparison. However, to corroborate the earlier SBA study's findings (SBAs' dominant belief patterns) it was necessary to examine whether different SBAs have similar or systematically different views. The new SBAs were telephoned and the study explained: to validate the earlier SBA study's findings and to compare the SIM and the PCM and FDM approaches' outcomes. Without exception, all agreed. In addition, the SBA study's respondents were also contacted and asked to participate in the evaluation of the resulting causal maps and the research process.

SIM comparison base

The SIM data was available in the SBA project, discussed in Section 7.2. However, to construct a comparable database, that is, one collected around the anchor topics *NMF success* and *NMF failure*, it was necessary to remove from the SBA study's NLU and NCU databases data elicited around the anchor topic *NMF-growth/smallness*. The condensed NLU database has 1,153 NLUs (62.9 per cent) and the NCU database 1,528 NCUs (56.2 per cent). It can be noted that elicitation around *NMF success/failure* took more time, approximately two-thirds of the total SIM interview time (M = 80.0 minutes, SD = 16.9 minutes), that is, approximately 50 minutes on average (see Section 7.2.2). Technically, the SIM, PCM and FDM data were handled as separate CMAP3 projects. The PCM and FDM projects had the same STV and NLU databases, but obviously different NCU data.

Concept pool

As was emphasized in Sections 3.1.4 and 3.6, the concept pool can be critical for the validity in structured CCM. The respondents first choose from the pool a subset of concepts, observing the criteria given in the instructions. The selected concepts (ideally) represent the participants' knowledge and beliefs about

---

3 The PCM/FDM SBAs' mean age is 51.1 years (SD = 9.49). There were four female and 11 male SBAs. Seven respondents double as SBAs and unit managers. The average SBA experience is 10.9 years (SD = 5.63). Eight SBAs have a master's-level and five a bachelor-level degree. Most SBAs have personal business experience, usually in managerial positions.

which phenomena exist in the context and which are relevant and important from the defined perspective of NMF success/failure. Conversely, concepts which are not selected—or not added to the list if this option is available—are assumed to be either unknown or not important enough for the shortlist.

When constructing the comparison study's concept pool, two aspects were observed. The first was to follow the models of previous structured CCM studies, in particular Markóczy and Goldberg (1995) and Clarkson and Hodgkinson (2005). The pool had 49 predefined concepts. The participants selected 14 concepts. With the preselected *NMF success/failure* the total number was N = 15. These are within the limits noted in the literature, especially considering that the causal links were not to be specified in this case. A general requirement is to ensure that the pool's concepts (not necessarily all) are representative, that is, familiar and relevant to the participants considering the selection task. Normally, this requires preliminary interviews and studies of context documents, literature, and so on. In this case, the SBA study at the background obviates this stage by clearly providing a large and representative repertoire of typical SBAs' notions, including information about their type and frequencies (Table 7.3).

Second, the concept pool now serves the dual objective of comparison and validation of the SBA study. Therefore, it must include concepts which allow the emergence of both similar and different belief patterns compared with the SBA study. As noted in Section 7.2, typical SBA thinking is focused on entrepreneur/actors and single NMF clients, de-emphasizing environmental factors and indirect local effects such as displacement of existing firms/jobs. Thus, in addition to the typical SBA notions, there had to be concepts which could be selected by participants representing also *different* belief patterns. For example, some might wish to emphasize the environmental factors or the social consequences of NMFs. Some could be more risk conscious, even risk averse, and stress consequences of an NMF failure. Finally, some SBAs could stress either the cause or the effect side or the public or private interests in NMF formation. Therefore, the pool included concepts which refer to factors in the economic and social environment and to local consequences such as job creation or existing firm displacement. In addition, NMF failure issues such as financial difficulties or stigmatization were included. Third, it was important to include *NMF-growth/smallness* to observe its emerging relative significance when it was not explicitly probed as was done in the SBA study. Fourth, concepts concerning an SBA's expertise, impact and resources and the FEA itself were included, although also they did not occur in the SBA study. Finally, significantly, the SBAs had the option of freely adding up to three personal, self-noted concepts to the pool and to select them instead of those in the predefined set.

The pool's concepts were the same as in the SBA study's standard term vocabulary, and, as noted in Section 7.2, close to the SBAs' original expressions. Some of the terms were reworded so that no acronyms or possibly unusual abbreviations were in the concept pool. The pool was imported into the projects' standard term vocabulary (STV) in CMAP3 (Section 5.3). A concept selection list (CSL) was created as an Excel worksheet and sent to the participants as an email-attached file. As shown in Figure 7.9, the concepts were presented using four columns. The text box (and the email text, too) contained the instructions to select *14 concepts* which the respondent considered "most important from the viewpoint of their typical clients', nascent entrepreneurs' and their firms' success and failure." The concept *NMF success/failure* was preselected. The respondents were explicitly encouraged to add/use their own concepts if they felt that something important was missing. There were counters to show the number of selected concepts. Finally, the respondent was asked to comment briefly on the CSL task, the concepts' clarity and how they performed the task and how long it took.

TEHTÄVÄ: Valitse seuraavasta käsitelistasta 14 tekijää/asiaa, jotka mielestäsi ovat **tärkeimmät** tyypillisten asiakkaidesi, alkavien **yritysten/yrittäjien menestymisen ja epäonnistumisen kannalta.** Ajattele silloin sekä siihen **vaikuttavia tekijöitä (syitä)** että niiden tuloksia **(seurauksia).** Valinta tehdään merkitsemällä **ykkönen (1) nollan (0) tilalle** valitsemasi asian/tekijän viereen **(peruutus = palauta nolla).** (Menestyminen/epäonnistuminen on valittu **valmiiksi:** kokonaismäärä = 15). Jos listasta mielestäsi puuttuu joku olennainen tekijä, kirjoita se/ne **Lisäkäsitteiksi** ja valitse. Lista on **satunnaisjärjestyksessä,** ja siksi hyvä käydä ajatuksella läpi kokonaisuutena ennen valintaa. Valintaa voi selkeyttää valitsemalla (= 1) ensin useampia asioita ja karsimalla (= 0) niistä lopullisen top-14 listan. Listan voi **tulostaakin.** Laskuri näyttää, montako on vielä valittavissa tai karsittava. Tutkimukselle on tärkeä valita **tavoitemäärä 14, ei yli eikä alle.** Kaikki harkitut, omaan tietämykseen perustuvat valinnat ovat yhtä oikeita. Kun olet valinnut, **tallenna Excel-tiedosto ja lähetä email-liitteenä** Mauri.Laukkanen@uef.fi. Saat 2. vaiheen tehtävän nopeasti saatuani 1. vaiheen vastauksesi. Lisätietoja: 040-5506552

KÄSITE	1/0	KÄSITE	1/0	KÄSITE	1/0	KÄSITE	1/0
kansantalouden tila/(nousu/taantuma)	1	yrittäjän sos.turva	0	toimeentulo/yrittäjä + perhe	0	yrityksen kilpailu/kilpailijat	1
yrittäjän sosiaal.arvostus	0	sattuma/onnekkuus/yrittäjä	0	yrittäjyys/yrittäjämäärä/alue	0	liiketoiminta- + alan osaaminen/yritt.	1
yrityksen kasvu/pieneksijäänti	0	liiketoimintaympäristö/-ehdot	1	asiakkaat/markkinat	1	yritysten menestys/epäonnist.	1
kilpailuhaitat/toimivien yritt.syrjäytym.	0	yrityspalvelut/neuvonta/alue	0	alueen vetovoima/kilp.kyky	0	liiketoiminta/yrittämistilaisuus	0
viranomaisbyrokratia	0	yrittäjän/perheen henk.k. vaikeudet	0	uusyrityskeskus/rahoitus/talous	0	luottokelpoisuus/yrittäjä	0
yrittäjän tavoitteet/motiivit	1	myynti/markkinointi	1	yrittäjän työllistyminen	0	lopetus/konkurssi	0
liiketoimintasuunnitelma/laatu	0	talous-/yritys-/yrittäjyyspolitiikka	0	yritystuet/avustukset	0	työllisyys/työpaikat/alue	0
vaurastuminen/yrittäjän	0	henkilöstö/yrityksen	0	yrittäjä-/yritysriskit/-vastuut	0	liikeidea/tuote/palv./toim.tapa	1
yrittäjyyskasvatus/yrittäjäkoulutus	0	yrittäjän taustat/ura/koulutus	1	verkostot/yrittäjän+yrityksen	1	yrittäjäominaisuudet/puute	1
riskivalmius/riskinkarttaminen/yrittäjä	0	yritysneuvoja/osaaminen+asent.	0	pakkoyrittäjyys/työttöm.uhka	0	EU/globaalit tekijät	0
yks.talouden vaikeudet/velkaant.	1	yrittäjän työehdot, -tuki	0	verotulot/hyvinvointi/palvelut	0	Lisäkäsite 1	0
yrittäjän leimaantum./eristyminen	0	yritysneuvoja/työehdot, -tuki	0	yritysverotus/-lait ja normit	0	Lisäkäsite 2	0
kannattavuus/tulos/yritys	1	rahoitus/resurssit/yrityksen	1	uusyrityskeskus/arvostus/imago/alue	0	Lisäkäsite 3	0
Valittu käsitteitä/sarake	5	Valittu käsitteitä/sarake	4	Valittu käsitteitä/sarake	1	Valittu käsitteitä/sarake	5
VALITTU (tavoite = 14 + 1 = 15)	15	VALITTAVISSA (= < 14)	0	KARSITTAVAA (> 14)	0		

Voisitko ystävällisesti vielä lyhyesti vastata näihin kysymyksiin - jatka kirjoittamalla ao. riville:
1) Oliko **tehtävä** selkeä vai epäselvä? Oliko se kiintoisa vai enemmän tylsä? Muuta? Suhteellisen selkeä tehtävä kun luki rauhallisesti ja ajatuksella ohjeistuksen.
2) Olisitko valinnut **enemmän kuin 14** käsitettä? - **mitkä** valitsemiesi lisäksi? En välttämättä olisi valinnut enempää, melkein vähempikin olisi riittänyt.
3) Olivatko **käsitteet** yksiselitteisiä vai vaikeita tulkita? Mitkä olivat vaikeita? **Pääsääntöisesti** käsitteet aukenivat (ainakin luulen niin)
4) Miten **toteutit tehtävän** (Excelissä, paperitulostus+Excel, valitsin useita ja karsit, suoraan kaikki, jne)? Tein tehtävän Excelissä. Valitsin ensin 14, joista sitten muutaman vielä vaihdoin
5) Kauanko tehtävään meni suunnilleen **aikaa** kaikkiaan? n. 10 minuuttia

Figure 7.9 **Concept selection list (CSL) in the PCM/FDM comparison study (S01)**

As a rule, the CSLs (with feedback) were returned very quickly by email. The CSL selection task's mean duration was M = 11.7 minutes (SD = 6.1). Next, the concept columns and selection data were copied (with the STAGs added) to create a CSL worksheet/book which conforms to the CMAP3 conventions (Section 5.3). The selected concepts were imported into the project's NLU database for each respondent.

The next step was to elicit data about the selected concepts' causal relationships. To enable the study's objective of method comparison, this was done first using the pairwise comparison method (PCM). In addition, after a period of two weeks, also a freehand drawing (FDM) task was administered to the same respondents. Because the respondents were all busy professionals, it was assumed that the memory impact of the PCM task would have waned by then and the FDM task appeared as a new and independent one. It may be noted that concerning the impact of the order when administering the tasks, Hodgkinson et al. (2004) examined the influence and did not observe any significant impact. Therefore, the PCM and FDM order was the same for all respondents.

Pairwise comparison method

The pairwise comparison of the concepts which a given respondent had selected was realized electronically using a matrix in worksheet format. As described in Section 5.3, CMAP3 creates the PCM matrices automatically when the participant's NLUs are available in the NLU database. Figure 7.10 displays the matrix for the same respondent (S01), whose CSL is shown in Figure 7.9 and whose causal maps will be examined below.

The matrix has the 14 concepts of S01 and the preselected (NMF success/ failure) in 15 concept columns and rows. In addition, there are counters for the Od and Id values. The instructions were given in the text box and the email. The respondents had to replace the cells' 0 with a 1 if they felt that the concept in the left "cause" column causally influenced one or more concepts in the "effect" columns to the right. The number of links was not restricted. Because the SBA study did not inquire about the relationships' characteristics, link specification was not done in the comparison study either. As in the CSL task, the respondents were asked to comment on the task's clarity, how easy or difficult it was, and how long it took (see below). After completion, the respondents emailed the worksheet back to the researcher. The PCM task took longer and the duration varied more than the CSL task (M = 34.2 minutes, SD = 25.9).

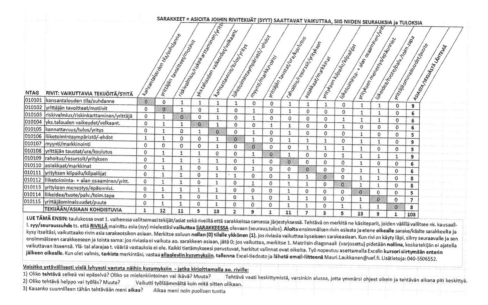

Figure 7.10   Pairwise comparison matrix worksheet (returned, S01)

To create an importable matrix, the returned matrices were copied (the Od/Id counter data removed) into a new worksheet following the CMAP3 conventions (Section 5.3). The NCUs were imported into the project's NCU database for each respondent. As in all structured CCM studies, there was no need to code/ standardize the NLU data because the respondents had to stay within the predefined concept pool. Moreover, slightly surprisingly, *no* SBA used the option of adding personal concepts, which would have required coding.

Freehand drawing (FDM)

The participants received a letter after approximately two weeks. It contained a reminder about the study, new instructions, and the FDM instrument: an A4 size paper sheet, on which that specific respondent's selected concepts had been printed, arranged in a neutral order, leaving room for drawing. There was also a brief A4 form for background data and a return envelope (with stamp). The instruction was to think carefully about the causal influence relationships among the concepts and to indicate them by drawing the corresponding connecting arrows from the causes to the effects. The number of links/ arrows was free and no specification of the arrows/links was required. After completion, the FDM sheet and the background data form were returned in the pre-stamped envelope. Most SBAs did so quickly; some had to be reminded by email. According to the participants' reports (N = 10), the FDM task took on average M= 18.5 minutes (SD = 12.5).

Instead of using manual drawing, it might have been possible to ask the respondents to scan and email the manual drawing or even perform the process using an application such as MS PowerPoint for drawing the arrows on a prepared template containing the selected concepts. However, the respondents' computer facilities and skills were unknown so such options were not used. Instead, the returned FDM sheets were converted (by the researcher) into PCMs and the NCU data imported into CMAP3 as usual.

7.3.2   INDIVIDUAL CAUSAL MAPS

We will first discuss the comparison study's results in concrete terms, using three typical individual cause maps, elicited by the compared methods. The point is that to understand the different methods' characteristics, an idea in visual form of what the methods typically seem to elicit from an individual participant is useful. After all, the individual causal maps will underlie the aggregate cause maps (ACM) and eventual conclusions. In the mind's eye, the reader can thus form a rough idea of what comes out when several more or less similar standardized individual cause maps (N = 15) which include both widely shared and less frequent, even unique, notions are aggregated in a cause map to represent the dominant belief patterns. The resulting ACMs will be examined later.

In this case, "typical" was defined as a cause map/respondent whose SNT base had relatively more core SNTs (CR => 8) and the highest C/D value (SNT based) in the project. Both indicate the degree to which a respondent's concept base is shared. The cause map in Figure 7.11 is that of S12 in the SBA study based on the SIM method. The other two cause maps are from S01 in the PCM/ FDM comparison study. The one in Figure 7.12 is based on the PCM method, and the cause map in 7.13 on the FDM method. Because the latter two come from the *same* respondent (S01), their comparison is especially interesting. In addition, numerical summary and average data will be presented (Table 7.5). The figure titles show the number of nodes (SNT), causal links (SCU) and reciprocal, two-way causal links (RSCU) in the maps.

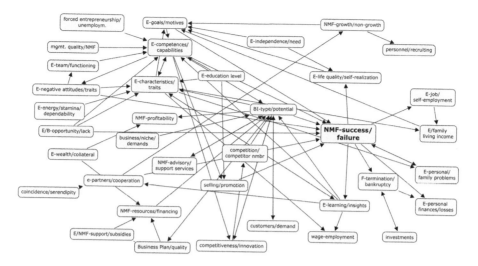

Figure 7.11 S12's SIM cause map (N/SNT = 37, N/SCU = 72, N/RCU = 12)

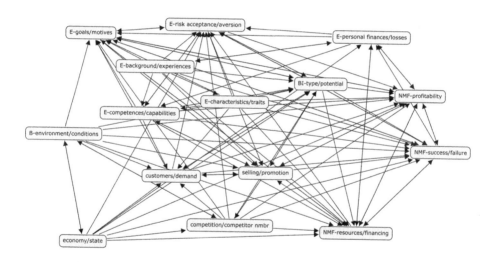

Figure 7.12 S01's PCM cause map (N/SNT = 15, N/SCU = 103, N/RCU = 40)

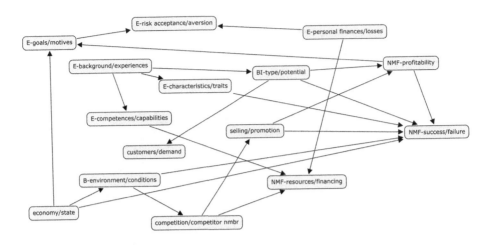

Figure 7.13 S01's FDM cause map (N/SNT = 15, N/SCU = 22, N/RCU = 0)

The differences in the individual cause maps are salient. It can be noted first that the number of cause map nodes, concepts, in the SIM cause map is significantly higher. The second difference is the PCM cause map's higher *relative* number of *causal links* (SCUs/arrows) and density as compared with the SIM and FDM cause maps. As shown in Table 7.5, the SCU/SNT relationship in the PCM map is 6.87. In the SIM map it is 1.95 and in the FDM map it is 1.47. The third and intriguing major difference, closely related to the SCU numbers, is the number and share of two-directional, *reciprocal* causal links (RSCUs). Almost 40 per cent of the PCM SCUs are RSCUs. In the SIM map there are 16 per cent RSCUs. The FDM map has no RSCUs.

There is also a fourth, less obvious difference. The causal relationships in the PCM and FDM cause maps include relatively more general "overarching" SCUs, especially those where a contextual variable such as *economy/state* or *B-environment/conditions* or the entrepreneurs' *characteristics* or general business functions such as *selling/promotion* is seen to influence *NMF success/ failure,* the focal issue As causal statements they are not necessarily dubious. Rather, they arguably represent causal shortcuts, which are typical in everyday discourses. However, compared with the SIM cause map, the SIM cause map gives a more detailed and arguably also a more logical view of the causal paths of mediating variables and thus of the productive *mechanisms* than the PCM and FDM maps, which stay at a more general level.

7.3.3 COMPARISON AT AGGREGATE LEVEL

The differences can be first examined in quantitative terms. The left columns in Table 7.5 summarize data of the above typical individual causal maps. The next three column groups show the main differences at the aggregate level of the SIM, PCM and FDM methods using the earlier discussed dimensions, which CMAP3 calculates. The following overt observations can be made.

Table 7.5   SIM, PCM and FDM comparison data

Measure	Typical CM (CD Max)			SIM F01 (N = 15)			PCM (N = 15)			FDM (N = 15)		
	SIM (S12)	PCM (S01)	FDM (S01)	Total	Mean	SD	Total	Mean	SD	Total	Mean	SD
SNT	37	15	15	92	37.80	7.63	38	15.00	0.00	38	15.00	0.00
SNT-%-Total	40.22	39.47	39.47	100.00	41.09	8.29	100.00	39.47	0.00	100.00	39.47	0.00
SNT-%-CR	81.08	66.67	66.67	45.65	75.71	8.64	28.95	57.33	12.29	28.95	57.33	12.29
SNT-Unique-%	0.00	0.00	0.00	13.04	2.02	2.37	13.16	2.22	4.11	13.16	2.22	4.11
SCU	72	103	22	583	71.80	21.06	671	112.00	28.96	180	19.67	5.64
SCU-%-Total	12.35	15.35	12.22	100.00	12.32	3.61	100.00	16.69	4.32	100.00	10.93	3.13
SCU-%-CR	18.06	33.98	13.64	3.43	17.99	6.46	6.41	24.15	8.57	1.67	9.97	4.15
SCU-Unique-%	22.22	8.74	27.27	67.24	35.10	8.17	50.07	18.92	15.29	67.22	40.58	13.80
DENSITY	1.72	14.65	3.13	13.93	1.71	0.50	95.45	15.93	4.12	25.60	2.80	0.80
SCU/SNT	1.95	6.87	1.47	6.34	1.87	0.27	17.66	7.47	1.93	4.74	1.31	0.38
NLU	83	15	15	1,153	76.87	19.81	225	15.00	0.00	225	15.00	0.00
NLU/SNT (M)	2.24	1.00	1.00		2.02	0.28		1.00	0.00		1.00	0.00
NCU	117	103	22	1539	102.60	29.09	1680	112.00	28.96	295	19.67	5.64
NCU/SCU (M)	1.63	1.00	1.00		1.44	0.15		1.00	0.00		1.00	0.00
R-SCU	12	40	0	132	8.80	3.61	1090	72.67	36.27	18	1.20	2.48
R-SCU/SCU	0.17	0.39	0.00		0.12			0.65			0.06	
CD/SNT M	0.45	0.49	0.52		0.398			0.411			0.450	
CD/SNT SD	0.06	0.13	0.18			0.076			0.119			0.187

First, the SIM method elicits a relatively high number of *distinct* phenomena (SNTs) (N = 92) which are (subjectively) proximately or distantly related to the focal issue of *NMF success/failure* in the SBA context. In the PCM and FDM methods the total number of concepts is much lower (N = 38). In addition, their concept selection shows more dispersion, as indicated by the lower share of common *core* SNTs.

Second, the average and total number of elicited *causal links* (SCUs) in the PCM method is much higher than in the other methods, in particular in FDM. The former elicited much more SCUs (112.0/19.7 = 5.7), which is also shown by the SCU-related indicator (Density, SCU/SNT relationship). As noted, a very salient difference is the number of *reciprocal* (two-way) SCUs (RSCUs). In the PCM case, on average almost two-thirds of all SCUs are RSCUs. All PCM respondents had those. The high dispersion (SD = 36.27, range 30–144) of PCM RSCUs' occurrence also suggests considerable individual variance when performing the PCM matrix task. In contrast, only four SBAs had two-directional RSCUs in the FDM task, two of them several. The SIM SCU database contains some RSCUs. All SBAs had some of them.

From a method and research design viewpoint, a major practical issue is the different CCM approaches' *substitutability*. Are they interchangeable alternatives? To assess this, it is necessary to assume that PCM and/or FDM are used for the same task as in the SIM-SBA study, in this case, to locate the SBAs' *typical* beliefs about *NMF success/failure*. This allows a comparison in aggregated *content* terms of the more intensive CCM approach (SIM) on the one hand, and of results of the administratively easier structured methods (PCM, FDM) on the other hand. In addition, the findings can tentatively validate or refute the SBA study.

On the SIM side, the comparison base is already available in the form of the SBA aggregate causal map, displayed in Figure 7.8. As noted, it was created as a full domain map (DMF) around *NMF success/failure*. The SIM ACM contains 35 SCUs and 29 SNTs, which are shared practically by all participants in the SBA study (TF median = 13). In principle, to have comparable PCM and FDM ACMs, they too should be generated as DMFs using TF => 7 to produce cause maps with nodes shared by the majority of the SBAs in the PCM/FDM study. As seen below, this did not work exactly like this.

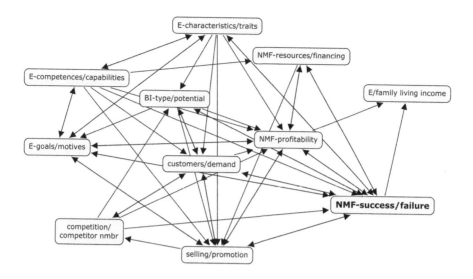

Figure 7.14   PCM domain map around *NMF success/failure* (N/SNT = 11, N/SCU = 54, N/RSCU = 34)

Figure 7.14 displays the PCM DMF generated around *NMF success/failure* using TF => 7. This produces an ACM, where the median TF of the SNTs is 12. Compared with the corresponding SIM cause map (Figure 7.8), the PCM ACM is very compact. It contains a much smaller number of SNTs (N = 11), which represent less than third of all concepts (N = 38) selected by the PCM/FDM study's SBAs. A visual inspection also shows that most causal links are two-way RSCUs (34/54).

The FDM ACM in Figure 7.15 was generated as a DMF around *NMF success/failure*. To create a representative ACM, that is, one containing the most frequently occurring phenomena (SNTs) as selected by the SBAs, however, a lower cut-off point (TF => 3) was necessary. This results in an ACM, where most included SNTs are highly shared (median TF = 11). In addition, the generation includes four less frequent SNTs (in *italics* in the ACM) with a lower TF (*Business plan/quality* TF = 7, *E-background/experiences* TF= 7, *B-environment/conditions* TF = 6, *E-risk acceptance/aversion* TF = 6). The FDM ACM has no RSCUs.

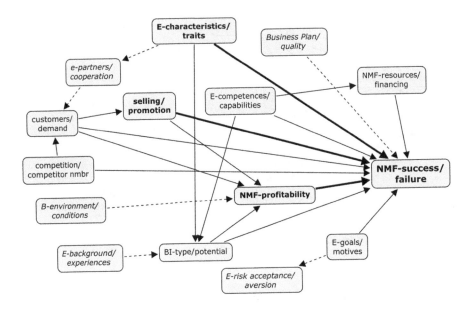

Figure 7.15   **FDM domain map around** *NMF success/failure* **(N/SNT = 15,**
N/SCU = 23, N/RSCU = 0)

The different generation parameters (TF) of the PCM and FDM ACMs
can raise the question about the appropriate inclusion threshold, defining
operationally what is considered typical or atypical. In a small N CCM study it
is not meaningful to define it statistically. On the other hand, it cannot be quite
arbitrary. It requires common-sense judgment, noting, first, that in CCM the
target phenomena (mental models) are volatile and vary across the respondents
and that random factors can influence data acquisition. Therefore, it is not
reasonable to demand fully shared ACMs but rather ACMs that represent
the respondents' majority. Second, it is also important which elements of the
target phenomena should be emphasized: the distinct phenomena, represented
by the concepts (SNTs) or their causal and temporal relationships (SCUs), as
perceived by the respondents, or both. Depending on the research interests,
either dimension can be important. In the FDM case, it is known that most
SBAs discern the ACM's phenomena/SNTs and, furthermore, judging by the
PCM, it can be assumed that *had* they been asked about them (or had they
used more time to think about the connections when drawing), they would
probably have connected the nodes for them more densely. As noted above,
had the FDM ACM been generated using TF => 7, it would have contained just
four SNTs and three SCUs, which obviously does not seem plausible at all.

Therefore, the ACM in Figure 7.15 appears more representative. This was also supported by the SBA feedback, as discussed below.

In addition to the numerical differences indicated by the relative numbers of SNTs and SCUs and derivative aspects such as density, the SIM ACM (Figure 7.8) and the PCM and FDM ACMs differ in *substantive* terms. As the individual PCM and FDM maps, the ACMs also contain several causal shortcuts and give overall a sparse and less coherent model of the causal factors and especially of consequences of the focal phenomenon (*NMF success/failure*) than the SIM ACM. This concerns especially the PCM ACM, which has many RSCUs. In contrast, the SIM ACM appears a rather detailed model of the causal paths and mediating variables and thus of the productive *mechanisms*. In particular, the SIM ACM includes some of the private and social consequences which are missing from the PCM and FDM maps, which focus on *explaining* NMF success/ failure at a general level.

7.3.4 UNDERSTANDING THE DIFFERENCES

The SIM, PCM and FDM CCM approaches produce markedly different data and results, which obviously can, depending on the case, lead to divergent and possibly erroneous conclusions. For example, a naïve interpretation could be that the PCM respondents are (or turn) cognitively different—more "complex" and knowledgeable—than those (or when) measured by the FDM task, the SIM respondents being the most knowledgeable of them all. This is, of course, absurd. Whilst some variance of the individual knowledge and inferential tendencies, probably also in data acquisition, must be assumed, differences of this magnitude can only result from the methods' psychometric and technical differences.

As for the technical factors, an obvious one is the different probing: SIM does not constrain the number of elicited notions (NLUs and thus of the emerging SNTs). Structured PCM/FDM *must* limit the number of selectable concepts (NLUs = SNTs). In this case the number was N = 15, which, as noted, represents the upper literature recommended limit, but was acceptable now because the causal links were not to be specified. It could perhaps be argued that the different probing makes the methods not comparable. However, when they are used for the *same* purpose—in this case locating the respondents' typical belief patterns—the methods can (must) be compared in those terms.

A first observation is that the limited number of selectable concepts can also influence how many distinct notions can emerge and thus the extent to which the focal domain or issue will be covered. SIM elicited 98 SNTs (as coded), PCM/FDM 38 SNTs. Technically, the latter could elicit an SNT number close to the pool/CSL (in this case N = 48), depending in addition on how many new concepts the SBAs add. Thus, the pool-based methods have an inherent focusing and constraining effect, which can preclude the emergence of a part of the respondents' knowledge base and their inference/reasoning. In this case the consequence is that the SIM DMF cause map around *NMF-success/failure* provides a more detailed and differentiated view of the SBAs' thinking both in terms of distinct phenomena and causal relationships than the PCM or FDM ACMs, which focus more on explaining factors alone. This can be useful or counterproductive, again depending on the research task.

Another difference, which concerns mainly PCM and FDM, is the number of elicited causal links (SCUs) and the respectively denser or sparser cause maps at individual and aggregate level. The grounds are probably psychometric and related to the technical procedures. Whatever the explanation, the density and sparseness also influence the results and the plausibility and usability of the respective methods in addition to their overall focusing and restricting effect noted above.

Hodgkinson et al. (2004) found that pairwise comparison produced approximately five times more causal links than FDM. This is surprisingly close to the present study's multiplier of 5.6. As to explanation, they suggest that the approaches launch different memory processes. More specifically, PCM would be dependent on *recognition* and FDM more on *recall*. When the concept pairs are presented successively using a questionnaire,[4] the respondents were assumed to recognize and then report those pairs which correspond to their causal model of the problem. When performing the FDM task, on the other hand, the respondents apparently did not systematically generate and evaluate all variable pairings, but "searched their memory of how they had modelled the problem, reporting only those causal relations that they recalled" (Hodgkinson et al. 2004, p. 17). As to the consequences, Hodgkinson et al. invoke the notion of two kinds of memory error: *errors of commission*, where something is reported although it does not actually exist or happen, and *errors of omission*, when things which exist or happened are not remembered. They conclude that PCM and FDM differ in their ability to capture mental representations—PCM

---

4   In the present PCM case, the concepts were presented as matrix rows and columns (Figure 7.10) and the respondent paired them successively for comparison. The FDM tasks were of course essentially similar in both studies.

having a tendency to overestimate and FDM to underestimate the complexity of representations.

Some support to this view is provided by the SBAs. They were asked for feedback (see below), whereby one item was an open question about why the number of SCUs was much higher in PCM than in FDM. Regrettably, many did not answer or answered something trivial. The thoughtful comments, first, suggested that the world simply *is* complicated and involves ambiguous reciprocal cause–effect relationships as in the PCM cause maps. However, the commentators did not notice or explain the obvious discrepancy that they had *not* expressed this very complexity in their FDM tasks as they did in the PCM. Perhaps more to the point, some SBAs noted that PCM did not require as much "thinking" (recall?) as FDM. Using FDM it was easier to visualize and conceptualize the causal directions than in the matrix, where the process was more mechanical, involving less conscious thinking (recognition?). Finally, some suggested that the differences could also simply result from lack of concentration and not observing the instructions.

Notably, the above explanation of the PCM/FDM differences defines the issue as a problem of memory recall and recognition, which can indeed lead to inaccurate representations of the actors' memory contents. However, it also implies that there exists a distinct memory entity, a (causal) mental model, which can be captured and measured, for example, in terms of its complexity. As noted in Section 2.5, this assumption may be valid sometimes but not necessarily always, perhaps not even as a rule. Instead, it must be assumed that the targets (mental models) are typically transitory and volatile, partly recalled from long-term memory, partly also generated ad hoc at the STM-LTM border. Different probing methods—not only PCM and FDM but also SIM or the more unstructured CCM ones—can be assumed to tap and activate the basic cognitive processes to varying degrees. Thus, the observed differences probably reflect not only memory effects but also differently activated generative ad hoc processes. In PCM, the respondents can be assumed to ask themselves first: "does A cause B directly?" or "is C a proximate consequence of B?" However, it seems probable that they could also frame the question more generally, asking essentially: "could there be *some/any* plausible connection or influence path, however distant, between A and B and so on?" Depending on the assessed concept pair, the answer to this question can be affirmative and result in a reported causal connection. The FDM task, although the same stimuli (A, B, C and so on) as in the PCM matrix are simultaneously visible, could instead foster a tendency to stay *within* the displayed frame as defined by the concepts on the paper, and thus to focus more on the *proximate* linkages only, which are then drawn as causal arrows. If these unambiguous linkages do not come to mind, the more speculative distant and indirect connections are not reported, even if they might be recalled.

There is a further aspect to consider. In Section 3.6 it was argued that methods like PCM and/or FDM should make sense in that there are indeed plausible and relatively proximate causal relationships and evoked models/mechanisms, where the listed phenomena, at least many of them, are logically connected. From this perspective, structured CCM methods can pose issues which are not adequately observed. The concept pool (CSL) can be too heterogeneous and contain concepts/phenomena which have little to do with each other. If/when the participants are asked to select a subset of concepts which they consider important (generally or from a given perspective), they usually can do that without difficulty, as indeed happened in the present study. That they can select, however, does not necessarily mean that the selected concepts, even if selected as subjectively "important", are also *logically connected* with each other causally or temporally, in other words, that actually they belong to a coherent causal (mental) model. In general, it can be presumed that the more general and ambiguous the selected "important" or predefined concepts are, the more likely they will be perceived as at least distantly connected to the other concepts. This concerns particularly PCM, where the respondents focus on *individual* node-node pairs at a time. In contrast, in FDM the concepts may be perceived more as a set of which the respondent tries to create a coherent, integrated whole as far as possible. The higher numbers of reciprocal causal connections (RSCUs) in PCM as compared with FDM would seem to fit this assumption.

Finally, differences of elicited data will reflect not only on the methods' demand characteristics but also on how they are applied technically. An obvious factor is probing *time*. Other things being equal, more available response time will foster both recall and ad hoc generation of notions and potential causal connections, resulting in broader and denser cause maps. Another factor is how the acquisition takes place: is it local and guided by an interviewer or less controlled, as when using mailed forms or electronic media? The response times and probably also the carefulness will vary more in the latter case. The overt impact, however, can differ. For instance, a short response usually indicates a quick and unthinking answer, but this can sometimes produce more, not fewer, connections in the PCM task.

7.3.5   ASSESSING REPRESENTATIVENESS

When comparing CCM methods, one could focus on cause maps' quantifiable aspects such as absolute and relative numbers of concepts and causal links and derivative measures like density as, for example, Hodgkinson et al. (2004) did. Whilst this too can be important, arguably more useful would be to assess the methods' ability to capture and represent the respondents' substantive beliefs (Nicolini 1999). However, this is difficult to quantify and requires judgment. In the present case, we will examine the resulting ACMs first in terms of their domain coverage and coherence as causal models of the focal phenomena. Second, there is some feedback data, where the participating SBAs evaluated the ACMs' representativeness.

Let us first return to the PCM ACM in Figure 7.14 and compare it with the SIM ACM displayed in Figure 7.8. To provide a background, it is useful to also examine once again the individual cause maps (Figures 7.11–7.13) and to remember that the SIM and PCM/FDM studies' respondents represent the same FEA SBA population. Furthermore, it can be recalled that the PCM/FDM method's CSL (concept pool) was constructed so that the concept selection enabled, in principle, the emergence of *similar* but also of systematically *divergent* belief patterns compared with the SIM study.

As already noted, the main overt difference is that the SIM approach elicits both individually and overall more *distinct concepts* from the respondents than the structured PCM and FDM approaches. This reflects, of course, the different probing discussed above. In terms of *domain coverage*, thus, the SIM ACM can provide a more detailed and differentiated view of the causes and consequences of NMF-success/failure, as perceived by the SBAs. Reflecting partly the constraining and focusing effect of the PCM/FDM concept selection, partly the underlying belief patterns, the PCM and FDM ACMs will contain much fewer concepts and focus (ideally) on the key factors of NMF-success/failure. This and the distribution of selected concepts in PCM/FDM (Table 7.3, right column) corroborates the SBA study's view of the basic SBA mindset, as summarized in Section 7.2.4, however, with the important difference that the PCM and FDM ACMs emphasize the *causes* of individual NMFs' *success*. The public and private *consequences* of success, let alone those of NMF failure, are not included in the dominant belief pattern, although they are very probably well-known to most SBAs in the comparison study.

The *internal coherence* of the ACMs is a more judgmental issue. We have argued that they should be consistent and make logical sense as *models* of the focal phenomena and mechanisms, in this case, the causes and consequences of NMF-success/failure. In this respect, the PCM ACM (Figure 7.14) seems really problematic mainly because of the many reciprocal causal links. On the one hand, some of the RSCUs are plausible and many at least conceivable, for example, as delayed feedback effects. On the other hand, believing and thinking that "everything depends on everything" (as argued by some SBAs) is less convincing because such mental models can hardly support cognitive tasks such as explaining phenomena, logical reasoning and purposive planning and decision-making. In practice, actors must assume (not necessarily accurately) that certain causal factors and mechanisms are primary and more relevant than some others, however imaginable in principle. Thus, the PCM ACM does not seem coherent, which also makes it less plausible as a representation of the SBAs' general *causal* thinking. The FDM and SIM ACMs appear more logical as models of the causal mechanisms.

A different view to the ACMs' validity is provided by the feedback data which was collected from the respondents of the SBA study (N = 15), the PCM/FDM comparison study (N = 15) and 15 other randomly selected SBAs. Thus, the sample (N = 45) represents roughly half of the FEA's current SBAs. They received (by email) a summary of the study, three typical cause maps, and a questionnaire inquiring (*inter alia*) which map corresponds to their own core thinking about *NMF success/failure*, and to typical SBA thinking, as they know it. Thirty-one completed responses were returned: a rather high rate of 68.9 per cent. The results are summarized in Table 7.6.

Table 7.6   SBAs' feedback data (%) on SIM, PCM and FDM cause maps
(N = 31)

	Equals my thinking	Not my thinking	Equals SBA thinking	Not SBA typical	Most informative	Least informative	Difficult, tangled
SIM map	45.2	16.1	35.5	6.5	51.6	3.2	6.5
PCM map	22.6	35.5	19.4	32.3	35.5	19.4	87.1
FDM map	29.0	22.6	45.2	12.9	9.7	32.3	3.2
None of them	3.2	25.8	0.0	48.4	3.2	45.2	3.2
(N = 31)	100.0	100.0	100.0	100.0	100.0	100.0	100.0

Table 7.6 suggests some broad conclusions. First, perhaps most importantly, all three ACMs seem accepted as representations of the SBAs' thinking, although there is a clear preference of the more detailed and causally coherent SIM map and (somewhat less) of the sparser but also logical FDM cause map. When the same is framed in rejection form (not corresponding or SBA typical), the response pattern is similar. Second, there is an interesting tendency to consider the more complicated and informative cause maps (SIM, to a lesser degree PCM) being closer to the respondent's own views and the simpler FDM map respectively mirroring better the typical thinking of "others". This can reflect that we feel usually more aware of our own thinking than of other people's ideas, which we can infer mainly through overt communication. Third, the PCM map with its numerous RSCUs is perceived as difficult and complicated and a less typical one. However, in spite of this, it was not widely rejected.

To summarize, the analysis of the ACMs and the individual cause maps together with the SBAs' feedback suggests, first, that it is not meaningful to ask which CCM method or causal map is "better" and more valid. All above maps originate with the SBAs and seem to represent (to them) their thinking, some more, some less accurately in subjective terms. On the other hand, as noted earlier, it cannot be assumed that there is a definite entity, which could be elicited and labelled as "the" SBA mental model, not even about such a relatively specific issue as NMF success/failure. Second, it seems that different CCM methods capture but also *generate* variably detailed and differentiated views of the SBAs' prevalent thinking. They have varying focusing and constraining impacts, which will be manifested in the resulting raw data and the different aggregated causal maps.

7.3.6 METHODOLOGICAL LESSONS

As to the lessons, the comparison study provides first some concrete observations about the different methods' response time and resource needs. These are sometimes important *practical* selection criteria. Furthermore, the study enables speculating about the eventual impacts if something essential would have been carried out differently. Third, the study enables at least provisional conclusions about the compared CCM methods' usability in general and in different contexts. Finally, the study experience can suggest new variants of CCM.

To begin with, the time that the respondents used for the different elicitation cases can be known relatively accurately. As noted, SIM required approximately 50 minutes of interview time. The concept selection task, which preceded PCM and FDM methods, had a mean duration of 11.7 minutes

(SD = 6.1). The PCM comparison task's mean was 34.2 minutes (SD = 25.9) and the FDM's 18.5 minutes (SD = 12.5). Thus, the FDM process, including the concept selection, took roughly half an hour and the SIM and PCM processes a quarter more. Whilst such differences are probably not very significant for the participants, from a researcher's point of view the methods differ markedly. SIM data must be acquired *in situ* and it also requires more time and effort in data processing and coding/standardization. However, it is important to note that this varies considerably depending on the number of respondents, focal topics, and type and level of coding, as discussed earlier. Moreover, had the PCM or FDM studies been realized *ab ovo*, that is, without the present SBA background, preliminary interviews and so on would have been necessary to build a valid concept pool (CSL). The number of preparatory interviews would vary depending on the issue and the respondents. For the present or similar cases a rough estimate can be inferred from by the SIM concepts' saturation process, discussed in Section 7.2.2.

As to the impact of a different technical realization of the study, at least four aspects can be considered. First, instead of the electronic (email) data acquisition an *in situ* administration could have been used. Whilst this would have nullified the very idea of the comparison, it would have most likely produced more consistent and less variable data. However, considering that the detected differences were so large, that would not have changed the main outcome and conclusions. Second, an *in situ* procedure would have enabled the more conventional card-based comparison technique (Markóczy and Goldberg 1995) or the questionnaire method (Hodgkinson et al. 2004, p. 8). It is difficult to assess whether this would have made a difference and to which direction. At least the present matrix method appears essentially similar to the questionnaire method. Both present all concept pairs simultaneously. Third, the pool concepts (CSL) could have been more general, combining, for example, most entrepreneur-related SNTs. Whilst this would have nullified the comparability of the three approaches, it would have had a focusing effect, probably increasing the SCUs' sharedness. Fourth, had the PCM and FDM also required the conventional SCU specification (weight, direction), a noticeably smaller set of selected SNTs (perhaps 10 instead of 15) would have been possible. Using the present pool/CSL, the most probable result would have been even more variance and less sharedness of the concepts and the causal links than in the present case.

The third point is the different methods' usability and their results' validity. This is obviously a complex issue, which depends also on the research type and mapping objectives (Huff 1990). A conclusion of this study is that when the objective is to elicit a detailed and logically coherent representation of the respondents' causal beliefs, the SIM approach performs better. The structured methods are constrained in their ability to elicit concepts and original notions. In addition, PCM seems to have a tendency to produce very dense and incoherent causal maps at individual and even more so at aggregate level. The free drawing method (FDM) seems to elicit plausible causal maps/models as far as it is possible within the preselected concept set. However, if the CCM research requires only comparing the participants in terms of cognitive complexity (Hodgkinson et al. 2004) or clustering them into distinct groups in terms of *a priori* known belief differences, structured approaches such as PCM or FDM can work,assuming they are appropriately prepared.

Furthermore, the comparison study shows that methods such as PCM or FDM, which *separate* the elicitation of concepts and causal links, can be sensitive to the composition of the concept pool (CSL). As discussed above, if the CSL contains concepts at different generality levels and from mutually distant subject spheres, it can lead to selecting concept subsets which do not correspond to any coherent causal mental model but trigger instead a recall of several models and ad hoc creative processes. As argued in Section 3.6, the studied belief systems and the method's operational characteristics, in particular the concept pool's composition, should match. In addition, the respondents should well-, ideally highly motivated to perform the tasks consistently. Ensuring this, however, usually requires *in situ* procedures, perhaps excepting cases where the respondents are very knowledgeable and experienced and understand the importance of the study's goals and its needs of dependability.

However, one could ask why use structured CCM methods which separate the eliciting of cause map nodes and the causal linkages and can thus inadvertently produce less coherent and dubiously representative cause maps? A ground could be an overriding nomothetic interest on structural aspects and distance and complexity measurement instead of emphasizing cause maps' contents. However, as shown here and in the Hodgkinson et al. (2004) study, quantitative measurement can/will be problematic when the underlying database is ambiguous and volatile. Assuming *in situ* acquisition, an obvious alternative is a method such as SIM, which to some extent can combine the advantages of unstructured and structured elicitation: rich and original data and relative efficiency in terms of less redundant data and time needs. However, if *in situ* procedures (or other interactive remote sessions) are not feasible, one might consider and devise approaches which *combine* concept selection and causal link elicitation and encourage thus a more coherent reporting of the causal beliefs. Some conceivable options, which are essentially FDM variants, were outlined in Section 3.1.6.

To conclude, it was recently observed that "there is currently no agreement concerning the most appropriate way to elicit actors' belief systems" (Clarkson 2007, p. 41). This could be taken to imply that such an agreement is possible and a universal CCM approach could eventually exist which is capable of eliciting and comparing several persons' causal beliefs for any conceivable research task. However, in view of the different CCM research contexts, tasks and researcher preferences, which are manifested in published studies, this does not seem likely. To reflect and support the diversity, different CCM methods and approaches are necessary. However, it would be important that more researchers actively develop and test new CCM methods and approaches, in particular those which use the new digital and internet-based technologies which are already available and seem to advance continually.

References

Ambrosini, V. and C. Bowman (2002). Mapping successful organizational routines. In: A.S. Huff and M.D. Jenkins (eds), *Mapping Strategic Knowledge*. Trowbridge, Wiltshire: SAGE Publications Ltd.

Anderson, J.R., D. Bothell, M.D. Byrne, S. Douglass, C. Lebiere and Y. Qin (2004). An integrated theory of the mind. *Psychological Review*. Vol. 111, No. 4, 1036–60.

Armstrong, D.J. (2005). Causal mapping: a discussion and demonstration. In: V.K. Narayanan and D.J. Armstrong (eds), *Causal Mapping for Research in Information Technology*. Hershey, PA: Idea Group, 20–45.

Aronson, E., T.D. Wilson and R.M. Akert (2012). *Social Psychology*. 8th edn. Boston: Pearson Higher.

Audretsch, D.B. and M. Keilbach (2006). Entrepreneurship, growth and restructuring. In: M. Casson, B. Yeung, A. Basu and N. Wadeson (eds.) *The Oxford Handbook of Entrepreneurship*. Oxford: Oxford University Press, 281–310.

Axelrod, R. (ed.) (1976). *Structure of Decision: The Cognitive Maps of Political Elites*. Princeton: Princeton University Press.

Bandura, A. (1986). *Social Foundations of Thought and Action*. Englewood Cliffs, NJ: Prentice-Hall.

Bandura, A. (2001). Social cognitive theory: an agentic perspective. *Annual Review of Psychology*. Vol. 52, 1–26.

Bartunek, J.M., J.R. Gordon and R.P. Weathersby (1983). Developing "complicated" understanding in administrators. *Academy of Management Review*. Vol. 8, No. 2, 273–84.

Bartunek, J.M., S.L. Rynes and R.D. Ireland (2006). What makes management research interesting, and why does it matter? *Academy of Management Journal.* Vol. 49, No. 1, 9–15.

Bazerman, M.H. and D.A Moore (2008). *Judgment in Managerial Decision Making.* 7th edn. Hoboken, NJ: Wiley.

Bennett, R.J. (2014). *Entrepreneurship, Small Business and Public Policy: Evolution and Revolution.* Padstow: Routledge.

Bettis, R.A. and C.K. Prahalad (1995). The dominant logic: retrospective and extension. *Strategic Management Journal.* Vol. 16, 5–14.

Bitonti, C. (1993). Cognitive mapping: a qualitative research method for social work. *Social Work Research & Abstracts.* Vol. 29, No. 1.

Bluhm, D.J., W. Harman, T.W. Lee and T.R. Mitchell (2011). Qualitative research in management: a decade of progress. *Journal of Management Studies.* Vol. 48, No. 8, 1866–91, December.

Bostrom, A., B. Fischoff and M.G. Morgan (1992). Characterizing mental models of hazardous processes: a methodology and an application to radon. *Journal of Social Issues.* Vol. 48, No. 4, 85–100.

Bougon, M.G. (1983). Uncovering cognitive maps: the self-Q technique. In: G. Morgan (ed.), *Beyond Methods.* Beverly Hills, CA: Sage, 173–88.

Bougon, M.G., K.E. Weick and D. Binkhorst (1977). Cognition in organizations: an analysis of the Utrecht Jazz Orchestra. *Administrative Science Quarterly.* Vol. 22, 606–39.

Bougon, M.G., N. Baird, J.M. Komocar and W. Ross (1990). Identifying strategic loops: the self Q interview. In: A. Huff (ed.), *Mapping Strategic Thought.* Chichester: Wiley, 327–54.

Brewer, M.B. (2001). Ingroup identification and intergroup conflict. In: R.D. Ashmore, L.J. Jussim and D. Wilder (eds), *Social Identity, Intergroup Conflict, and Conflict Reduction.* Oxford: Oxford University Press.

Bridge, S., K. O'Neill and S. Cromie (2003). *Understanding Enterprise, Entrepreneurship and Small Business.* New York: Palgrave Macmillan.

Brown, J.S. and P. Duguid (2001). Knowledge and organization: a social-practice perspective. *Organization Science*. Vol. 12, No. 2, 198–213.

Bryson, J.M., F. Ackermann, C. Eden and C.B. Finn (2004). *Visible Thinking: Unlocking Causal Mapping for Practical Business Results*. Chichester: Wiley.

Budhwar, P. (2000). The use of visual card sorting technique to study managers' belief structure. an international comparative study. *Journal of Managerial Psychology*. Vol. 15, No. 5, 440–59.

Budhwar, P.S. and P.R. Sparrow (2002). Strategic HRM through the cultural looking glass: mapping the cognition of British and Indian managers. *Organization Studies*. Vol. 23, No. 4, 599–638.

Buehner, M.J and P.W. Cheng (2005). Causal learning. In: K.J. Holyoak and R.G. Morrison (eds), *The Cambridge Handbook of Thinking and Reasoning*. Cambridge: Cambridge University Press, 143–68.

Byrne, R.M.J. (2002). Mental models and counterfactual thoughts about what might have been. *Trends in Cognitive Sciences*. Vol. 6, No. 10, October, 426–31.

Carbonara, N. and B. Scozzi (2006). Cognitive maps to analyze new product development processes: a case study. *Technovation*. Vol. 26, 1233–43.

Carley, K. (1997). Extracting team mental models through textual analysis. *Journal of Organizational Behavior*. Vol. 18, 533–58.

Carley, K. and M. Palmquist (1992). Extracting, representing and analyzing mental models. *Social Forces*. Vol. 70, No. 3, 601–36.

Cassell, C. and G. Symon (eds) (1994). *Qualitative Methods in Organizational Research*. London: SAGE Publications Ltd.

Chaney, D. (2010). Analyzing mental representations: the contribution of cognitive maps. *Recherche et Applications en Marketing (English Edition)*. Vol. 25, 95–115.

Chell, E. (2004). Critical incident technique. In: C. Cassell and G. Symon (eds), *Essential Guide to Qualitative Methods in Organizational Research*. London: Sage, 45–60.

Chi, M.T.H. and S. Ohlsson (2005). Complex declarative learning. In: K.J. Holyoak and R.G. Morrison (eds), *The Cambridge Handbook of Thinking and Reasoning*. Cambridge: Cambridge University Press, 371–99.

Clarkson, G. (2007). Causal cognitive mapping. In: R. Thorpe and R. Holt (eds), *The SAGE Dictionary of Qualitative Management Research*. London: Sage Publications Ltd, 40–42.

Clarkson, G.P. and G.P. Hodgkinson (2005). Introducing Cognizer™: a comprehensive computer package for the elicitation and analysis of cause maps. *Organizational Research Methods*. Vol. 8, No. 3, 317–41.

Clarkson, G.P. and G.P. Hodgkinson (2006). *Making Sense of Workplace Performance*. London: Advanced Institute of Management Research Publications.

Claxton, G. (1998). Knowing without knowing why. *The Psychologist* (May 1998), 217–20.

Collins, J. and M.T. Hansen (2011). *Great by Choice: Uncertainty, Chaos, and Luck – Why Some Thrive Despite Them All*. New York: Harper Business.

Conover, P.J. and S. Feldman (1984). How people organize the political world: a schematic model. *American Journal of Political Science*. 1984, 95–126.

Corbin, J.M. and A.C. Strauss (2008). *Basics of Qualitative Research: Techniques and Procedures for Developing Grounded Theory*. London: SAGE Publications.

Cossette, P. (2002). Analysing the thinking of F.W. Taylor using cognitive mapping. *Management Decision*. Vol. 40, No. 2, 168–82.

Cressy, R. (2006). Determinants of small firm survival and growth. In: M. Casson, B. Yeung, A. Basu, and N. Wadeson (eds), *The Oxford Handbook of Entrepreneurship*. Oxford: Oxford University Press, 161–93.

Cunningham, Q.W., V.K. Narayanan and M.T. Schultheis (2013). Neuroscience tools in management research: extending organizational research to new questions. Paper, *BAM 2013 Conference*. Liverpool, UK, September.

Deng, X. (1993). *Deng Xiaoping Wenxuan* [Selected Works of Deng Xiaoping]. Beijing: Renmin Chubanshe [The People's Publishing House]. Vol. 3.

Diesner, J. and K.M. Carley (2004). *AutoMap1.2—Extract, Analyze, Represent, and Compare Mental Models from Texts*. CASOS Technical Report, CMU-ISRI-04-100. Carnegie Mellon University, School of Computer Science, January.

Doyle, J.K. and D.N. Ford (1998). Mental models concepts for system dynamics research. *System Dynamics Review*. Vol. 14, No. 1 (Spring), 3–29.

Dueck, C. (2004). New perspectives on American grand strategy: a review essay. *International Security*. Vol. 28, No. 4, 197–216.

Eden, C. (1992). On the nature of cognitive maps. *Journal of Management Studies*. Vol. 29, No. 3, May, 261–5.

Eden, C. and F. Ackermann (1998). Analysing and comparing idiographic causal maps. In: C. Eden and J.-C. Spender (eds), *Managerial and Organizational Cognition: Theory, Methods and Research*. London: SAGE, 193–209.

Eden, C. and F. Ackermann (2004). Cognitive mapping expert views for policy analysis in the public sector. *European Journal of Operational Research*. Vol. 152, 615–30.

Eden, C., F. Ackermann and S. Cropper (1992). The analysis of cause maps. *Journal of Management Studies*. Vol. 29, No. 3, May, 309–24.

Eden, C. and J.-C. Spender (eds) (1998). *Managerial and Organizational Cognition: Theory, Methods and Research*. London: SAGE.

Einhorn, H.J. and R.M. Hogarth (1987). Decision making: going forward in reverse. *Harvard Business Review*. January–February, 66–70.

Eisenhardt, K.M. and M.E. Graebner (2007). Theory building from cases: opportunities and challenges. *Academy of Management Journal*. Vol. 50, No. 1, 25–32.

Ericsson, K.A., N. Charness, P. Feltovich and R. Hoffman (eds) (2006). *Cambridge Handbook on Expertise and Expert Performance*. New York: Cambridge University Press.

Eriksson, P. and A. Kovalainen (2008). *Qualitative Methods in Business Research*. London: Sage.

Evans, J.St.B.T. (1988). The knowledge elicitation problem: a psychological perspective. *Behaviour and Information Technology*. Vol. 7, No. 2, 111–30.

Evers, J.C., K. Mruck, C. Silver and B. Peeters (eds) (2011). The KWALON experiment: discussions on qualitative data analysis software by developers and users. *Forum: Qualitative Social Research*. Vol. 12, No. 1, http://www.qualitativeresearch.net/index.php/fqs/issue/view/36.

Fahey, F. and V.K. Narayanan (1989). Linking changes in revealed causal maps and environmental change: an empirical study, *Journal of Management Studies*. Vol. 26, No. 4, 361–78.

Feng, H. (2007). *Chinese Strategic Culture and Foreign Policy Decision-making: Confucianism, Leadership and War*. London: Routledge.

Fiske, S. and S.E. Taylor (2013). *Social Cognition: From Brains to Culture*. 2nd ed. London: SAGE Publications.

Ford, J.D. and W.H. Hegarty (1984). Decision makers' beliefs about the causes and effects of structure: an exploratory study. *Academy of Management Journal*. Vol. 27, No. 2, 271–91.

Forrester, J.W. (1971/1995). Counterintuitive behavior of social systems. *Technology Review*. Vol. 73, No. 3, January 1971, 52–68. (Updated 1995 version at: http://clexchange. org/ftp/documents/system-dynamics/SD1993-01CounterintuitiveBe.pdf).

Frederiksen, C.H. (2004). Propositional representations in psychology. In: N.J. Smelser and P.B. Bates (eds), *International Encyclopedia of the Social and Behavioral Sciences*. Oxford: Elsevier, 12219–24.

Friedberg, A.L. (2005). The future of US-China relations: is conflict inevitable? *International Security*. Vol. 30, No. 2, 7–45.

Gadenne, V. (2001). Causation (theories and models): conceptions in the social sciences. In: N.J. Smelser and P.B. Bates (eds), *International Encyclopedia of the Social and Behavioral Sciences*. Oxford: Elsevier, 1561–7.

Gallistel, C.R. (2002). Psychology of mental representations. In: N.J. Smelser and P.B. Bates (eds), *International Encyclopedia of the Social and Behavioral Sciences*. Oxford: Elsevier, 9691–5.

Gavetti, G. and J.W. Rivkin (2005). How strategists really think: tapping the power of analogy. *Harvard Business Review*. April, 54–63.

Gelman, S.A. and C.H. Legare (2011). Concepts and folk theories. *Annual Review of Anthropology*. Vol. 40, 379–98.

Gentner, D. (2004). The psychology of mental models. In: N.J. Smelser and P.B. Bates (eds), *International Encyclopedia of the Social and Behavioral Sciences*. Oxford: Elsevier, 9683–7.

George, A.L. (1969). The "operational code": a neglected approach to the study of political leaders and decision-making. *International Studies Quarterly*. Vol. 13, No. 2, 190–222.

Ghyczy, T.V. (2003). The fruitful flaws of strategy metaphors. *Harvard Business Review*. September, 86–94.

Gioia, D.A., K.G. Corley and A.L. Hamilton (2013). Seeking qualitative rigor in inductive research: notes on the Gioia methodology. *Organizational Research Methods*. Vol. 16, No. 1, 15–31.

Goldstein, A. (2005). *Rising to the Challenge: China's Grand Strategy and International Security*. Stanford: Stanford University Press.

Goldstein, E.B. (2011). *Cognitive Psychology*. 3rd edn. Independence, KY: Wadsworth Cengage Learning.

Good, B.J. (2001). Anthropology of belief. In: N.J. Smelser and P.B. Bates (eds), *International Encyclopedia of the Social and Behavioral Sciences*. Oxford: Elsevier, 1137–41.

Gordon, S.E. (1992). Implications of cognitive theory for knowledge acquisition. In: R.R Hoffman (ed.), *The Psychology of Expertise: Cognitive Research and Empirical AI*. New York: Springer.

Gruber, H. (2004). Acquisition of expertise. In: N.J. Smelser and P.B. Bates (eds), *International Encyclopedia of the Social and Behavioral Sciences*. Oxford: Elsevier, 5145–50.

Haas, P.M. (2001). Policy knowledge: epistemic communities. In: N.J. Smelser and P.B. Bates (eds), *International Encyclopedia of the Social and Behavioral Sciences*. Oxford: Elsevier, 11578–86.

Hall, R.I. (1976). A system pathology of an organization: the rise and fall of the old *Saturday Evening Post*. *Administrative Science Quarterly*. Vol. 21, 185–211.

Hall, R.I. (1984). The natural logic of management policy making: its implications for the survival of an organization. *Management Science*. Vol. 30, No. 8, August.

Hebert, R.F. and A.N. Link (2006). Historical perspectives on the entrepreneur. *Foundations and Trends in Entrepreneurship*. Vol. 2, No. 4, 261–408.

Hine, D.W., C.J. Montiel, R.W. Cooksey and J.H. Lewko (2005). Mental models of poverty in developing nations: a causal mapping analysis using a Canada-Philippines contrast. *Journal of Cross-Cultural Psychology*. Vol. 36, No. 3, 283–303.

Hirschfeld, L.A. and S.A. Gelman (eds) (1994). *Mapping the Mind: Domain Specificity in Cognition and culture*. New York: Cambridge University Press.

Ho, M.W.Y. (2005). *Employment System Mental Models in Organisation Building: Founder's Mental Models of Employment in New Zealand Biotechnology Start-ups*. Auckland: University of Auckland, New Zealand.

Hodgkinson, G.P. and G.P. Clarkson (2005). What have we learned from almost 30 years of research on causal mapping? In: V.K. Narayanan and D.J. Armstrong (eds), *Causal Mapping for Research in Information Technology*. Hershey, PA: Idea Group Publishing, 46–79.

Hodgkinson, G.P., A.J. Maule and N.J. Bown (2004). Causal cognitive mapping in the organizational strategy field: a comparison of alternative elicitation procedures. *Organizational Research Methods*. Vol. 7, No. 1, 3–26.

Hodgkinson, G.P., E. Sadler-Smith, L.A. Burke, G. Claxton and P.R. Sparrow (2009). Intuition in organizations: implications for strategic management. *Long Range Planning*. Vol. 42, 277–97.

Hodgkinson, G.P and M.P. Healey (2008). Cognition in organizations. *Annual Review of Psychology*. Vol. 59, 387–417.

Hoffmann, A.N. (2007). A rough guide to entrepreneurship policy. In: D.B. Audretsch, I. Grilo and A.R. Thurik (eds), *Handbook of Research on Entrepreneurship Policy*. Cheltenham: Edward Elgar, 140–71.

Hoffman, R.R. and G. Lintern (2006). Eliciting and representing the knowledge of experts. In: K.A. Ericsson, N. Charness, P. Feltovich and R. Hoffman (eds), *Cambridge Handbook on Expertise and Expert Performance*. New York: Cambridge University Press, 203–22.

Holsti, O. (1976). Foreign policy formation viewed cognitively. In: R. Axelrod (ed.), *Structure of Decision: The Cognitive Maps of Political Elites*. Princeton: Princeton University Press, 18–54.

Huff, A.S. (1990). Mapping strategic thought. In: A.S. Huff (ed.), *Mapping Strategic Thought*. New York: John Wiley, 11–49.

Huff, A.S. and K.E. Fletcher (1990). Conclusion: key mapping decisions. In: A.S. Huff (ed.), *Mapping Strategic Thought*. New York: John Wiley, 403–12.

Huff, A.S. and M. Jenkins (eds) (2002). *Mapping Strategic Knowledge*. Trowbridge, Wiltshire: SAGE Publications Ltd.

Huntington, S.P. (2002). *The Clash of Civilizations and the Remaking of World Order*. Reading, Berkshire: Simon & Schuster.

Hutchins, E. (2001). Distributed cognition. In: N.J. Smelser and P.B. Bates (eds), *International Encyclopedia of the Social and Behavioral Sciences*. Oxford: Elsevier, 2068–72.

Inglehart, R. and C. Welzel (2005). *Modernization, Cultural Change, and Democracy: the Human Development Sequence*. Cambridge: Cambridge University Press.

Johnson-Laird, P.N. (1983). *Mental Models*. Cambridge: Cambridge University Press.

Johnson-Laird, P.N. (2004a). Reasoning with mental models. In: N.J. Smelser and P.B. Bates (eds), *International Encyclopedia of the Social and Behavioral Sciences*. Oxford: Elsevier, 12821–4.

Johnson-Laird, P.N. (2004b). The history of mental models. In: K. Manktelow and M. Chung (eds), *Psychology of Reasoning: Theoretical and Historical Perspectives*. Hove, East Sussex: Psychology Press, 179–212.

Johnson-Laird, P.N. (2005). Mental models and thought. In: K.J. Holyoak and R.G. Morrison (eds), *The Cambridge Handbook of Thinking and Reasoning*. Cambridge: Cambridge University Press, 185–208.

Johnson-Laird, P.N. (2008). *How We Reason*. Oxford: Oxford University Press.

Johnston, A.I. (1998). *Cultural Realism: Strategic Culture and Grand Strategy in Chinese History*. Princeton: Princeton University Press.

Jones, N.A., H. Ross, T. Lynam, P. Perez, and A. Leitch (2011). Mental models: an interdisciplinary synthesis of theory and methods. *Ecology and Society*. Vol. 16, No. 1, 46. http://www.ecologyandsociety.org/vol16/iss1/art46/ (Accessed November 28, 2013).

Kahneman, D. (2011). *Thinking, Fast and Slow*. London: Penguin Books.

Kearney, A.R. and S. Kaplan (1997). Toward a methodology for the measurement of knowledge structures of ordinary people. *Environment and Behavior*. Vol. 29, No. 5, 579–617.

Khong, Y.F. (1992). *Analogies at War: Korea, Munich, Dien Bien Phu, and the Vietnam Decisions of 1965*. Princeton: Princeton University Press.

Kitchin, R. (2001). Cognitive maps. In: N.J. Smelser and P.B. Bates (eds), *International Encyclopedia of the Social and Behavioral Sciences*. Oxford: Elsevier, 2120–24.

Klein, G. and R.R. Hoffman (2008). Macrocognition, mental models, and cognitive task analysis methodology. In: J.M. Schraagen, L.G. Militello, T. Ormerod and R. Lipshitz (eds), *Naturalistic Decision Making and Macrocognition*. Aldershot, UK: Ashgate Publishing Ltd, 57–80.

Krippendorff, K. (2004). *Content Analysis: An Introduction to its Methodology*. 2nd edn. London: SAGE.

Langan-Fox, J., S. Code and K. Langfield-Smith (2000). Team mental models: techniques, methods, and analytic approaches. *Human Factors.* Vol. 42, 242–71.

Langan-Fox, J., J. Anglim and J.R. Wilson (2004). Mental models, team mental models, and performance: process, development, and future directions. *Human Factors and Ergonomics in Manufacturing.* Vol. 14, No. 4, 331–52.

Langfield-Smith, K. (1992). Exploring the need for a shared cognitive map. *Journal of Management Studies.* Vol. 29, No. 3, 349–68.

Larson, D.W. (1994). The role of belief systems and schemas in foreign policy decision-making. *Political Psychology.* 17–33.

Laukkanen, M. (1990). Describing management cognition: the cause mapping approach. *Scandinavian Journal of Management.* Vol. 6, No. 3, 197–216.

Laukkanen, M. (1992). Comparative cause mapping of management cognitions. *A Computer Database Method for Natural Data.* Helsinki School of Economics and Business Administration, Publications D-154, Helsinki.

Laukkanen, M. (1994). Comparative cause mapping of organizational cognitions. *Organization Science, Special Issue on Managerial and Organizational Cognition.* Vol. 5, No. 3, 322–43.

Laukkanen, M. (1996). Comparative cause mapping of organizational cognitions. In: J.R. Meindl, C. Stubbart and J.F. Porac (eds), *Cognition Within and Between Organisations.* London: SAGE.

Laukkanen, M. (1997). Towards understanding the impact of management cognitions: the case of SME winners and losers. Paper, *5th International Workshop on Managerial and Organizational Cognition,* Facultés Universitaires Notre-Dame de la Paix, Namur, Belgium, September 3–5.

Laukkanen, M. (1998). Conducting cause mapping research: opportunities and challenges. In: C. Eden and J.-C. Spender (eds), *Managerial and Organizational Cognition: Theory, Methods and Research.* Thousand Oaks, CA: SAGE, 168–89.

Laukkanen, M. (2000). Cognitive maps of entrepreneurship: describing policy makers' subjective models of local development. Paper presented at: *ICSB World Conference 2000,* Brisbane, Australia, June 7–10.

Laukkanen, M. (2001a). Maintaining the cognitive grip: managing and learning in a crisis. In: B. Hellgren and J. Löwstedt (eds), *Management in the Thought-full Enterprise: A Socio-cognitive Approach to the Organization of Human Resources.* Oslo-Bergen: Fagbogforlaget.

Laukkanen, M. (2001b). How does a rural community work? Unveiling social systems by comparative cause mapping. Paper: *8th Workshop on Management and Organization Cognition,* EIASM—ESCP-EAP Paris, France, May 30–June 1.

Laukkanen, M. (2003). Exploring academic entrepreneurship: drivers and tensions of university-based business. *Journal of Small Business and Entrepreneurship Development.* Vol. 10, No. 4.

Laukkanen, M. (2008). *Comparative Causal Mapping with CMAP3: A Method Introduction to Comparative Causal Mapping and a User's Manual for CMAP3.* Kuopio, Finland: University of Kuopio.

Laukkanen, M. (2012). Comparative causal mapping and CMAP3 software in qualitative studies. *Forum: Qualitative Social Research.* Vol. 13, No. 2, Art. 13. Available at: http://nbn-resolving.de/urn:nbn:de:0114-fqs1202133 (accessed June 26, 2012).

Laukkanen, M. and H. Niittykangas (2010). Fostering entrepreneurship and sound small business? Exploring start-up-advisors' mindsets. Paper, *BAM Conference 2010,* Sheffield, UK.

Laukkanen, M. and P. Eriksson (2013). New designs and software for cognitive causal mapping. *Qualitative Research in Organizations and Management.* Vol. 8, No. 2.

Layne, C. (1997). From preponderance to offshore balancing: America's future grand strategy. *International Security.* Vol. 22, No. 1, 86–124.

LeBoeuf, R.A. and E.B. Shafir (2005). Decision making. In: K. Holyoak and B. Morrison (eds), *The Cambridge Handbook of Thinking and Reasoning.* Cambridge: Cambridge University Press, 243–65.

Leslie, A.M. (2001). Theory of mind. In: N.J. Smelser and P.B. Bates (eds), *International Encyclopedia of the Social and Behavioral Sciences.* Oxford: Elsevier, 15652–6.

Levi, A. and P. Tetlock (1980). A cognitive analysis of Japan's 1941 decision for war. *Journal of Conflict Resolution.* Vol. 24, No. 2, 195–211.

Levins, A. and C. Silver (2007). *Using Software in Qualitative Research: A Step-by-Step Guide.* London: SAGE Publications.

Linstone, H.A. and M. Turoff (eds) (2002). *The Delphi Method: Techniques and Applications.* Newark, NJ: Information Systems Department, New Jersey Institute of Technology. (Available at: http://is.njit.edu/pubs/delphibook/index.html).

Lundström, A. and L.A. Stevenson (2005). *Entrepreneurship Policy: Theory and Practice.* New York: Springer.

Maoz, Z. and A. Shayer (1987). The cognitive structure of peace and war argumentation: Israeli prime ministers versus the Knesset. *Political Psychology.* Vol. 8, No. 4, 575–604.

March, J. and H. Simon (1958). *Organizations.* New York: Wiley.

Marfleet, B.G. (2000). The operational code of John F. Kennedy during the Cuban Missile Crisis: a comparison of public and private rhetoric. *Political Psychology.* Vol. 21, No. 3, 545–58.

Markman, A.B. and E. Dietrich (2000). Extending the classical view of representation. *Trends in Cognitive Sciences.* Vol. 4, No. 12, 470–75.

Markman, A.B. and D. Gentner (2001). Thinking. *Annual Review of Psychology.* Vol. 52, 223–47.

Markóczy, L. and J. Goldberg (1995). A method for eliciting and comparing causal maps. *Journal of Management.* Vol. 21, 305–33.

Maxwell, J.A. (2004a). Using qualitative methods for causal explanation. *Field Methods.* Vol. 16, No. 3, 243–64.

Maxwell, J.A. (2004b). Causal explanation, qualitative research, and scientific inquiry in education. *Educational Researcher.* March, Vol. 33, No. 2, 3–11.

Maxwell, J.A (2010). Using numbers in qualitative research. *Qualitative Inquiry.* Vol. 16, No. 6, 475–82.

Maxwell, J.A. (2012). *Qualitative Research Design: An Interactive Approach*. 3rd edn. Thousand Oaks, CA: Sage Publications.

McDonald, S. (2005). Studying actions in context: a qualitative shadowing method for organizational research. *Qualitative Research*. Vol. 5, 455–73.

McDonald, S. and B. Simpson (2014). Shadowing research in organizations: the methodological debates. *Qualitative Research in Organizations and Management: An International Journal*. Vol. 9, No. 1.

McNamara, G., R.A. Luce and G.H. Thompson (2002). Examining the effect of complexity in strategic group knowledge structures on firm performance. *Strategic Management Journal*. Vol. 23, 153–70.

Meindl, J.R., C. Stubbart and J.F. Porac (eds) (1996). *Cognition Within and Between Organisations*. London: SAGE.

Merriam, S.B. (2009). *Qualitative Research: A Guide to Design and Implementation*. San Francisco, CA: Jossey-Bass.

Miller, G.A. (2003). The cognitive revolution: a historical perspective. *Trends in Cognitive Sciences*. Vol. 7, No. 3, March.

Mohammed, S., R. Klimoski and J.R. Rentsch (2000). The measurement of team mental models: we have no shared schema. *Organizational Research Methods*. Vol. 3, No. 2, 123–65.

Montemari, M. and C. Nielsen (2013). The role of causal maps in intellectual capital measurement and management. *Journal of Intellectual Capital*. Vol. 14, No. 4, 522–46.

Mooi, E. and M. Sarstedt (2011). *A Concise Guide to Market Research*. Berlin: Springer-Verlag.

Morgan, M.G., B. Fischhoff, A. Bostrom and C.J. Altman (2001). *Risk Communication: A Mental Models Approach*. Cambridge: Cambridge University Press.

Morin, C. (2011). Neuromarketing: the new science of consumer behavior. *Society*. Vol. 48, No. 2, 131–5.

Nadkarni, S. and V.K. Narayanan (2005). Validity of the structural properties of text-based causal maps: an empirical assessment. *Organizational Research Methods*. Vol. 8, No. 9, 9–40.

Nadkarni, S. and V.K. Narayanan (2007). Strategic schemas, strategic flexibility, and firm performance: the moderating role of industry clockspeed. *Strategic Management Journal*. Vol. 28, No. 3, 243–70.

Narayanan, V.K. (2005). Causal mapping: an historical overview. In: V.K. Narayanan and D.J. Armstrong (eds), *Causal Mapping for Research in Information Technology*. Hershey, PA: Idea Group, 1–19.

Narayanan, V.K. and D.J. Armstrong (eds) (2005). *Causal Mapping for Research in Information Technology*. Hershey, PA: Idea Group Publishing.

Nelson, K.M., S. Nadkarni, V.K. Narayanan and M. Ghods (2000). Understanding software operations support expertise: a revealed causal mapping approach. *MIS Quarterly*. Vol. 24, No. 3, 475–507.

Nicolini, D. (1999). Comparing methods for mapping organizational cognition. *Organization Studies*. Vol. 20, No. 5, 833–60.

Nystrom, P.C. and W.H. Starbuck (1984). Managing beliefs in organizations. *The Journal of Applied Behavioral Science*. Vol. 20, No. 3, 277–87.

Pick, H.L., Jr. (2001). Psychology of mental maps. In: N.J. Smelser and P.B. Bates (eds), *International Encyclopedia of the Social and Behavioral Sciences*. Oxford: Elsevier, 9681–3.

Pinker, S. (1997). *How the Mind Works*. New York: W.W. Norton & Co.

Pinker, S. (2008). *The Stuff of Thought: Language as Window into Human Nature*. New York: Penguin Books.

Porac, J., H. Thomas and C. Baden-Fuller (1989). Competitive groups as cognitive communities: the case of Scottish knitwear manufacturers. *Journal of Management Studies*. Vol. 26, 397–416.

Porac, J.F., Y. Mishina and T.G. Pollock (2002). Entrepreneurial narratives and the dominant logics of high-growth firms. In: A.S. Huff and M. Jenkins (eds), *Mapping Strategic Knowledge*. Trowbridge, Wiltshire: SAGE Publications Ltd, 112–36.

Prahalad, C.K. and R.A. Bettis (1986). The dominant logic: a new linkage between diversity and performance. *Strategic Management Journal*. Vol. 7, 485–501.

Priem, R.L. and J. Rosenstein (2000). Is organization theory obvious to practitioners? A test of one established theory. *Organization Science*. Vol. 11, No. 5, 509–24.

Prietula, M.J. and H.A. Simon (1989). The experts in your midst. *Harvard Business Review*. January–February, 120–24.

Renshon, J. (2008). Stability and change in belief systems the operational code of George W. Bush. *Journal of Conflict Resolution*. Vol. 52, No. 6, 820–49.

Renshon, J. (2009). When public statements reveal private beliefs: assessing operational codes at a distance. *Political Psychology*. Vol. 30, No. 4, 649–61.

Roberts, F.S. (1976). Strategy for the energy crisis: the case of commuter transportation policy. In: R. Axelrod (ed.), *Structure of Decision: The Cognitive Maps of Political Elites*. Princeton, NJ: Princeton University Press, 142–79.

Rouse, W.B. and N.M. Morris (1986). On looking into the black box: prospects and limits in the search for mental models. *Psychological Bulletin*. Vol. 100, No. 3, 349–63.

Sandelowski, M. (2001). Real qualitative researchers do not count: the use of numbers in qualitative research. *Research in Nursing & Health*. Vol. 24, 230–40.

Schafer, M. and S. Crichlow (2000). Bill Clinton's operational code: assessing source material bias. *Political Psychology*. Vol. 21, No. 3, 559–71.

Schafer, M. and S.G. Walker (eds) (2006). *Beliefs and Leadership in World Politics: Methods and Applications of Operational Code Analysis*. Basingstoke: Palgrave Macmillan.

Seale, C. and D. Silverman (1997). Ensuring rigour in qualitative research. *European Journal of Public Health*. Vol. 7, 379–84.

Shane, S.D. (2009). Why encouraging more people to become entrepreneurs is bad public policy. *Small Business Economics*. Vol. 33, No. 2, 141–9.

Sheetz, S.D., D.P. Tegarden, K.A. Kozar and I. Zigurs (1993). *A Group Support Systems Approach to Cognitive Mapping*. Denver: University of Colorado, Graduate School of Business Administration (http://www.acis.pamplin. vt.edu/faculty/tegarden/wrk-pap/JMIS-1.PDF).

Silverman, D. (2006). *Interpreting Qualitative Data: Methods for Analysing Talk, Text and Interaction*. London: Sage.

Simon, H.A. (1987). Making management decisions: the role of intuition and emotion. *Academy of Management Executive*. February, 57–64.

Simon, H.A. (2001). Psychology of problem solving and reasoning. In: N.J. Smelser and P.B. Bates (eds), *International Encyclopedia of the Social and Behavioral Sciences*. Oxford: Elsevier, 12120–23.

Sims, H.P., Jr. and D.A. Gioia (eds) (1986). *The Thinking Organization*. San Francisco, CA: Jossey-Bass.

Sloman, S.A. and Y. Hagmayer (2006). The causal psycho-logic of choice. *Trends in Cognitive Sciences*. Vol. 10, No. 9, 407–12.

Spender, J.-C. (1998). The dynamics of individual and organizational knowledge. In: C. Eden and J.-C. Spender (eds), *Managerial and Organizational Cognition: Theory, Methods and Research*. Thousand Oaks, CA: SAGE, 13–39.

Starbuck, W.H., A. Greve and B.L.T. Hedberg (1978). Responding to crisis. *Journal of Business Administration*. Vol. 9, 111–37.

Stein, J.G. (2013). Threat perception in international relations. In: L. Huddy, D. Sears and J. Levy (eds), *The Oxford Handbook of Political Psychology*. 2nd edn. Oxford: Oxford University Press.

Sternberg, R.J. and K. Sternberg (2012). *Cognition*. 6th intl. edn. Independence, KY: Wadsworth Publishing.

Stone, R. and M. Young (2009). The content and intersection of identity in Iraq. In: R. Abdelal, Y.M. Herrera, A.I. Johnston and R. McDermott (eds), *Measuring Identity: A Guide for Social Scientists*. Cambridge: Cambridge University Press.

Storey, D.J. (1994). *Understanding the Small Business Sector*. London: Routledge.

Storey, D.J. (2006). Evaluating SM policies and programmes. In: M. Casson, B. Yeung, A. Basu and N. Wadeson (eds), *The Oxford Handbook of Entrepreneurship*. Oxford: Oxford University Press, 248–78.

Swaine, M.D. and A.J. Tellis (2000). *Interpreting China's Grand Strategy: Past, Present, and Future*. New York: Rand Corporation.

Tetlock, P.E. (2001). Counterfactual reasoning: public policy aspects. In: N.J. Smelser and P.B. Bates (eds), *International Encyclopedia of the Social and Behavioral Sciences*. Oxford: Elsevier Publishers, 2864–9.

Tetlock, P.E. (2005). *Expert Political Judgment: How Good Is It? How Can We Know?* Princeton: Princeton University Press.

Thompson, M. (2005). Structural and epistemic parameters in communities of practice. *Organization Science*. Vol. 16, No. 2, 151–64.

Tolman, E.C. (1948). Cognitive maps in rats and men. *The Psychological Review*. Vol. 55, No. 4, July, 189–208.

Tyler, B.B. and D.R. Gnyawali (2009). Managerial collective cognitions: an examination of similarities and differences of cultural orientations. *Journal of Management Studies*. Vol. 46, No. 1, 93–126.

Vári, A. (2004). *The Mental Models Approach to Risk Research—An RWM Perspective*. Nuclear Energy Agency, OECD, NEA/RWM/FSC(2003)7/REV1.

Walker, S.G., M. Schafer and M.D. Young (1998). Systematic procedures for operational code analysis: measuring and modeling Jimmy Carter's operational code. *International Studies Quarterly*. Vol. 42, No. 1, 175–89.

Walker, S.G. and M. Schafer (2000). The political universe of Lyndon B. Johnson and his advisors: diagnostic and strategic propensities in their operational codes. *Political Psychology*. Vol. 21, No. 3, 529–43.

Walsh, J.P. (1995). Managerial and organizational cognition: notes from a trip down memory lane. *Organization Science*. Vol. 6, No. 3, 280–321.

Wassink, H., P. Sleegers and J. Imants (2003). Cause maps and school leaders' tacit knowledge. *Journal of Educational Administration*. Vol. 41, No. 5, 524–46.

Weick, K.E. (1969/1979). *The Social Psychology of Organizing*. 1st/2nd edn. Reading, MA: Addison-Wesley.

Weick, K.E. and M.G. Bougon (1986). Organizations as cognitive maps. In: H.P. Sims, Jr. and D.A. Gioia (eds), *The Thinking Organization*. San Francisco, CA: Jossey-Bass, 102–35.

Wendt, A. (1999). *Social Theory of International Politics*. Cambridge: Cambridge University Press.

Wenger, E. (2001). Communities of practice. In: N.J. Smelser and P.B. Bates (eds), *International Encyclopedia of the Social and Behavioral Sciences*. Oxford: Elsevier, 2339–42.

Wenger, E.C. and W.M. Snyder (2000). Communities of practice: the organizational frontier. *Harvard Business Review*. January–February, 139–45.

Wiginton, K.L. (1997). Cognitive mapping: its use as an assessment tool for client education. *Journal of American College Health*. Vol. 45, No. 4.

Wrightson, M.T. (1976). The documentary coding method. In: R. Axelrod (ed.), *Structure of Decision: The Cognitive Maps of Political Elites*. Princeton, NJ: Princeton University Press, 291–332.

Wu, G. (1995). 'Documentary politics': hypotheses, process, and case studies. In: S. Zhao (ed.), *Decision-making in Deng's China*. New York: ME Sharpe, 23–38.

Yan, J. (1995). The nature of Chinese Authoritarianism. In: S. Zhao (ed.), *Decision-making in Deng's China: Perspectives from Insiders*. New York: ME Sharpe.

Young, M.D. (1996). Cognitive mapping meets semantic networks. *The Journal of Conflict Resolution*. Vol. 40, No. 3 (September), 395–414.

Young, M.D. and M. Schafer (1998). Is there method in our madness? Ways of assessing cognition in international relations. *Mershon International Studies Review*. Vol. 42, No. 1, 63–96.

Zhao, S. (2004). *A Nation-state by Construction: Dynamics of Modern Chinese Nationalism*. Stanford: Stanford University Press.

Zheng, B. (2006). *China's Peaceful Rise: Speeches of Zheng Bijian, 1997–2005*. Washington, DC: Brookings Institution Press.

Zheng, Y. (1999). *Discovering Chinese Nationalism in China: Modernization, Identity, and International Relations*. Cambridge: Cambridge University Press.

Index

accuracy *see* validity/validation
Ackermann, F. 1, 7, 80
adjacency (square) matrix 6, 48, 81, 83
aggregation/aggregated causal map
  (ACM) 4, 9, 27, 34, 48ff, 66ff, 72,
  75, 78, 82, 91, 182ff
anchor theme/topic
  interview notes sheet (INS) 54
  number of 51
  in SIM interviews 49–54
argumentation structure 159, 162, 171
artificial intelligence (AI) 29
attribution 19–20, 58, 158–9
audit trail in CCM 100
Auto increment command 112
AutoMap 57
automated causal mapping 57
availability bias 20
Axelrod, R. 1, 6, 8, 14, 39, 41, 44, 72,
  80ff, 157–8, 164

Backup/Duplicate command 132
Bandura, A. 20
belief patterns
  aggregation, comparison 8, 40
  capturing 71–2
  evaluation of validity 77–9
  unification 23
  what if analysis 76
beliefs/knowledge, *see* knowledge/
  beliefs
belief system xvii, 4, 8, 13–15, 19,
  22–8, 34–8, 41, 44, 83–8, 91–5,

  142, 145, 149, 151, 158, 160–62,
  169, 171–3, 182, 207, 208
Bennett, R.J. 174, 184
Bougon, M.G. 1, 6, 14, 42, 45, 95, 84

Carley, K. 14, 23, 26, 57
Cassell, C. 80, 89
causal knowledge/beliefs/ideas, *see*
  knowledge/beliefs
causal/cause map
  aggregation 4, 66, 182
  cognitions as target phenomena 3
  coherence 93
  complexity 84
  comprehensiveness 84
  database format 6
  definitions 2
  differentiation 84
  evaluation of validity 77–9
  format criteria 7
  indicators/measures 80, 148ff
  matrix format 6
  modellability 93
  nodes/arrows 2
  pictorial/visual format 2
  systems as target phenomena 3
  text form 5
  terminological issues 14
  visual vs. non-visual formats 4
  vs. cognitive map 14
causal/cognitive mapping, *see*
  comparative causal mapping
  (CCM)

causal propositions 6, 18, 33, 38, 53,
      55, 57
causal reasoning
   factors in 20
   processes 19
   with mental models 14
causal relation/link type
   direct/inverse, entry of 108
   weight value, entry of 109
causality
   controversiality 21
   in different languages 164
   eliciting causal ideas 94
   as everyday premise 21
   in mental models 18
   regularity vs. process
      interpretation 21
   visual reprentation 155
C/D index
   analysis, interpretation 150
   calculation in *CMAP3* 81, 150
   in cluster analysis 152
   correspondence/distance indicator
      81
centrality
   of causal maps 82
   of concepts/nodes 82
Clarkson, G.P. 14, 26, 45ff, 48, 65, 80,
      87, 93ff, 188, 208
clusters
   comparison/distance 85
   of concepts/nodes 169
   displaying 139ff
   hierarchical cluster analysis 85–6
   predefining in *CMAP3* projects
      105, 115
   in Statistics module 147, 150ff
CMAP3
   acronyms/conventions 108–9

CCM indicators/measures 148
C/D Index matrix 150
CMAP2 xii
   downloading URL xii
   installing 102
   origins xi
   overview 99
   printing data 101–2, 113, 127, 151
   Project Log, editing of 104
   Run as Administrator 102
   Statistics & C/D Index module
      147, 151
   Windows compatibility 102
CMAP3 project
   backup/duplicate 106
   database, compacting 104
   parallel *CMAP3* projects 87, 101,
      106, 132, 151
   removing, deleting 106
   setting up/defining 103
CmapTools
   downloading URL 153
   using with *CMAP3* 101–2, 118 ,
      141–4, 146, 152–4, 166, 169, 182,
      183
coding/standardizing
   assessing, *see* validation
   basic logic of 59, 65
   coding scheme (STV) 59, 100, 132
   collapsing/compression effect
      63–4, 176
   commonality effect 63–4, 176
   consistency 132
   data compression effect 60
   ex post coding 70
   example, SBA study case 176
   in inductive STV construction 127
   inductive vs. deductive 63
   iterative process 65, 110, 125

levels of coding/standardizing 62,
  127
misconceptions about 65
in raw data entry 109, 100
standard term vocabulary(STV)
  59, 100, 132
standardized/output data,
  generating 132
subjectivity in 65
tasks/objectives of 59
tentative/provisional coding/
  standardizing 125
cognitions
  biases 20, 24, 39, 44, 158
  cognitive grip 27
  cognitive "misers" 24
  contextual factors in 33
  idiosyncratic vs. shared 4
cognitive complexity 17, 26–7, 44,
  84–6, 88, 90, 158–9, 207
  vs. cognitive grip 27
cognitive control
  sense of security 22
cognitive data
  retrieval vs. *ad hoc* generation 33
cognitive factors/processes 11, 16, 19,
  29–30, 31, 37, 52, 201
  methodological implications 17
cognitive grip 12, 27–8
cognitive map/ping, *see* comparative
  causal mapping
  in cognitive psychology 13
  in cognitive studies xxii, 1, 39, 87,
    93, 159
  as a map of cognitions 14
  metaphorical meaning 35
  spatial interpretation 13
  terminological alternatives 35
  terminological issues 3, 13–14

as a visualizing tool 14
  vs. mental models 14, 29
cognitive style
  "foxes" vs. "hedgehogs" 26
collective belief 40, 66, 83–5, 159, 173
community
  community of practice 17, 23, 72
  epistemic community 23
comparative causal mapping (CCM)
  advantages/objectives 4, 7
  comparison for aggregation 66
  comparison of methods 185
  decision support 7
  document-based causal mapping
    (DBCM) 157–60, 164, 173
  method approaches/alternatives
    37ff
  method selection criteria 89
  methodological constraints 31
  origins 1
  research applications 1
  research interests in 30
  shortcut techniques 55
  study cases 157ff
  substitutability of 196
  systemic/holistic description 7
  technical method, platform 96
  understanding result differences
    199
  visual cause map findings 196
composite causal map/mapping 41,
  62–3, 67, 101, 104, 123, 151, 157,
  162, 165–6, 168–9, 173
computerizing
  CAQDAS software 9, 63, 97
  in CCM 96
  in coding/standardization 65
  Cognizer 48, 97
  office applications in CCM 96

using *CMAP3* 99ff
concept development 61
concept/idea mapping 5, 96
concept pool/method, *see* structured
    CCM methods
concept selection list (CSL)
    creating, importing in structured
        CCM 120
    in the PCM/FDM comparison
        study 189
confirmability 69
confirmation bias 20
CORE TF
    defining for SNT/SCU generation
        134–5
    in SBA study 192
    in Statistics 148
counterfactual thinking 8, 16, 39
    see also What if analysis
critical incident analysis 38
CUT-W
    use in SCU generation 135
CXL file format
    Domain Map export 146
    Focal Map export 144
    SCU export to *CmapTools* 141

data in CCM
    accuracy 75
    authenticity 72
    dependability 34
    dimensions of data quality 72
    factual correctness 75
    methodological issues 35
    primary data, elicitation of 33
    sincerity 72
    subjective factors in elicitation 34
    trustworthiness 34
    validity, reliability 34

data acquisition in CCM
    alternative methods 37ff
    cognitive processes in 17, 29ff,
        201
    contextual factors in elicitation 34
    data quality 69ff
    main strategies 31
    "overproduction" 34, 74
    recognition vs. recall processes
        200
    shortcut methods 55
data entry in *CMAP3*
    conventions in data import 110
    data import 116ff
    erasing of 116
    keyboard entry of raw data/RDS
        111
    preparing raw data for entry 107
    Raw Data Sheet (RDS) 107
DBCM 157–60, 164, 173
Deng Xiaoping 157–8, 160–61
decision-making 8, 15, 22, 28, 34, 39,
        82, 158ff, 204
Delphi method in CCM 56
density
    indicators of 80
    Statistics module 148
dependability
    assessing in SBA study 181
    criteria in CCM studies 70
    preconditions of, in CCM 71
    qualitative criteria/definition 69
    see also validity, reliability
digraph theory 6
direct /indirect methods
    in MOC studies 38
    in cognitive psychology 29
discourse
    analysis 173

as CCM data 33
in everyday communication 7, 31, 60
distance/similarity indicators in CCM
C/D index 80
distance ratio 84
documentary data
in CCM studies 39ff
in international relations (IR) studies 158
processing, analysis in CCM 41
pros/cons in CCM studies 39
representativeness, comparability issues 40
Domain Map (DM)
Domain Map Browser 145
exporting to *CmapTools* 146
types of, creation 145
visual form/display 146
drawing causal maps, *see* visual/ graphic causal maps

Eden, C. 1, 7, 14, 26, 80
electroencephalography (EEG) 30
epistemic community 23
error of comission/omission 200
everyday beliefs
conflicting, mistaken 22
evocative/explorative CCM studies 90
expertise 17

face validity
assessing of 78, 132
in CCM 69–70, 89
of coding/standardizing (STV) 78
fixed-list method in CCM 45
Focal Map (FM)
browsing SCU database 143
creating 145

export to *CmapTools* 144
visual cause map analysis 144
folk (naïve) theories 15
foreign policy 8, 26, 157, 160, 161
frame of reference 15
freehand drawing method (FDM)
in CCM 117, 123, 185
comparison with PCM 48
in SBA study 185, 191ff
functional magnetic resonance imaging (fMRI) 30
fundamental attribution error 20

Gentner, D. 14ff, 19–20, 29ff
George, A. 159
Gioia, D.A. 1, 89,
GTF/Generating Total Frequency 134

Hodgkinson, G.P. 1, 22, 26, 34, 45, 48, 70, 87, 190, 200, 203ff
homonyms 60
Huff, A.S. 1, 77, 95, 206
hybrid method, *see* structured CCM methods

Id, Od and Td values
generation of 133
in SNT browsing 142
impact of cognitions
mediating processes 27
importing raw data 116
indegree (Id) 81
indirect methods 38
incidence of SNT/SCUs
calculation in output generation 133
influence paths/mechanisms
influence (causal) path 6
in system causal maps 83
inter-coder reliability/agreement 132

internal coherence
  of causal maps 203
Interview Note Sheet (INS) 107
international relations (IR) 157, 158,
    159, 165
interviewing in CCM
  low-structured, open 42
  semi-structured (SIM) 49ff
  sincerity/insincerity 73

Jenkins, M.D. 1, 38,
Johnson-Laird, P.N. 12ff,
Johnston, A.I. 159

knowledge/beliefs
  accuracy, validity 27
  acquisition/eliciting, *see* data/
    acquisition in CCM
  adoption/formation 19
  aggregation, comparison 8
  divergence/similarity 151
  division of labor 22
  eliciting data 31, 37ff, 55, 57
  evaluation of validity 74–5, 77–9,
    205ff
  experiential learning 20
  general vs. domain-specific 17
  illusory 17
  impact of 16, 25
  isomorphism 27
  organizational, professional 23
  pathological 28
  phenomenological 3, 18, 83
  in policy and decision making 22
  pragmatic instrumentality 22
  propositional vs. procedural 32
  psychological and social roles 22
  reciprocal causal beliefs (RSCU)
    140
  representation 83–4, 92, 154, 182,
    205ff

sharedness 131
social mechanisms of formation 20
social phenomena 28
social unification 23
stability vs. change 23
stability/volatility 34
  as target phenomenon in CCM 4,
    18–19
    causal 3, 18–19, 83
    conflicting 17
    correlational, temporal 18
  types of 18
  verification of 24
knowledge adoption/change/
    formation
  attrition, forgetting of 25
  belief change 23–5, 44, 90, 155
  causal explanation 19
  epistemological problems 24
  functional logic 25
  functional role 22
  individual and social factors 24
  stability vs. change 23, 34
Krippendorff, K. 39, 43, 63, 78, 132

learning
  contents, underlying factors 22
  experiential 19
  social processes 20
  vicarious 19
level of generalization 61–6, 165
long-term memory (LTM) 15
low-structured interviewing *see*
    interviewing in CCM

managerial cognitions
  cognitive studies 27
  in crisis studies 28
  LSEs 27
  Management and Organization
    Cognition (MOC) 1

mediation path 26
small/owner-managed firms 27
Markóczy, L. 45ff, 76, 81, 84, 87, 93ff,
    188, 206
Maxwell, J.A. 1, 21, 43, 65, 69, 74, 78,
    80, 89, 96,
means-end 82–3, 172
mental models
    analogies and metaphors 16
    basic notion: "simulacrum" 12
    in causal mapping/CCM 18
    causal models/reasoning 15
    characteristics of 18
    coherence 93
    comparative analysis of 86
    conceptual background 12
    conflicting 17
    direct/indirect methods 29–30
    frame/of reference 15
    illusory 22
    impact mechanisms 16
    interpretations 14
    logical models/reasoning 15
    metaphorical use/sense 35
    "modellability" 93
    professionals' mental models 173
    relation to knowledge/beliefs 17
    schema/ta xvii, 13–15
    script 15
    terminology/alternatives 35
mental simulation 8, 15
    see also counterfactual thinking
metrics in CCM studies, see
        quantifying in CCM studies
mind mapping 5
modellability 93
MS Excel
    cause map datatable 6
    in CMAP3 102, 141ff

data entry/import 111, 116, 118ff,
    122ff, 127, 162ff, 189
data exporting 113, 141–2, 118ff,
    151, 162ff, 189
printing CMAP3 data 100–102,
    113, 127, 151
MS PowerPoint 55ff, 101ff, 154

n/N
    defining in SNT/SCU generation
        (GTF) 134
    respondent/data source (S)
        number in CMAP3 101
Narayanan, V.K. 1, 26, 43–4, 76,
    80–82, 84, 159
narratives
    in MOC studies 38
natural causal unit (NCU) data
    importing 116ff
    manual entry of 114
    natural causal unit (NCU) 99
natural language unit (NLU) data
    importing 116ff
    manual entry of 111
    natural language unit (NLU) 99
Nicolini, D. 42, 73–4, 203
NLU database
    batch deleting of 115
    browsing and sorting 113
    copy/paste of NLU data 113
    exporting 113
    printing of 113
    spreadsheet format 113
NLU/SNT Matrix
    in STV construction 129–31, 168
NLU/STAG Batch Replacement 131
Node Data & Standardizing module
    112
nomothetic research 48, 69, 90, 101,
    186, 207

NTAG
    definition/components 109
    of natural language units (NLU)
        99
    numbers in CCM studies *see*
        quantifying CCM studies

observation
    observation methods in MOC
        studies 38
    of overt behaviors 31
operational code 159
organizations, cognitive aspects 20
outdegree (Od) 81
output language, *see* standard
    language

pairwise comparison method (PCM)
    pairwise comparison matrix
        (PCM) 117
    comparison with FDM/SIM 48,
        195ff, 199
    creating/importing in structured
        CCM 121
    in SBA study 190
    reciprocal causal links 140, 194
parameters
    defining for SNT/SCU generation
        134
participant feedback
    in data acquisition 122
    feasibility of 77
    in SBA study 204
    validity assessment 77, 181, 204
political psychology 158–9
pre-existing beliefs/knowledge 7, 16,
    24
preliminary interview 51
Profiler Plus 57

Project Manager
    of *CMAP3* 103
Project Statistics
    in *CMAP3* 147ff
    in SBA study 179
psychometric methods/emulation in
    CCM 69

quantifying in CCM studies
    heuristic uses in CCM 89
    indicators/metrics/numbers in
        CCM studies 80
    in mapping belief systems/mental
        models 83
    maxim of "counting the
        countable" 89
    meaningfulness in CCM 87, 159,
        203
    quantifying causal maps 79ff
    quantitative indicators/ measures
        in CCM 80
    of socio-technical systems 81
    Statistics & C/D Index module in
        CMAP3 147ff

RDS/RDWS techniques
    in DBCM studies 167
    in primary data processing/entry
        107ff
realist position 21
reciprocal SCUs (RSCU) 80, 140, 148,
    192ff
reliability, *see* dependability,
    trustworthiness
    assessing/evaluation 78, 132
    audit trail as precondition 100
    coding/standardizing 65, 68–70
    conformability 69
    conventional definition 69

in DBCM 164–6, 173
low-structured inteviewing 43
repeatability/stability 69
in structured CCM 47
research objectives
in CCM studies 90
respondents/data sources (S)
max. number of 104

saturation
assessing in SBA study 181
in CCM research/design 4, 79, 91,
104, 176
of concepts in CCM 79
as validity indicator in CCM 79
schema xvii, 14–15, 159
SCU/SNT datatables
analysis of 142
exporting 141
SCU/SNT module 137
using filters 140
selection of CCM methods
criteria 89ff
labor intensitivy issue 65, 95–6
subjectivity issue 65
self-evaluation
in CCM studies 77
Self-Q interview 42
semi-structured interviewing (SIM)
in SBA study 176
semi-structured interviewing
method (SIM) 49, 185
SIM interviews note-taking,
recording 53
SIM-interviews practical aspects
in 52
shadowing 38
short-term memory (STM) 15, 33
SIM/PCM/FDM comparison
comparison study 185ff

methodological lessons 205
participants' feedback 204
similarity/dissimilarity
C/D index 81, 150
of individual causal maps 84
strategies for determining 67
simulation/modeling
qualitative vs. quantitative 8
sincerity 72–5, 161, 181
small business advisors (SBA)
causal maps of mental models 174
small business advisor (SBA) 11
social construction 42
socio-technical systems,
causal mapping of 81
specifying causal links/maps in
CMAP3
appropriateness 47
direct/inverse (+/–) 115
"overspecifying" 47
weighting (W) 115
STAG
use in *CMAP3* 100
in coding/standardizing 109ff,
124ff, 126, 165
in data entry 109ff, 123ff
need/components of 110
NLU/STAG Batch Replacement
131–132
in structured CCM methods 118ff,
123
Standard Causal Unit (SCU) 100
browsing, sorting 138
generation of in *CMAP3* 133
standard language
practices 126
primary language (STERM) 126,
135
secondary language (STENG) 135

selection for SNT/SCU generation
135
see also standard term vocabulary
(STV)
Standard Node Term (SNT)
browsing, sorting 138, 141
standard node term (SNT) 100
standard term vocabulary (STV) 59,
100
inductive construction of 127
provisional, initial 125
technical aspects in creating 123ff
standardizing/ation, *see* coding/
standardizing
statistics in CCM studies, *see*
quantifying in CCM studies
Storey, D.J. 174, 184
structured CCM methods
applicability criteria 48, 91ff
in *CMAP3* 101ff, 123
Cognizer 48, 97
concept pool, criteria 92, 202
concept pool/hybrid method 45ff,
56, 62, 66, 68
data elicititation in 45
data import in *CMAP3* 116ff
freehand drawing approach 48
implicit assumptions in 93
low communality/aggregability
93ff
methodological implications 91
non-equivalence 48
"overspecifying" 47
paired comparison approach 48,
185ff
in SBA comparison study 185ff
shortcut alternatives 55ff
standard term vocabulary (STV)
in 118ff

validation/validity issues 76, 91,
93ff
subjectivity in CCM 43, 65–6
symbolic thinking 21
synonyms 60

tacit knowledge/beliefs
in CCM data elicitation 30, 34
cognitive contents/processes 16
conversion into explicit 35
decision-making 34
Tetlock, P. 26, 158
text-based causal map/mapping
(TBCM) 43
theory development 61
theory of mind 37
thinking/thought process, *see*
cognitive process/ing
shared, role of 22
thought experiment 16
Tolman, E.C. 13
total degree (Td) 81
transferability 69
trustworthiness
assessing in SBA study 181
criteria in CCM studies 70
preconditions of, in CCM 71
qualitative criteria/definition 69
see also validity, reliability
two-way SCUs (RSCU) 140

validity/validation
accuracy 18, 24, 27, 72, 75, 132
audit trail 100
in CCM studies 27–8, 31, 66, 69–79
132, 176, 181
coding/standardizing 65, 165
conventional definition 69
in DBCM 40

impact of aggregation 34, 72, 75
in low-structured CCM 42
participants' feedback 77, 181, 204
peer feedback/review 77, 204
qualitative definition 69
in quantifying CCM 87
replication 77
saturation 181
in SBA study 181
semantic validity 132
sharedness as indicator 79, 181
in structured CCM 49, 68, 91, 187
of STV/standardizing 132
validation strategies 77–8
Verstehen 8, 39
visual/graphic causal maps
in *CMAP3* 97, 99, 101, 126, 142, 152ff, 154
conventions 154–5, 169
in DBCM study 166, 169ff, 173
in SBA study 182ff

simulating with Focal Maps 143ff, 152
using *CmapTools* 101, 141–2, 144, 146, 153
using drawing/graphic applications 97, 101, 154
visual vs. non-visual presentation in CCM 4ff, 7, 13–14, 38–9, 57, 83, 96, 142, 144

W (weight) value
in *CMAP3* 47, 109
setting in output generation 135
specification in data 47, 84
Weick, K.E. 1, 6,
What if analysis 8, 16, 39
Windows, *CMAP3* compatibility with 102
working/short-term memory (STM) 15, 33
WorldView 57

For Product Safety Concerns and Information please contact our EU representative GPSR@taylorandfrancis.com Taylor & Francis Verlag GmbH, Kaufingerstraße 24, 80331 München, Germany

Printed and bound by CPI Group (UK) Ltd, Croydon, CR0 4YY

01/05/2025

01858414-0011